SEARCH FOR SECURITY

A Study in Baltic Diplomacy, 1920-1934

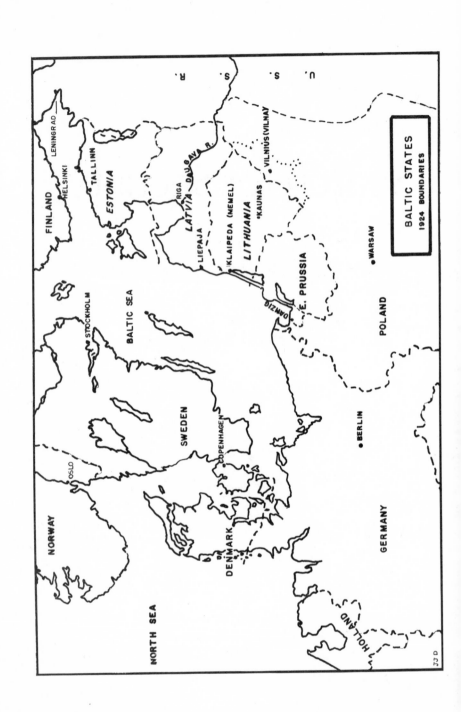

BALTIC STATES
1924 BOUNDARIES

NORWAY

NORTH SEA

OSLO

SWEDEN

STOCKHOLM

BALTIC SEA

FINLAND

HELSINKI

LENINGRAD

TALLINN

ESTONIA

U. S. S. R.

RIGA

LATVIA DAUGAVA

LIEPAJA

KLAIPEDA (MEMEL)

LITHUANIA

KAUNAS

VILNIUS (VILNA)

DENMARK

COPENHAGEN

DANZIG

E. PRUSSIA

BERLIN

POLAND

WARSAW

GERMANY

HOLLAND

JJ D

Search for Security

A Study in Baltic Diplomacy, 1920-1934

BY
Hugh I. Rodgers

ARCHON BOOKS
1975

Library of Congress Cataloging in Publication Data

Rodgers, Hugh I
    Search for Security.

    Bibliography: p.
    1. Baltic States—Foreign Relations. 2. Baltic Entente,
1934. I. Title
DK511.B3R54   327.47′4   74-16366
ISBN 0-208-01478-0

Printed in the United States of America

for

Sandra and Barton

You realize for what imperative European reasons we must follow the development of this Baltic microcosm in its international life. It reproduces all those causes of fear and hope, all those interests and ideals which, by reversing the magnifying-glass, we can see spread over the whole of Europe.

Count Carlo Sforza, 1928

Contents

Preface

Karlis Ulmanis, the University of Nebraska graduate and some-
time Texas creamery operator who eventually became prime
minister and last president of the Latvian republic, once remarked
in a press conference that all Latvia's foreign policy could be
placed under two headings: economics and security. Both topics
included matters vital to the survival of the Baltic countries but
problems of security were of overwhelming importance.

Hardly any region of Eastern Europe offered more serious
diplomatic problems than did the strip of territory along the
eastern coast of the Baltic Sea. Before World War I the Russian
and German empires divided this coast between themselves. By
1920, however, Soviet Russia and Weimar Germany found their
portions drastically reduced as five new states had appeared:
Finland, Estonia, Latvia, Lithuania, and Poland. Preserving
this territorial adjustment which secured the existence and
integrity of the new states constituted the major theme of Baltic
diplomacy between the two world wars.

The dramatic military and diplomatic events connected with
the emergence of the Baltic states in the aftermath of World War
I and with their demise in the prelude to World War II have been
the subject of several scholarly investigations. Much less attention has been paid by Western scholars to the diplomatic activity
of the independence era. There are a number of reasons for this
lack of attention.

Many aspects of interwar diplomacy seem dated and old-fashioned to a generation used to the drama of Cold War, great power, atomic diplomacy. Even during the 1920s and 1930s the Baltic area was little studied by Western diplomats and journalists. The statesmen of these small countries were, to borrow a phrase from Pierre Renouvin, "condemned to all the pathetic guiles of the weak." Consequently, they furnish us with few attractive examples of statecraft practiced on a grand scale.

Yet, for all its paltry deviousness, a study of the diplomacy of the Baltic region is unexpectedly rewarding. The practice of diplomacy had a compelling urgency about it for these minor statesmen. For twenty years the Baltic states existed upon the edge of a volcano that could erupt at any moment. Here in the Baltic the ideological forces of the twentieth century met and collided. A study of the Baltic's situation, far from being an exercise in antiquarianism, affords one a unique perspective on larger European events.

Small states, like the poor of Biblical aphorism, are apparently with us always. There are today 137 members of the United Nations organization. The overwhelming majority of these states are "small" by any definition and many are former colonial dependencies. The parallels to the condition of the Baltic states in the earlier postwar era are numerous and instructive. In the 1920s and 1930s the Baltic states experienced to the full the frustrations of being new, small, poor, weak, and "emerging nations" in a world dominated by the interests of the great powers.

But in the Baltic situation were certain ironlike, unyielding actualities for which one finds few parallels among contemporary small powers. These actualities, with which this study is concerned, solidified by the end of 1927 and confronted Baltic diplomats with tasks of heroic proportions. Indeed the tragic element always threatened to break through in Baltic affairs; the energy with which Latvian statesmen in particular pursued their difficult labors calls to mind not the figure of Hercules but that of Sisyphus. The Baltic experience—especially the Latvian version—thus contains certain unique diplomatic elements even as it exhibits something of the universal in its human aspect. I have tried to keep sight of both in the pages which follow.

The study of Baltic history is rendered difficult by the inaccessibility of the archives, by the scattered nature of other research materials, and by the several languages in which these occur. Some valuable memoir literature has appeared among Baltic emigrés, and one Soviet Latvian historian with access to the archives in Riga has published a useful if decidedly biased study of "bourgeois" Baltic diplomacy. Fortunately for the historian, there exist enormously rich resources for the study of Baltic affairs in German diplomatic archives, and in memoirs, public documents, and newspapers. The archives and documentary publications of other countries have also yielded up much of value. Inevitably, there are certain risks in filtering the beams of Baltic evidence through these non-Baltic prisms. Yet the existence of multiple sources of documentation (including significant Baltic materials) has permitted the reconstruction and analysis of events and policies. Consequently, the opening of the Baltic republics' archives in the future could alter this study only in minor details.

In undertaking this work I have had the encouragement and advice of Professor Oliver H. Radkey of the University of Texas at Austin. Professor Edgar Anderson of California State University at San José, who almost singlehandedly founded Baltic studies in the United States, was a valuable guide to Baltic bibliography and personalities. Cheerfully and tirelessly Mr. and Mrs. Romans Jansons assisted me with key materials in the Latvian language. Thanks go to James J. Dwyer for preparing the map of the Baltic States. To all the above and to my wife I owe much. They are, of course, free of responsibility for any errors of fact or judgement which appear in this work.

H. I. R.

Columbus College,
Columbus, Georgia

SEARCH FOR SECURITY

A Study in Baltic Diplomacy, 1920-1934

1

Latvia and the Baltic Security Problem

Latvia, along with the other modern Baltic republics, occupies a bitterly contested region in northern Europe. The territories where Latvians lived, Livonia and Courland, have been the objects of great power conflicts which overwhelmed the unfortunate inhabitants. From the thirteenth to the sixteenth century German clerics, knights, and merchants controlled the *Baltikum* and turned the Baltic Sea into a German lake. With the decline of the Teutonic Order in the fifteenth and sixteenth centuries, however, Livonia and Courland passed to the Polish crown. Sweden assumed control of Baltic affairs during the seventeenth century, but in 1721 Russia, under Peter the Great, obtained most of Livonia and ended Sweden's century of glory. A portion of eastern Livonia retained by Poland, Latgale, was annexed by the Russian Empire in 1772 at the time of the First Partition. Russia added Courland to her Baltic possessions in 1795, thus bringing all territory inhabited by Latvians into her empire.[1]

The economic and social conditions of the Latvians in the Russian Empire changed very slowly. The Baltic-Germans retained a privileged position on the land, in the cities, and in the Lutheran Church. However, between 1816 and 1819, serfdom was abolished in Livonia and Courland, an event which marks the beginning of the rise of the modern Latvian nation. One hundred years later, as a result of World War I and the Russian Revolution, the Latvians were able to form an independent state.

As a new participant on the European diplomatic scene Latvia suffered several disabilities. Her 25,399 square miles spread strategically around the Gulf of Riga into which the important Western Dvina (Daugava) River flowed from the Russian hinterland. Although comprising an area approximately the size of Belgium and the Netherlands combined, Latvia did not have impressive population resources. The war and liberation struggle had taken such a heavy toll that even in 1935 the population numbered only 1.9 million. Of this total, non-Latvian minorities accounted for 24.5 percent.[2] Somewhat less than one-third of the population lived in Latgale, a province bordering on Soviet Russia and Poland. Differing from the rest of the population in religion and dialect, and with substantial concentrations of Russians and Poles, Latgale produced both internal and foreign policy anxieties in the capital of the new republic.[3]

The problem of this small and diverse population was compounded by Latvia's war-wrecked economy. Despite lack of resources, industries on Latvian territory had produced four percent of the prewar Russian Empire's total industrial output. But this industrial complex, built with foreign capital and supplied with foreign raw materials, was destroyed or evacuated by the Russians following military reverses in 1915. The number of industrial workers in Latvia fell from 93,000 in 1910 to 20,000 in 1920, a drop reflecting, in part, the industrial collapse.[4] Such catastrophic losses could not be quickly restored. Instead, the land provided the foundation for a reconstruction on a new basis.[5] Through a series of land reform acts initiated by Karlis Ulmanis in the Latvian Constituent Assembly in 1920, the 1,338 large estates (mostly owned by Baltic-German nobility) accounting for 48.1 percent of the arable land in Latvia were broken up, and, along with certain State lands, were redistributed so that 77 percent of the Latvian peasantry became landowners.[6] This reform laid the social, political, and economic foundations of the new republic.

The economy of this country of peasant proprietors became characterized by intensive and specialized agriculture, the products of which were destined for export.[7] Latvia's economic security was thus dangerously dependent upon the price stability of agricultural products and the willingness of industrial countries to absorb these goods. By 1930, Germany and Great Britain were together accepting 55 percent of Latvia's total export. Anything threatening good relations with either country endangered the Latvian state. But Latvia had to compete for these markets with her Baltic neighbors who were exporting the same type of products. A formidable barrier to political and economic collaboration among the Baltic states thus existed from the beginning of the independence era.[8]

The lack of an industrial base together with a limited population made the raising, equipment and supply of defense forces difficult.[9] At the end of the liberation struggle in 1920 Latvia had a maximum of 75,000 men under arms. According to the military service law of 1923, all male citizens between the ages of seventeen and fifty were subject to compulsory service. But during the independence era the size of the standing army never exceeded twenty thousand officers and men. A kind of *ad hoc* rural militia, the Home Guard, numbering around 24,000 men, could supplement the regular army and reserves in an emergency. Small naval and aviation units rounded out the defense structure.[10] Needless to say, the defense tasks of this small force far exceeded its capabilities. The Latvian armed forces could fight a serious delaying action in the face of an invasion from the east, but foreign support would be necessary in the end. Seeking such support would be a major diplomatic activity.

The economic and military problems of the new state were a serious drain on the thought and energy of Latvia's novice politicians who had also to establish the republic's political machinery. The Latvian Constitution, adopted February 15, 1922, featured universal suffrage, proportional representation, a one chamber parliament (the Saeima), and a weak executive authority. Numerous political parties, encouraged by a constitutional provision allowing any group of 100 citizens to present a list of candidates in elections, made for a lively and interesting parliamentary life. They also made stable majority government impossible.

The average life of a coalition cabinet was nine months; between 1922 and 1934, Latvia had fourteen different governments but only four parliamentary elections.[11] At critical moments the multiplicity of parties could paralyze the government. The end result was a *coup d'état* in 1934 and the establishment of a mild dictatorship.

Despite the number of parties, only two important political concentrations existed: the Farmers' Union to the right of center and the Social Democrats on the left.[12] In a general way one may say that the agrarian party supported collaboration with Poland and the other Baltic states and looked to Great Britain for international backing. The Social Democrats were less sympathetic to a Baltic bloc containing Poland and, while also westward-looking, hoped to be a bridge between a Social Democratic Germany and Bolshevist Russia.

The agrarian parties along with bourgeois center groups supplied all but one of Latvia's ten different foreign ministers. Individuals will be considered in detail later but it may be noted here that Latvia's foreign service personnel, with a few exceptions, were young, inexperienced, and untrained amateurs. Young men of middle class or well-to-do peasant backgrounds who might in an earlier day have followed legal, medical, academic, or journalistic careers now entered politics and government service.[13]

The Latvian Foreign Ministry reproduced, on a small scale to be sure, the organizational structure of a typical European foreign office. In addition to the foreign minister, between 1919 and 1923 a succession of vice-ministers also existed. Such officials were made necessary by the exigences of Latvian party politics. In 1923, a permanent official called the Secretary General was installed. This official managed the foreign minister's office routine and served as temporary minister when necessary. A forty-four year old lawyer, Hermanis Albats, was appointed to this influential office in 1923; he held it for ten years.[14]

The foreign ministry consisted of the administrative, political, and legal departments. The important political department contained the Baltic States section, Western Powers section, Eastern Powers section, and the press section. By 1938 the foreign ministry in Riga had a total of thirty-three officials. In addition, Latvia maintained sixteen legations abroad and several important consulates.[15]

Modesty in the foreign ministry's size did not prevent Latvia's young politicians and officials from voicing an intensely self-conscious nationalism that often inhibited international co-operation. The struggle for liberation had been long and costly and Latvians were quite sensitive about their new sovereignty.[16] Exaggerated national pride made every piece of territory seem important. A characteristic issue was the dispute between Latvia and Estonia over the railroad junction town of Valka (Walk). Both countries claimed that without Valka they would be "cut off" and "strangled." Fortunately, the British were able to arbitrate the dispute, but the Latvian Constituent Assembly was so angry over the loss of the town the foreign minister had to resign as a gesture of protest.[17]

Being a young and untried diplomat was a heady thing in an Eastern Europe from which Germany and Russia seemed excluded. Some Latvian statesmen may have dreamed of playing a role in the larger field of European politics.[18] Latvians at first had a tendency to see things in simple terms, to utter Wilsonian slogans and clichés, to trust in the continued good will of Britain and France, in the efficacy of conferences, treaties, and solemn assurance, and in the League of Nations.[19] Latvian diplomats were in a constant flurry of activity, much of it of no lasting consequence. But serious work would be attempted as the nature of Latvia's security problem became fully appreciated.

Latvia thus exhibited many of the characteristics of the new postwar state: a heightened nationalism, political inexperience and instability, a small population on strategic ground, an agrarian economy dependent upon foreign markets, and unrealistic foreign policy attitudes. But despite major internal difficulties, Latvia gradually attained an ordered civic life and a tolerable standard of living.[20] This was achieved without the foreign assistance so lavishly extended to the emerging states of the post-World War II era. Even with its weaknesses, failures, and mistakes, the record of the small Latvian republic is impressive.

The very existence of a small state, however, and the kind of role it plays in international affairs depends largely on the policy of the big powers.[21] Of course, a small state is usually the object rather than the initiator of action and, given her political geography, Latvia could not be a detached spectator. While not a factor of primary importance in European affairs, Latvia nevertheless was situated "in the midst of world political combinations."[22] What precisely was the international constellation surrounding the new Baltic republic? What, in brief, was the Baltic security problem?

It will be useful at the outset to determine the attitudes of Latvia's potential friends and enemies. The overwhelming menace came, of course, from Soviet Russia. The Bolsheviks aimed at the reincorporation of the *Baltikum* into the Russian state from which it had so recently escaped. Shortly after the proclamation of Latvian independence in November, 1918, the Soviets had launched an invasion of Latvia, announced the formation of a Latvian Soviet Republic, and had called for its voluntary union with Soviet Russia.[23] With the aid of German military elements and British and French naval forces and the Polish army, the Latvians drove out the Red Army. On August 11, 1920, the Soviets signed a peace treaty "unreservedly" recognizing the independence and sovereignty of the Latvian Republic and "voluntarily and forever renounc[ing] all sovereign rights over the Latvian people and territory."[24]

But the new masters of Russia viewed the Soviet retreat from the *Baltikum* as merely a temporary necessity.[25] Moscow re-graded the region as a "special sphere of Russian interest if not as future Russian territory."[26] Latvian officials recognized that the Soviets would try to reach their goal "through propaganda and agitation where they have failed to achieve it by bayonets."[27] Soviet diplomatic ploys during the 1920s and 1930s varied but always in the background lurked the threat of physical absorption. Such was the grievous weight pressing down upon the new republic. To whom could the Latvians turn for help?

Germany might appear at first glance to have been a likely patron of the new Baltic states. The long history of German involvement in the *Baltikum* and the Reich concern about the significant German minority there pointed in that direction. But Latvian independence was achieved in defiance of original German plans for the *Baltikum*. These plans had called for the attachment (in some fashion) of Lithuania, Courland, Livonia, and Estonia to the German Reich.[28] Defeat on the western front and revolution at home had interrupted such schemes.

In the confused aftermath of the world war, the Allied Powers had authorized certain German military units present in the Baltic region to prevent the conquest of the area by Bolshevik forces. The German elements, swollen with volunteer formations from the Reich early in 1919, soon constituted a grave threat to the new Latvian state. They had to be forced out of Latvia in late 1919 by Allied pressure and by the Latvian army.[29]

The legacy of German involvement was a tremendous amount of bitterness on both sides. Many leading German figures saw the new border states as hindrances to the establishment of close ties with Soviet Russia. The possibility that the two pariah nations might come to "an understanding over the bodies of the Baltic States" was real enough.[30] General Hans von Seeckt condemned the "false border state policy" which had produced a dividing wall of countries between Germany and Russia.[31] The German foreign minister in 1921 accused the Western powers of inhibiting German-Russian trade by erecting as barriers "small economically artificial formations" between them.[32] These expressions of German hostility convinced certain segments of the Latvian press that Germany wished the destruction of the Baltic states.[33]

Ultimately, calmer spokesmen prevailed in the eastern division of the German foreign ministry.[34] There the realization grew that since the Baltic states were destined for independence for a "number of years," German policy must seek to influence the new states and capture their markets.[35] The major advocate of this policy was Wilhelm Theodor Erich Wallroth, German minister to Riga from 1921 to 1923.[36] Latvia, Wallroth argued, because of its location and excellent harbors and railway system, was the natural intermediary for German-Russian relations. Germany ought to make conciliatory gestures in order to secure for her use the Latvian bridge site (*lettländische Brückenstellung*).[37] Others picked up Wallroth's bridge theory. One official in the Reich economic ministry, after a tour of the Baltic, concluded that "Latvia was predestined to serve as the entry area for all economic activity with Russia."[38]

But the optimism of the "bridge theory" collapsed against the hard reality of the Soviet manipulation of its trade policy for political ends. Latvia, despite her own sincere efforts, never became the economic bridge between Soviet Russia and Weimar Germany.[39]

As it turned out, Germany did not need the Latvian bridge: Germany and the Soviet regime established a working relationship well symbolized by the Rapallo Treaty of 1922. Germany's major aim in East Europe was the isolation of Poland. While maintaining formally correct and occasionally cordial relations with Riga and other Baltic capitals, Germany sought to prevent the formation of an alliance system that would group the Baltic states with Poland. Soviet Russia also shared this concern; the interests of Germany and Russia thus coincided completely in the Baltic.[40]

Consequently Germany and Soviet Russia cooperated to prevent the formation of a Baltic alliance system which included Poland. This German-Soviet policy, successfully pursued for at least ten years, constituted the basic power factor in Baltic and border state affairs. It was the great mountain up which the Latvian Sisyphus toiled.

In the view of many Latvians the only state in the region capable of mounting significant resistance to Soviet Russia was Poland. The Poles indeed desired to assume the predominant position in a regional alliance system. Pilsudski even spoke of a federation composed of Poland, White Russia, and the Ukraine, which would then confederate with Lithuania, Latvia, Estonia, and Finland. This unlikely structure, Pilsudski claimed, would be able to withstand the pressures of both Soviet Russia and Germany.[41] The Poles also had in mind specific territorial adjustments.

Warsaw hoped, in brief, to restore the Polish boundaries of 1772 inside of which would fall the Latvian province of Latgale. In the spring of 1920, the Polish envoy in Riga flatly declared that the Latvian district of Latgale belonged to Poland.[42] In addition, Poland coveted the fine Latvian harbors of Liepāja (Libau) and Riga, especially as Poland did not acquire control of Danzig.[43] As late as 1922, the Latvian foreign minister revealed to Berlin that "next to the possession of Daugavpils (Dünaburg) . . . the major desire of Poland remained, despite all protestations to the contrary, the possession of the excellent Latvian port of Liepāja. With this fact every important policy in Latvia must be concerned."[44] Poland's territorial aspirations threatened the integrity of the Latvian state, and, while Latvian military figures often called for a close military alliance with Poland, the Baltic republic's civilian policy makers moved quite cautiously in this direction.

Faced with the Soviet threat, with an enigmatic Germany, and with land-hungry Poland her only possible protector, Latvia turned longing eyes toward the western powers. The attitude of the western powers toward the emerging border states of Eastern Europe was at first favorable and benevolent. But, rhetoric about self-determination of peoples aside, these powers, especially the United States, had been slow to act. Britain had led the way by extending *de facto* recognition on November 11, 1918. When the Soviets had invaded early in 1919, the British despatched a squadron to Liepāja (Libau). France and the United States also had sent military missions.[45]

The western powers had expected that the Baltic states, along with other border countries, would form a *cordon sanitaire* against the Bolshevik infection. The western diplomats had hoped that before long the Bolsheviks would be overturned and a democratic and federated Russia reconstituted. In the meanwhile, no formerly Russian territory was to be permanently alienated (except for Poland and Finland). Now Latvian authorities had willingly accepted the common struggle against the Bolsheviks in the hope that the western powers might grant *de jure* recognition and help with postwar reconstruction. Unfortunately, the great powers refused to take such positive action.[46] Faced with this attitude, Latvia had withdrawn from the anti-Bolshevik front and had signed a peace treaty with the Soviet regime.[47]

Although the Soviets had extended the prize of *de jure* recognition, Latvia still wanted such acknowledgement by the great powers of the west and membership in the League of Nations as confirmation by the international community of her status. Accordingly, in December, 1920, Latvia and the other Baltic states applied to the League of Nations for acceptance. Admission to the League meant that members would have to guarantee the territorial integrity of Latvia. But as one spokesman put it: "Now who will be ready to go to aid in the defense of those Baltic States? Let those who vote to admit them first make sure their governments are ready to send troops to defend them."[48] No one wished to risk a confrontation with Soviet Russia should that state move upon the Baltic countries, and so the League Assembly rejected the Baltic application.

By the winter of 1920-21, however, it was obvious that the Soviets had won the civil war in Russia; there would be no "restoration." Accordingly, the Allied Supreme Council, meeting in Paris, in January, 1921, overcame British reluctance and extended the coveted *de jure* recognition.[49] In the following months Germany and the lesser powers followed suit and on September 22, 1921, Latvia became a member of the League of Nations. Finally, in the summer of 1922, the United States also recognized the Baltic states.[50]

After *de jure* recognition, at least the possibility of a political or military commitment from one or more of the western powers existed. Political considerations aside, however, distance and geography militated against any western assumption of obligations toward Latvia and the other Baltic states. In some respects, Latvia resembled Belgium and the Netherlands. In both instances there were powerful neighbors who might wish to control the mouths of rivers and the coastal harbors. Unlike the Low Countries, however, the Baltic states did not have Great Britain as an interested friend across the sea. Sweden could not be the Britain of the Baltic Sea. The geography of the Baltic Sea is also such that access to Latvia from the west could easily be interrupted by a hostile Germany or Russia.[51]

Further limiting the possibility of a western commitment to Latvia was the development of a moderate rivalry between Britain and France for influence in the new states. Some Englishmen urged an active policy in the Baltic area in order to prevent its going "by default as a French sphere, so to speak, or as a region where Germany may do as she likes unchallenged."[52] In the spring of 1923, Latvia and Britain concluded a commercial treaty to which the Latvians attached a "far-reaching political significance."[53] But German observers interpreted English activity in the Baltic merely as a counter to French involvement with Poland and other border states.[54]

This mild rivalry worked against the formulation of any joint policy of support to the new states. As the initial postwar interest in the Baltic as an anti-Bolshevik beachhead waned, no western commitments to the new states were forthcoming.

Such were the elements of the Latvian security problem. The thrusts of a revolutionary and subversive Soviet Russia, the half-veiled threat of Polish expansionism, a German policy tending toward cooperation with Russia in the *Baltikum*, the general indifference of the Western powers—all combined to present Latvian diplomats with a frightful task. These elements appeared at the beginning of the new state's life and remained fairly constant throughout the period of independence.

By the end of 1922 Latvia stood fully clothed in the robes of legitimacy. Her status as an independent state was affirmed by treaty with Soviet Russia, recognized by all the great powers, and confirmed by membership in the League of Nations. Such security as treaties and international sanction could bestow had been won. Nevertheless, the circumstances in which the Latvian republic existed boded a highly uncertain future. Diplomats of the new state quickly sought to secure its hard-won but precarious independence.

2

In Pursuit of the Baltic League Chimera:

From Bulduri to Warsaw, 1920-1922

The formation of a league or regional alliance system providing for mutual assistance in case of attack was an obvious security measure for the Baltic states to take. A number of schemes for such an alliance system appeared during the independence struggle and the realization of their own physical weaknesses kept the idea alive among the Baltic area states from 1920 onward.

Diplomatic and military cooperation during the liberation and anti-Bolshevik conflicts of 1918-1919 provided precedents for future collaboration among the Baltic states. Estonia had assisted Latvian forces in the decisive battle of Cēsis (Wenden) in June, 1919, while Polish forces helped clear Latgale of Bolshevik forces late in 1919 and early 1920. Diplomats of the new states had cooperated in London and Paris to seek recognition and assistance from the western powers.[1]

In line with this general trend, Kaarel Robert Pusta, a member of Estonia's Paris delegation, had put forward a plan for a Baltic League in November, 1918. His project had called for a series of political and economic alliances among three groups of states: the Scandinavian (Denmark, Norway, Sweden); the eastern Baltic (Finland, Estonia, Latvia); and the southern Baltic (Lithuania and Poland). Pusta had also projected a joint supreme command for coordination of war fleets and a common armed force for the Baltic area. Pusta envisaged his "Baltic League" as a kind of subgroup of the League of Nations.[2]

Despite the merits of such plans as Pusta's, the Scandinavian

14

kingdoms consistently rejected any involvement with the defense problems of the dangerous eastern Baltic coast. Pusta's project died aborning. Even on the quite practical level of coordinating a common response to the Soviet peace overtures of 1919 the new Baltic countries found it difficult to agree. A series of conferences at the Baltic capitals during the fall and winter of 1919 culminated in a meeting at Helsinki in January, 1920. But neither a common policy toward the Soviet peace offensive nor a common military convention could be achieved. On the contrary, these meetings revealed how far apart were the interests of Poland, the three Baltic states, and Finland.[3]

Dramatic events stirred Eastern Europe in 1920. Josef Pilsudski and the Poles launched an offensive against the Reds which carried them to Kiev by June. But in the summer the Soviets began a drive to the West which swept them to the gates of Warsaw by mid-August. While Poland fought, the Baltic states negotiated, first armistices and then peace treaties, with Moscow —Estonia in February, Lithuania in July, and Latvia in August. It was against this background that Latvia's foreign minister, Zigfrīds Anna Meierovics, arranged a Baltic diplomatic conference for August at the resort of Bulduri near Riga.

Meierovics, described by an unsympathetic German journalist as "one of the most interesting phenomena of postwar Europe," was born in 1887 in Durben near Liepāja (Libau). His father, a converted Jewish physician, and his mother, who came from a "Germanized" Latvian family, maintained a middle class household of the German type. Orphaned at an early age, Meierovics was reared by an uncle, a country school teacher. In this environment, the young Zigfrīds soon left behind his parents' German culture and identified himself completely with his Latvian associates.

After a commercial education in Riga, Meierovics embarked on a successful career in an agrarian banking institution. The outbreak of World War I found Meierovics a member of the liberal and patriotic All-Russian Municipal Union which despatched him to Rezekne in Latgale (Vitebsk province) to organize food supplies for the northern front. Later, when the revolution occurred in March, 1917, Meierovics shared the hopes of his bourgeois contemporaries for a Latvian future inside a democratic Russia.[4]

Meierovics, then thirty years old, plunged into the stormy political sea that was Vidzeme (the Lettish-speaking part of Livonia and still, in early 1917, not in German military hands). He became a member of the Provisional Livonian Provincial Council and also participated in the founding congress of the Latvian Farmers' Union.[5] In November, 1917, various political and civic groups of Latvians constituted the Latvian National Council. Zigfrīds Meierovics, who rather reluctantly embraced the cause of Latvian independence, joined the Council's department for foreign relations with headquarters in Petrograd.[6] With one interlude, Meierovics, from that point until his death, cautiously guided the course of Latvian diplomacy.

As he presided over the small Latvian foreign office after the establishment of independence, Meierovics looked the part of the elegant statesman. Contemporary photographs reveal a handsome, sharply profiled, smooth shaven, faultlessly dressed young man. A German newspaperman found him rather like a "young Honourable," a member of the British House of Lords or the Carleton Club. Perhaps Meierovics had picked up the aura of the British upper classes in 1918 while on his first diplomatic mission in London. He once remarked that Lord Balfour, the man who introduced him to diplomatic society and protocol, was his "real tutor."[7] Contemporaries agreed that Meierovics possessed the "gifts and finesse" of the born diplomat.[8]

Older studies of Baltic diplomacy have tended to celebrate Meierovics as the leading exponent of a Baltic alliance system including Finland and Poland.[9] Indeed, he devoted much labor to that end. Yet closer examination reveals a much more complex and circuitous pursuit of Latvian security. During most of the spring and summer of 1920, Meierovics's primary concern was the conclusion of a peace treaty with the Soviets (signed on August 11, 1920) which would recognize the independence and sovereignty of Latvia. The parallel prosecution of alliance talks with other Baltic states provided a safe secondary action which might also impress the Bolsheviks. As he told the Latvian Constituent Assembly, in order to gain the respect of the great neighbors to the East and West, it was necessary for Latvia to reach "agreement with all our immediate neighbors to the North and South."[10]

Meierovics may have occasionally dreamed of making Latvia the linchpin of an alliance system curving from Oslo through Stockholm, Helsinki, Tallinn, Riga, Kaunas, and Warsaw. (Riga in those days was often grandly styled the "Paris of the Baltic"). But Meierovics was realistic and perceptive enough to understand that Latvia could play only a limited role in the game of power politics. Setting aside talk of a "Baltic Commonwealth,"[11] Meierovics pursued instead limited agreements. As the initiator and leading personality of the Bulduri Conference which opened on August 6 and lasted until September 6, 1920, what did Meierovics hope to accomplish?

While the foreign minister's own party organ, *Brīvā Zeme* (Free Land) called for military union in defense of the Baltic states, Meierovics himself noted that there would be no rapid adoption of formal political and military alliances. Pointing to the recently concluded peace treaty with Soviet Russia, Meierovics stated it would "be superfluous to conclude an agreement against Russia as we have nothing to fear from Russia."[12] The aim of the Baltic conference was to "solve a series of practical problems." An economic rapprochement among the states would precede the gradual evolution of a political entente. As Meierovics suggested, the participating states would pass through "successive stages" before reaching a firm political agreement.[13]

Meierovics's caution proved quite in keeping with the events. The Scandinavian states refused to send representatives to the Bulduri meeting, although delegations from the non-Bolshevik White Russian and Ukranian regimes appeared requesting admission to the conference.[14] The Polish delegation was headed by Leon Wasilewski, Pilsudski's advisor on eastern policy and chargé d'affaires in Tallinn. Wasilewski was, in Meierovics's eyes at least, a notorious advocate of the Poland of 1772, an entity that had included the Latvian provinces of Courland and Latgale.[15] With the Red Army standing upon the banks of the Vistula the Poles were understandably anxious for a Baltic military alliance system. An old advocate of Baltic unity, Kaarel Robert Pusta, led the Estonian delegation. Finland and Lithuania also sent representatives.

After the opening plenary sessions, presided over by Karlis

Ulmanis and Meierovics, the conference divided into several
working commissions and did not meet again in a plenary session
until August 20. The commissions performed a great deal of
technical work on financial, economic, communications, sani-
tation, and labor problems. Recommendations for a Baltic monetary union, a convention on communications, a Baltic Economic
Council, and an arbitration convention came out of this work.[16]

The political commission, entrusted with the preparation of a
general treaty, submitted a draft document on August 31. Under
the terms of the projected treaty, the participating states bound
themselves not to permit the formation on their territories of
"undertakings" hostile to another signatory nor to permit passage of military forces hostile to a participant. The proposed
treaty also obligated the signatories to abstain from agreements
with third powers directed against a state represented at the conference. The heart of the treaty was Article V, according to which
"the participating states agree to draw up without delay a defensive military convention."[17]

The Estonian and Polish delegations warmly urged the necessity of the "Baltic Union" as a guarantee of the independence of
the Baltic states and the peace of Eastern Europe. Meierovics
presented the text of the treaty and put it to a vote paragraph by
paragraph. The conference adopted the treaty, subject to ratification by December 15, 1920, although Poland and Lithuania
made reservations that neither accepted the treaty as binding with
the respect to the other. At the request of the Finns the treaty was
kept secret.[18]

The political treaty adopted by the Bulduri conference constituted a start toward a realistic common defensive system.
Would its implementation have increased the security of the
Baltic countries? In the 1920s a Soviet army would have faced
a combined force of around 360,000 men if Poland, Latvia,
Estonia, Finland, and Lithuania could properly unite their military resources.[19] It might be well to recall that in the winter of
1939/40, Finland, with a population of about 4 million and an
army of 126,000 defended its independence against a Soviet force
of 473,000. According to one calculation, Estonia, Latvia, and
Lithuania could have maintained, by that time, a standing combined army of 100,000 men. Such a force properly armed might
have been able to hold off a Soviet invasion.[20]

Assuming the solution of the technical problems of implementation, the treaty would have increased the security of the Baltic states. Why then did no state ratify the treaty by the stipulated deadline? In the first place, there was more than incongruity in the fact that as the common enemy pressed upon the capital of one of the conferees (Poland), two of the conference participants (Latvia and Lithuania) made peace with that enemy. There existed serious differences in policy aims to say the least.

In the second place, the growing Lithuanian-Polish conflict produced the failure of the Bulduri instrument. The Soviet Russians had ceded the city and surrounding district of Vilna to Lithuania by the treaty of peace between these two in July, 1920. But during the Polish counteroffensive of late August the fate of Vilna was again in the balance as fighting broke out between the Poles and Lithuanians in the Suvalki district. At the insistence of the Allied Supreme Council, the two disputants signed the Convention of Suvalki on October 7, 1920, which awarded Suvalki to Poland and Vilna to Lithuania. Unfortunately for the amity of the Baltic, on October 9 General Lucjan Zeligowski marched his Polish force into Vilna and seized it.[21] Lithuania, irreconcilable to the loss of her ancient capital, rejected all attempts at a Baltic alliance system which included Poland.

But the action by Zeligowski alarmed the Latvians as well. Latvian political and military leaders concluded that Poland might next raise claims to Kurzeme (Courland) and Latgale ("Polish Livonia").[22] Meierovics carefully warned Warsaw that Lithuanian independence was absolutely essential to Latvia's independence and security. If Poland threatened to destroy Lithuania's independence, then Latvia would help protect that country's sovereignty by all possible means.[23]

In seizing Vilna, Poland administered a *coup de grâce* to the treaty adopted at Bulduri. Suspicions of Poland drove the Latvian Constituent Assembly, especially the Social Democratic members, to bloc ratification of the treaty.[24] In fact, no state attending the Bulduri conference had ratified the document by December 15, the stipulated deadline. In the words of a Latvian foreign ministry official, the Bulduri treaty had "quite lost its significance."[25]

Thus in 1920 the five new states on the Baltic lost a golden opportunity to establish a common security arrangement. If

Polish action was mainly responsible for this eventuality, other factors nevertheless played a part. The Baltic states had all concluded peace treaties with the Soviet Russians, easing somewhat, as they believed, the immediate military danger. And, despite the proclaimed desire for close association, the relationships between the Baltic states were "in fact marked by jealousies, petty bickerings, and the almost deliberate placing of obstacles in the paths of their neighbors."[26] Under such circumstances, a political and military alliance could not be constructed.

Meierovics was not altogether displeased with the outcome of the Baltic conference at Bulduri. His ambivalent attitude toward an alliance system with Poland was revealed when, at the end of 1920, new Soviet threats appeared. Late in that year, the Soviet Russians, violating certain guarantees pledged in the Finnish-Soviet peace treaty, began a fierce institution of the Soviet system in Eastern Karelia. The Finnish and Estonian alarm thus produced was soon shared by Latvia.

During the month of December rumors flooded Riga about Soviet troop movements and preparations for a blow against Latvia. The correspondent of the *New York Times*, Walter Duranty, predicted that within three months all three Baltic states would be incorporated into the Soviet federation.[27] The German chargé in Riga melodramatically reported that "the strength of the people is shattered and the country lies before Bolshevism paralyzed as a rabbit before a snake."[28]

Despite the fears and rumors, however, Meierovics rejected a Polish suggestion for another conference to create a five-state alliance. Meierovics's position was a highly delicate one. He could not afford to alienate Poland if the threat from the east became directly serious. On the other hand, Soviet dangers had not quieted Meierovics's suspicions about Poland. He temporarily kept the Poles at bay by suggesting that the Bulduri treaty ought first to be ratified before a new conference was held. Then Meierovics sought an alliance with Estonia and Lithuania with a view to later *en bloc* negotiations with Poland.[29]

In pursuit of his program, Meierovics met Ants Piip of Estonia at Valka early in July, 1921, and worked out the framework of a political and military alliance. On July 7, the general staffs of the two countries signed a military convention. But at a conference of the foreign ministers of Latvia, Estonia, and Lithuania, held on July 12-13, in Riga, the Lithuanians insisted upon directing the proposed treaty against Poland rather than Soviet Russia. This was unacceptable to Meierovics as it was to the Estonians who had no desire to be dragged into Lithuania's quarrels. A triple alliance could not be achieved.[30]

Once again the Vilna controversy had barred the door to Baltic cooperation. But it must be pointed out that the Polish-Lithuanian conflict also provided Meierovics an excellent excuse for avoiding inconvenient military commitments to Poland. An occasion arose in July, 1921, to use the Vilna excuse. Meierovics, responding to French urgings and repeated Finnish invitations, along with Estonian and Polish representatives, went to Helsinki to consider a common response to the threat posed by Soviet action in Eastern Karelia.[31] Just before the conference opened on July 25, however, Moscow sent strong identical notes to Riga and Tallinn warning that an alliance between Latvia and Estonia on the one side with Finland or Poland on the other would be regarded as a *casus belli*.[32]

Soviet intimidation of the border states hung like a pall over the Helsinki conference. Meierovics dared not provoke a clash with the Russians. Instead, he virtually torpedoed the conference when he demanded Lithuania's inclusion in any alliance system. A number of secret deliberations could not come up with a formula for a military convention, although the conferees agreed to hold another meeting later in Warsaw.[33] Meierovics had postponed the problem.

Soviet belligerence did not mitigate during the interval between the Helsinki and Warsaw conferences. Meierovics was forced to pick his way carefully between Polish pressures and Muscovite dangers. The Karelian question once again in 1921-22 provided the Latvian foreign minister with his familiar dilemma.

In the fall of 1921 the Eastern Karelian Finns rose in a revolt against the Soviets and on November 20, 1921, proclaimed a non-Bolshevik government. When Latvia and Estonia supported Finland's transmission of an appeal by the new Karelian government to the League of Nations, the Soviets accused these countries of "entering the ranks of the hostile states in favor of attacking the R.S.F.S.R." Latvia was warned that involvement in

attacks on Soviet Russia could be "fatal."[34] The fate of the Eastern Karelians was sealed in February, 1922, at which point Poland
issued invitations to Latvia, Estonia, and Finland for a meeting
of foreign ministers in Warsaw to begin on March 13, 1922.

Meierovics was reluctant to join the conference without
Lithuania's presence, despite a French suggestion that he align
his policy with Warsaw.[35] He told the American envoy in Riga
that he was "frankly pessimistic" about the Warsaw meeting.
Before anything could be accomplished, the Vilna issue must
be settled. Meierovics stated emphatically that Latvia could not
undertake any military assistance to Poland "so long as the
present Polish-Russian frontier is maintained." In case of invasion a Latvian response could only be considered after the
Soviets had crossed the Curzon line.[36]

Yet, in public at least, the ambivalent Meierovics did an about
face when he arrived in Warsaw. Latvia, he told the Polish press,
had basically two policy choices. One was a "vertical orientation" putting Latvia in a common arrangement with Finland,
Estonia, Poland and Rumania. The second possibility was a
"horizontal orientation," a policy of rapprochement toward
Germany and Russia. "This latter does not conform to our
desires at all," Meierovics stated, "and, therefore, we are doing
everything . . . to create a lasting agreement with the four
states [at the conference]."[37]

He rejected a German-Russian orientation, he said, because
these two states were pursuing an anti-peace policy. To go along
with them, Meierovics maintained to the press, would "mean
hitching on to a war chariot."[38] While Meierovics was making
these remarks, doubtlessly well received by the Poles, he hinted to
Moscow that he would like an invitation to visit the Soviet leaders after the Warsaw meeting![39]

Moscow, however, turned a deaf ear to Meierovics's overtures
and made warlike noises. Just as the border states' diplomats
assembled in Warsaw, the Soviets announced "discovery" of a
plot between Poland and Roumania to attack Russia. Latvia and
Estonia were cautioned against supporting such schemes. During
the course of the conference, Moscow pointedly warned the

Baltic capitals that Soviet Russia would consider a military convention among them "an unfriendly act."[40]

Soviet threats served to reinforce Meierovics's reluctance to become involved in possible Polish-Russian disputes. Although accompanied, as were the other foreign ministers, by general staff personnel, no military convention was drawn up. Instead, the participants of the Warsaw conference signed a "Political Accord."

Under the terms of the accord, the signatories pledged a benevolent neutrality should any one of them come under attack and promised immediate consultation on common measures to meet the emergency. In addition, no signatory would conclude any treaty or agreement directed against any of the four members of the accord.[41] This weak instrument was properly named; it was simply an "accord" and not a political alliance. It barely went beyond a pledge of neutrality.

Meierovics found this modest agreement satisfactory. He had avoided offending the Soviet Russians yet had made a gesture toward border state cooperation. Even this arrangement encountered stiff opposition in Riga. Reports circulated in the Latvian capital that General Zeligowski of Vilna fame planned some kind of annexationist move in conjunction with the Polish minority in Latgale. The rumors, which may have been Soviet inspired, were well attuned to Latvian suspicions of Polish ambitions.[42]

In the Latvian Constituent Assembly, the Social Democrats, led by Felikss Cielēns, argued that while Poland's power was not great enough to protect Latvia, her ambitions could bring danger. Poland, Cielēns warned, coveted the role of a great power in Eastern Europe and her imperialism could lead to wars with Soviet Russia or Germany or both. Latvia, therefore, should abstain from any alliance with Poland.[43] Even some of Meierovics's own party members, averse to his "grand style" diplomacy, wanted to restrict his activities.[44] Nevertheless, Meierovics, persuasive when necessary, overcame the opposition, and obtained ratification of the Warsaw Accord.

Estonia also ratified the agreement but the Finnish parliament

rejected it.[45] Finland's rejection of the Accord marked the end
of her close association with the other Baltic states. The instrument, weak at best, was further reduced in its range. To be effective
all the Baltic powers including Lithuania should have been
involved in the agreement. The Political Accord of Warsaw provided only tenuous links among Latvia, Estonia, and Poland
and was therefore of little consequence.

Between 1920 and 1922 a Baltic or border states' alliance system,
despite profusive rhetoric, passed from the realm of probability
into the kingdom of chimeras. In the first place, Meierovics
held that the conclusion of peace with the Soviets rendered
superfluous such an alliance. Secondly, the Vilna controversy
aroused Latvian suspicion of Poland and made the achievement
of a league highly difficult at best. Finally, when the Soviets
made it painfully obvious that they would not tolerate a firm
political and military alliance system among the Baltic states
and Poland, Meierovics was forced upon a twisting and zigzag
course toward the goal of Latvian security. He could accommo-
date the Warsaw Accord to this policy but not anything firmer.

Meierovics scrupulously avoided giving Moscow any pretext
for taking offense, while through the Warsaw Accord he preserved a vague link to Warsaw. This loose association of Latvia
with Poland and Estonia barely kept alive the possibility to
adding military flesh to the chimera that was the Warsaw Accord.
Yet the Latvian foreign minister could enjoy only momentary
respites in his tortuous diplomatic struggles. Like a desperate
swimmer moving through a stretch of rough water he surmounted
one wave only to encounter another. The year 1922 was not
merely the date of the Warsaw Accord; it was above all the year
of Rapallo.

3

The Collapse of the Baltic League Idea, 1922-1925

Meierovics's frenetic circumspection at Warsaw did not lull the suspicions of Moscow. The Soviets condemned the Warsaw Accord as part of a French plot to surround Russia with military alliances. Chicherin, passing through Riga on his way to the European Economic Conference at Genoa (April 10-May 19, 1922), demanded—and got—a meeting with representatives of Latvia, Estonia, Finland, and Poland.[1] Chicherin wished, in the words of a Soviet historian, "to split up the unified front of the Baltic states and to blunt the anti-Soviet point of the Warsaw Accord."[2]

The Soviet commissar's task was facilitated by the fact that the new border states, no less than Soviet Russia, opposed French and British efforts to saddle them with portions of the Tsarist debt. Meierovics and the other representatives agreed to follow a common line on this question at Genoa and further committed themselves to support a Soviet arms limitation proposal.[3] Chicherin thus scored a minor coup. In Germany the Riga conversations were hailed as a "foil to the plans for a Baltic League under Polish leadership."[4]

Shortly after the encounter with Chicherin, Meierovics and his staff traveled to Genoa, or, more precisely, to their lodgings in Rapallo. Meierovics hoped that, along with releasing Latvia from any obligation to the Tsarist debt, the Conference powers would grant *de jure* recognition to the Soviet boundaries and issue a declaration regarding the independence of the small border states. The Latvians at the least expected to share in the proposed economic reconstruction of Europe and saw an important role for themselves should normal trade relations be resumed between Western Europe and Russia.[5] These hopes were to be cruelly disappointed.

The Genoa Conference was stripped of its potential significance, when, on Easter Sunday, April 16, 1922, Germany and Soviet Russia astounded the world by signing a treaty at Rapallo. Meierovics immediately grasped the implications of the Rapallo agreement. He feared the new partners would stifle Latvia economically by excluding her from the prospective Russian trade and, in a despairing mood, he even suspected indirect German support for a future Russian expansionist policy.[6] Maneuvering to counter such effects, Meierovics immediately joined the Estonian and Lithuanian foreign ministers in "confidentially" offering their services as friendly intermediaries in economic matters between Germany and Russia.[7] The Germans somewhat smugly concluded that the Warsaw Accord was now completely illusory and that the Baltic states found it necessary to be a "completely open and honest bridge between Germany and Russia."[8]

Meierovics's anxieties were reinforced in June when he talked with the German foreign minister, Walter Rathenau, in Berlin. Rathenau stressed that Germany, stripped of her colonies, had only one avenue for expansion and it led eastward; "We have no other opportunity," he told the Latvian diplomat.[9] A German thrust to the East, in an economic sense, came into view. Clearly the Rapallo treaty, by facilitating German-Russian relations, constituted a potential danger for Latvia and the other Baltic states.

The Rapallo treaty led Meierovics to embrace unambiguously a Baltic League. "The Treaty of Rapallo clearly demonstrated the necessity of the Warsaw political accord," Meierovics wrote in May.[10] The Baltic states and Poland must play the role of barrier, not bridge, between Germany and Russia if these two countries tried to form a political and military alliance. "We have to create a counterweight and for this reason a Baltic League (*Staatenbund*) is necessary." Creating that league was, in Meierovics's opinion, the primary task of the Latvian government.[11]

The Latvian press resounded with calls for alliances. Even

the German language *Rigasche Nachrichten* of December 29, 1922, demanded a defensive Baltic Union: "The organization of resistance against the latent aggressive imperialism of Russia . . . and the creation of a united economic front of the Baltic states ought to be the task of the hour."[12] But if Rapallo made clear the need for a regional alliance system, the prospect for its realization was dim.

Curiously enough, a Soviet invitation to a disarmament conference provided the Baltic and border states with yet another testing of their desire to collaborate jointly in security matters. In June, 1922, Litvinov sent identical letters to the governments of Poland, Latvia, Estonia, and Finland (the Warsaw accord states), and subsequently to Roumania and Lithuania, proposing the conference for December.[13] Litvinov suggested that the conference take up such matters as the establishment of a demilitarized zone and a mutal reduction in armed forces. Latvia and the other states could not ignore a matter so vital to their security; the problem was how to coordinate a common approach.

At a series of preliminary conferences it became clear that the Baltic states, Poland, and, when she joined them, Roumania, could not agree on specific responses. For example, the Kremlin's proposal for a demilitarized zone along the frontier with Soviet Russia was agreeable to Latvia, Estonia, and Finland, but not to Poland and Roumania. Poland's eastern regions contained large numbers of non-Poles who might threaten the integrity of the Polish state if military forces were withdrawn. Roumania had the Bessarabian problem and could not reduce her frontier forces.[14]

While all the conferees agreed in principle to render mutual assistance to a victim of aggression, they could not agree on the method. Poland suggested that in case of a Soviet attack, all the armies come under Polish command. Latvia reluctantly accepted this proposal, Finland rejected it, while Estonia reserved her decision.[15] Poland and Roumania already had treaties providing for mutual aid. Thus willingness to extend military aid varied directly with the distance of the perceived threat. Finland and the Baltic states obviously did not wish to be drawn into a conflict over the eastern regions of Poland and Roumania.

The Baltic states and Poland finally did agree to present the Soviets with a common counterproposal: a mutual defense, nonaggression, and arbitration pact was to be adopted before considering any reduction of armaments and the drawing of a demilitarized zone.[16] But taking a familiar position at the Moscow Disarmament Conference, the Soviets insisted upon disarmament *before* undertaking political agreements. Thus the conference was a complete failure.[17] Yet just this brief show of unity convinced one observer that a "League of the Border States" was a possibility.[18]

But none of the obstacles with which Meierovics had wrestled in the preceding months had changed—at least not for the better. Moscow's hostility toward any combination of border states was now echoed by Germany. Poland's ill-expressed ambition to lead the smaller Baltic countries still alarmed more than it assured the Latvians. The vagueness of any Western interest had not clarified during or immediately after the Genoa conference. These circumstances had frustrated bloc building before and nothing indicated the rapid formation of any "Baltic League."

Indeed, such a dispiriting reading of Latvia's foreign political situation was obtained in August, 1922, when Meierovics held a general stock-taking at the Latvian foreign ministry. The Latvian diplomats reached five conclusions: (1) the Scandinavian states were definitely not interested in a political or military alliance with the Baltic states; (2) Finland was increasingly oriented toward the Scandinavian countries and would probably never ratify agreements such as the Warsaw Accord of 1922; (3) the Rapallo Treaty between Germany and Soviet Russia indicated the possibility of their cooperation against the interests of Latvia and the Baltic states; (4) Polish imperialism and Lithuanian romanticism over Vilna prevented any general Baltic alliance system; (5) under existing circumstances only a Latvian-Estonian arrangement was possible.[19] Events over the next ten years confirmed this sober assessment.

But achievement of even the most limited agreement with Estonia alone proved difficult, and a desultory round of talks in the spring and summer of 1923, which included Lithuania, reached no conclusions whatsoever.[20] At the end of July

Meierovics limply admitted that Baltic political and economic cooperation had not reached a state where positive results could be expected.[21]

Gradually, the sense of urgency produced by the Rapallo treaty faded and the quest for a strong Baltic alliance slowed down. The sluggish pace of diplomacy was partly due to the exigencies of Latvian domestic politics. The first Saeima (parliament), elected the previous autumn, contained deputies from twenty-two different parties and neither the Social Democrats nor Meierovics's Farmers' Union could organize a cabinet.[22] Meierovics retained his portfolio in the "impartial" cabinet formed in January, 1923, but shared responsibility with a vice-minister, the Social Democrat, Felikss Cielēns.[23]

Cielēns, the most important figure on the Latvian left, and a formidable member of all the Saeimas from 1922 to 1933, was usually chairman of the foreign affairs commission. He had quite definite foreign policy views. Cielēns had already denounced the "Warsaw conference policy" of 1922. It was a "complete fiasco" he charged, and Meierovics, under the "hypnotic impress" of that agreement, had become "the psychological vassal of Poland." A broad alliance system including Poland and directed against Russia was, in his opinion, both impractical and dangerous.[24] Cielēns labored to give Latvia a new foreign policy orientation: "The nucleus of such a new orientation would be an equally good relationship with Germany and Russia."[25]

It was not Cielēns's exertions, however, but the pressure of events far beyond Latvia's influence that first revived the search for a security system and then destroyed the chances of achieving it. Germany and Soviet Russia provided both the stimulus and the depressant.

Unrest in Germany following the French occupation of the Ruhr reached a climax on October 23, 1923, with the communist rising in Hamburg. Soviet Russian agencies eagerly called for the overthrow of bourgeois institutions in Germany and for the establishment of a communist regime.[26] At the same time Soviet troops massed along the eastern frontiers of Poland and the Baltic states. The press organ of Meierovics's party, *Brīvā Zeme*, speculated that the Soviets wanted to "neutralize" the border states in order to have a free hand to "help the revolutionary class in Germany."[27] Would the Soviets demand unrestricted passage to Germany? And what effect would this have on Baltic independence and sovereignty?

Victor Kopp, former Soviet representative in Berlin and now policy director for border states' affairs in the foreign commissariat, arrived in Riga the week of the Hamburg rising. Kopp asked Meierovics directly whether Latvia would permit unhindered transit for Russia in case of "war developments" and whether Latvia would preserve its neutrality regardless of domestic events in Germany.[28] Soviet Russia, according to Kopp, had no desire to attack the Baltic states but would be forced to take action if these countries tried to keep socialist Russia and "socialist" Germany apart.[29]

Kopp's brutal demands and his threat of direct Soviet action sent an aroused Meierovics to Tallinn where he found the Estonians also ready to act. Under the weight of Soviet pressure, Meierovics and Friedrich Akel of Estonia concluded six agreements, the most important of which was a Treaty of Defensive Alliance, signed on November 1, 1923.

The treaty provided that if one of the signatories suffered an unprovoked attack the other would consider itself in a state of war and would furnish armed assistance. In such a case, neither party would conclude separate treaties or armistices. The signatories also agreed not to conclude an alliance with a third power without the consent of the other. The treaty was to be in force for ten years from the date of the exchange of ratification instruments (February 24, 1924).[30]

The alliance aimed at preserving the two Baltic lambs from the Soviet wolf. It was potentially, at least, a nucleus for a larger border-state combination. Along with a preliminary customs union agreement, it represented a step toward the gradual economic and political unification of Estonia and Latvia. To be sure, the military forces at the disposal of the Latvian and Estonian republics were not impressive. (Together the two countries had armies totaling 40,000 men. They were supported by 250 artillery pieces, 18 tanks, 91 airplanes with 747 airmen, and a naval force of 14 warships and 1280 men.)[31] However, in view of the determined fighting qualities of the two peoples, such forces were not altogether negligible, provided they had foreign support.

Meierovics urgently sought the backing of the anti-Bolshevik western powers. Indeed at the time of Rapallo he had appealed for general European collaboration to prevent a Russian-German combination. He now pressed the British to demand the withdrawal of Soviet troops from Latvia's frontiers and asked for a clarification of the British position should the Soviets actually attack the Baltic states.[32]

He put similar questions to France. But to these desperately crucial questions, the replies of the western powers were disappointingly evasive. The British and French stressed their lack of alliance obligations to Latvia and Estonia. Only if the League of Nations should take action could Britain and France offer assistance. France strongly urged an alliance with Poland as a safety measure.[33] In short, the Baltic states were on their own. The western powers no longer had any real interest in an anti-Bolshevik beachhead on the Baltic, and would not support, at least not directly, any collective security measures in that area.

As the diplomatic withdrawal of the western powers from the Baltic became known, Latvia and Estonia found their audacious treaty exposed to a characteristic Soviet reaction. Chicherin blandly warned in a press statement:

> These attempts to form combinations of border states will never solve the problem of their healthy development, which can come about only through friendly economic and political agreement with Russia, of course with complete preservation of their own independence.[34]

To prevent any further consolidation of the Baltic states, Moscow offered nonaggression pacts to each of them separately. The offer contained a number of pitfalls the wary Latvians readily recognized (there was no provision for compulsory arbitration of disputes, for instance). When Riga insisted on the arbitration clause the Soviets "temporarily" broke off the negotiations.[35] But the Kremlin, as we shall see, returned repeatedly in the course of the decade to this kind of proposition; it was an excellent way to divide the border states by separately committing them to pacts of neutrality.

"Bourgeois" Germany, the object of the Third International's wrath, shared the Soviet hostility to any common Baltic security system. In November, 1923, Germany's Baltic envoys concluded that Berlin had no further interest in supporting the Baltic states as dams against Bolshevik Russia. Her major concern must be the prevention of an alliance which assembled the Baltic states under Polish leadership. Germany must on no account allow herself to become involved by the Baltic states in any kind of differences with Russia while "welcoming any conflict between Russia and Poland."[36]

Germany's minister in Riga, the very able Dr. Adolf Koester, strongly emphasized that, on the matter of keeping the Baltic states separated from Poland, "German and Russian interest coincide completely." A Baltic-Polish alliance could be expected to come under French direction and would constitute a threat to both Russia and Germany.[37] Thus, although one of the Rapallo partners sought to foment revolution in the other, a common line of action could nevertheless be pursued in the Baltic area. Riga got the same message from both Moscow and Berlin: stay clear of Warsaw.

Such pressures reduced the possibility of expanding the Latvian-Estonian treaty into a large Baltic security system. The chances narrowed further when Lithuania added to her diplomatic liabilities by occupying the Memel territory in 1923.[38] This action involved the Lithuanians in numerous disputes with Germany, with whom Riga and Tallinn had no serious quarrels, and the latter capitals did not respond to Lithuania's overtures for inclusion in the Latvian-Estonian alliance.[39]

As for Poland, her diplomatic and territorial ambitions merely furthered the German-Soviet policy of keeping the border states apart. Poland's real intentions were probably more modest than suggested by the tactless language of her diplomats, but it was overt behavior rather than intentions with which contemporaries had to deal.

In March, 1923, the Poles raised Latvian tempers by advancing claims to six Latvian villages in the Illūkste district below Daugavpils (Dünaburg, Dvinsk).[40] Polish military circles made no secret of their desire to obtain Daugavpils itself, an important river city and railroad junction, while Polish ambitions regarding Liepāja and Latgale were old stories in Riga.[41] Consequently, Warsaw's overtures, with French support, about expanding the

Latvian-Estonian treaty did not automatically generate enthusiasm in the Latvian cabinet.

But the Polish minister in Riga initiated a campaign in the press and among pro-Polish politicians for a conference of Finland, Estonia, Latvia, and Poland to work out a Baltic League.[42] Unmoved by this barrage, Meierovics told the Saeima that if such an alliance were actually proposed by Warsaw, Latvia must reject it. His attitude deeply annoyed Polish and French circles in Riga.[43]

Yet the Latvian foreign minister was only being realistic. Meierovics was already in 1923 at the crux of the frustrating Baltic security problem: German-Soviet cooperation, Polish high-handedness, and western indifference. To pursue a Baltic security alliance in the face of Russian and German opposition and without western backing would verge on the suicidal.

Could Meierovics salvage anything from the specific complexities of 1923? On the one hand there was heavy Soviet pressure for a nonaggression and neutrality pact.[44] Then came Lithuania's request for inclusion in the Latvian-Estonian defense treaty followed rapidly by Poland's demand for the construction of a broad alliance system under her aegis. Meierovics, fully aware of the Russian attitude toward such plans, resolved upon a decisive stroke. He proposed a meeting in Riga of representatives of the Baltic states, Poland, and Soviet Russia to work out a "common platform" of peace and security for the Baltic area.[45] The conflicting proposals and demands might thus be resolved.

The Soviet Russians would rarely agree to negotiate *en bloc* with the border states, but Moscow, willing to undercut Polish ambitions, accepted Meierovics's invitation. Lithuania also announced willingness to attend. But Poland, furious at Meierovics for making overtures to Russia without Warsaw's prior approval, rejected his invitation. Then Tallinn notified the Latvian foreign minister that Estonia could not participate in a conference with the Soviets unless Poland attended as the three Baltic states alone were too weak to deal with Russia.

The Polish and Estonian rejections effectively sabotaged Meierovics's proposed conference and his hoped-for "common platform of peace." The failure of the conference together with Poland's skillful intrigue among pro-Polish politicians in Riga destroyed Meierovics's slender majority in the Saeima and forced the resignation in mid-January, 1924, of his cabinet.[46] Soviet diplomatic pressure and Polish arrogance triumphed over the Latvian foreign minister.

The double blow was a bitter personal loss to Meierovics, who refused to participate in the negotiations for a new cabinet and for the first time since the Republic's founding was not its foreign minister. The treatment he had received at Poland's hands soured Meierovics completely on Warsaw. He spoke about Poland to the German minister in terms "which would have been unthinkable a few months ago."[47]

The coolness between Riga and Warsaw did not improve while Meierovics was out of office and Ludvigs Sēja was foreign minister.[48] Sēja met with representatives of Finland, Estonia, and Poland in Warsaw in February, 1924, to consider a common arbitration treaty, but when the Poles tried to turn the conversations toward a Baltic defensive alliance, Sēja, as firmly as Meierovics, rejected the idea.[49] The conferees did agree to meet again in Helsinki to discuss further the proposed arbitration convention but the Finns put off holding the conference until January, 1925. Except in Tallinn, the Poles had not improved their position with the other Baltic states.

Latvian reserve toward Poland increased as the diplomatic position of the Western powers fully revealed itself. On February 1, 1924, Great Britain recognized the Soviet regime as the "*de jure* rulers of those territories of the old Russian Empire which acknowledge their authority."[50] The rather elastic language of the formula aroused some concern in the Latvian foreign ministry. Then came French *de jure* recognition of Soviet Russia on October 28, 1924. The action of Paris particularly "made a strong impression on all political circles in Latvia." *Brīvā Zeme*, organ of the Farmers' Union, expected the Soviets would try to disinterest France in the fate of the Baltic states.[51]

Recognition of the Soviet regime certainly underscored the western powers' lessened interest in and support of the border states including Poland. Meierovics reached this conclusion after a private visit to the British Foreign Office in July, 1924. Under-Secretary Arthur Ponsonby told Meierovics that the Soviet-Polish boundary was just as insupportable as the Polish-German frontier. In both instances "natural necessity" would force an alteration. Ponsonby then warned Meierovics against adhering to a Polish or Franco-Polish alliance. Still, Ponsonby hinted that British naval support would be furnished to Latvia in the event of a Soviet attack.[52] As it turned out the hint of support was merely bait designed to lure the Baltic fish away from the French angler.

But the French were apparently looking for bigger fish. Early in January, 1925, the new French envoy to Moscow, Jean Herbette, passed through Riga on his way to the Soviet capital. Meierovics asked Herbette what France might do in case of hostilities between Latvia and Russia. Herbette indicated that only "moral support" would be forthcoming. When Meierovics asked whether it was true that France did not guarantee the existing *eastern* frontiers of Poland, Herbette answered affirmatively; Poland's eastern border might be revised.[53]

These expressions by the French diplomat strongly influenced Meierovics's position respecting Poland. He clearly understood that if Poland got into difficulty with Russia over her frontiers, western aid was not guaranteed. Since Poland in this instance was just as isolated from the western powers as the Baltic states, the dangers resulting from a Polish alliance outweighed the advantages.

A dramatic exposé of the new attitudes of the powers was provided by the attempted communist *coup d'état* in Tallinn on December 1, 1924. Communist propaganda and subversive activities in the Baltic states were conducted on a large scale in the 1920s. The American legation in Riga had "complete and ample evidence" that Soviet diplomatic, consular, and trade mission personnel in Latvia and Estonia worked to overthrow these governments and establish communist regimes.[54]

Agitation became so blatant in Tallinn that authorities there arrested 149 individuals in November, 1924, for preparing an armed uprising. When the leader of this group was executed, the local Soviet Legation protested energetically. On December 1, 1924, probably with the assistance of special Soviet agents, the communists attempted to seize power. Several government buildings were occupied and the minister of transport shot. The Estonian army reacted swiftly and forcefully; General Johann

Laidoner suppressed the insurgents, arrested some three hundred, and instituted military tribunals which rapidly approved thirty executions.[55] But the attempted coup frightened the Estonians into ardently championing a Baltic alliance with Poland.

Also alarmed by developments in Tallinn, the Latvian foreign minister anxiously put the familiar question to the American, British, French, and Italian envoys in Riga: could Latvia expect help from their governments in case a similar communist attempt were made in Latvia? The powers supplied the usual answer which contained the familiar phrase, "moral solidarity." The British did not, as requested, send a fleet to the Baltic as a demonstration of support to the Latvian and Estonian republics. Since London would not make even this gesture, the other governments of Western Europe felt no obligation.[56]

At this moment of fearful isolation, a cabinet crisis in Riga brought the Farmers' Union back into power and once more installed Meierovics in the foreign ministry. Latvian military and conservative circles strongly favored the idea of a Polish alliance, but, as we have seen, Meierovics had not warmed toward Poland during his absence from the foreign ministry.[57] The crucial matter was western support; without it a Polish alliance was too dangerous for Latvia.

Poland nevertheless thought the time ripe for achieving her old dream of a Polish-led Baltic collective security pact. Her foreign minister, Count Alexander Skrzynski, proposed formal negotiations for such an alliance at the forthcoming Helsinki conference, now finally scheduled for mid-January, 1925. Warmly endorsing this idea, Estonia's foreign minister, Kaarel R. Pusta, came to Riga early in January in an attempt to convert Meierovics. The Latvian diplomat, however, threw cold water on Pusta's efforts. Meirovics admitted to "misgivings and a dread of Polish hegemony"; his government "categorically opposed such an alliance."[58]

In any event, the importunings of Poland and Estonia were nullified by a merciless pressure upon Meierovics from Moscow, a pressure which steadily mounted during December, 1924, and January, 1925. Chicherin noted that France was encouraging the Baltic states to seek security with Poland, but he warned these countries against participation in plans to "encircle" the Soviet

State. "We know that the most far-sighted Baltic politicians rightly regard this as a dangerous game," he ominously concluded.[59] Early in January the Soviet envoy in Riga stated in no uncertain terms that a military agreement between Latvia and Poland would be understood in Moscow as a hostile act.[60]

In the face of such pressure and in the absence of British or French support, Meierovics capitulated. On January 7 Meierovics told the Soviet envoy, Semen Ivanovich Aralov, that he realized a Polish alliance would "make an unfavorable impression and would significantly complicate our mutual relations. The same alliance [he continued] would also complicate relations even with Germany, and the German government is viewing the news of this alliance with extreme concern."[61] Without Western backing, the Latvian diplomat could not risk offending his powerful neighbors.

Meierovics thus continued his resistance to Estonian and Polish efforts for Baltic alliance negotiations at the Helsinki conference. When Count Skrzynski called in Riga on his way to the Helsinki meeting, Meierovics rushed the Polish foreign minister through a round of receptions and dinners and gave him no time for detailed diplomatic talks. The Latvian minister did not call on Pusta in Tallinn while himself en route to Helsinki.[62] Nor did the Finns evince any enthusiasm for an alliance with the more southerly Baltic states. The Finnish press greeted the arriving diplomats warmly but almost unanimously rejected the idea of Finnish participation in an alliance system.[63]

Thus the prospect of a general Baltic security system was dead even before the Helsinki conference opened; the subject of an alliance was not placed on the official agenda of the conference. An arbitration convention and few minor consular agreements closed out the conference, the final protocol of which glittered with the usual generalities which signified, as usual, nothing.[64]

The Baltic League idea provided Meierovics with no effective means for coping with the nettlesome dangers in which Latvia and her Baltic neighbors existed. These dangers increased in the period just surveyed: the fact of German-Soviet cooperation signified by the Rapallo treaty of 1922; the brutal Soviet demands in the fall of 1923; and, the electrifying threat of the communist coup at Tallinn in December, 1924. British and French recognition of the Soviet government in 1924 with its implication of western withdrawal from the Baltic added to the dangers. Complicating the picture was a nervous Polish ambition to lead the Baltic states, an ambition which expressed itself in flamboyant statements, extravagant territorial aims, and in destructive jealousy of the Latvian foreign minister.

As the inexorable pressure from Moscow increased; as the concern of the western powers declined; and as Poland's own isolation became apparent, Meierovics gave up completely the idea of a Baltic security arrangement including Poland. The danger of the Polish connection outweighed any advantages. The ghost of the "Baltic League" vanished at the Helsinki conference in 1925. The few threads of its shroud which remained would occasionally tempt Baltic diplomats into restoration projects but these would prove just as vain as the original efforts. The problem of Baltic security remained to be solved.

4

In Pursuit of the Great Powers:
Meierovics's Gamble

Following the utter collapse of the Baltic bloc concept, what options for Latvian security remained? One foreign ministry spokesman expressed the Latvian quandry to the American minister in Riga by saying: "We can either orient our policy with that of Poland and the Entente, or else—but we do not quite know with what."[1]

Latvia's experiences over the past two years, however, indicated that the Entente powers, especially Britain, were little concerned with the security problems of Poland and the Baltic states. British press articles pointing to the "absurdity" of Poland's frontiers could only have confirmed this conclusion. One such article went so far as to suggest the return of Polish provinces east of Brest to Russia. The Latvian newspaper which picked up this British article warned that "the process of restitution may be carried even further and at the expense of the Baltic states."[2]

Germany and Russia, not Poland, were now the recipients of British interest. Gustav Stresemann was struck by Britain's indifference to Polish frontier problems and in April, 1925, the German foreign minister concluded:

> Poland finds herself in the same position towards Germany as she is towards Russia, because Russia also does not recognize her frontiers with Poland. Affairs in the East are by no means settled. As soon as Russia decides whether she is prepared to remain permanently within these frontiers or not,

and when she raises the question of Poland and the Baltic states, then a new era will open up in European history.[3]

Thus Poland could offer no real protection to the Baltic states. Meierovics was *realpolitisch* enough to understand that Latvia's welfare required a certain coolness toward Warsaw. By 1925 the Latvian foreign minister was prepared to give proof of his independence of Warsaw.[4] Meierovics looked to the only power capable of counter-balancing the Soviet weight—Germany. Could Riga associate her security interests with one or both of the Rapallo partners now being courted by Britain? Meierovics concluded that Latvia's only hope for long term security lay in reaching some understanding with her giant neighbors.

The maximum for which Latvia could hope was a joint Soviet-German guarantee of her independence and territorial integrity. This objective was enticing but improbable, for the real question was how far it was in Russia's and Germany's interests to offer such assurances. The only way to attract the favorable attention of either power was to play upon their resentment of Poland.

In late March, 1925, Meierovics waved the Polish flag before the Teutonic bull in the course of a long conversation with the German minister in Riga, Dr. Adolf Koester. The Latvian remarked upon the apparent formation of blocs of states in Europe: there was a western bloc made up of England, France, Belgium, and Germany; a southeastern bloc composed of France, Poland, and the little Entente; and the French aimed at establishing yet a third or northeastern group composed of Poland, Latvia, Estonia, and later, Lithuania. Eventually, Meierovics hinted, Latvia would have to link up with one or another of these power combinations. Since a direct connection with the "western bloc" was, in the light of recent events, obviously out of the question, there remained only the French-sponsored Polish arrangement. After stressing his desire for a connection which involved Germany and England, Meierovics requested Koester's views.[5]

The suggestion of Latvia's association with Poland immediately aroused the German minister who still believed that a Polish-led alliance system was a serious possibility. In his subsequent report to Berlin Koester noted that ever since French recognition of Soviet Russia in October, 1924, and particularly since the west pact talks (which would lead to the Locarno agreements) had begun, Polish activity in the border states had increased. As the general aim of German policy in the Baltic, therefore, Koester advised "as soon as possible. . .guarantee treaties between the three northern border states and Germany on the one side and these states and Russia on the other side."[6] Koester mentioned as much to Meierovics who must have been delighted for he embraced the idea of a German-Russian guarantee as his own.[7]

The *Wilhelmstrasse*, however, was not as easily seduced as its representative in Riga. Berlin agreed that prevention of an alliance of states from Riga to Bucharest was of the highest importance since, under Polish leadership, such a bloc would create an additional military threat to Germany's eastern frontier and, as head of such an alliance, Poland might enhance her position in the League of Nations and create difficulties about Germany's entrance to that body. But, it was "questionable how far Germany's interests require the stabilization of the border states as long as the Polish Corridor question is unsolved."[8] Also the Memel issue would make a guarantee formula difficult, if not impossible, to find.[9]

As a consequence of the foregoing considerations, Stresemann's reaction to Riga was one of cool reserve. Berlin instructed Koester to tell Meierovics "unofficially" that Germany was interested in his ideas and that Berlin welcomed Latvia's favorable disposition toward Germany. But Germany could not participate in any general security arrangements in Eastern Europe. On the other hand, Germany would welcome any agreement between Latvia and Russia as a contribution to the peace of Eastern Europe. Berlin strongly advised against any Polish ties. "In the view of the German government, Latvia's interests—considered over the long run—lie in the direction of agreement (*Verständigung*) with her two great neighbors."[10]

Obtaining an honest understanding with Soviet Russia was, of course, the *summum bonum* toward which Latvia pressed. And here, the Germans were prepared to be helpful since a Russo-Latvian understanding would help isolate Poland. When the Latvian minister in Berlin, Oskars Voits, complained to State Secretary von Schubert that Latvia always felt threatened by Soviet Russia, Schubert revealed "in strictest secrecy" that Germany was "prepared to influence the Russians *(auf die Russen einzuwirken)* into giving definite guarantees to the border states, especially Latvia concerning their independence." Schubert indicated that the German ambassador in Moscow, Count Brockdorff-Rantzau, was already instructed to work to this end. The astonished Voits received this information with visible satisfaction; he asked for and got permission to inform his government.[11]

After receiving such encouraging nudges from Berlin, Meierovics in the early summer of 1925, sought to coordinate an approach of the three Baltic states to Russia and Germany. But when the Lithuanian foreign minister agreed to receive his Latvian and Estonian counter-parts in Kaunas in June, the Polish minister in Riga put heavy pressure on Meierovics to cancel the meeting. Polish pressure on Tallin was more successful. When Kaarel R. Pusta made "great difficulties" about attending a three-state conference, Meierovics went ahead with Lithuania alone.[12]

His meeting with Lithuanian officials in Kaunas produced very little. The two foreign ministers signed a protocol calling for conclusion of an arbitration convention, various economic agreements and for a conference of the three Baltic foreign ministers. This protocol was, in the words of an American observer, not a treaty, but "an agreement to agree—a form of diplomatic instrument which perhaps has a certain future in the Baltic."[13] Upon publication of this innocuous document, a "not very friendly exchange took place between Meierovics and the Polish minister in Riga"[14] Meierovics had demonstrated to Berlin and Moscow his independence of Warsaw but had at the same time angered Estonia. This latter circumstance prevented any common Baltic approach to Russia and Germany not to speak of a Baltic triple alliance.

The Latvian foreign minister found his task rendered more complex by the diplomatic world's preoccupation with the western guarantee (Locarno) pact negotiations then in progress. Meierovics, disturbed by the rumored omission of eastern European boundaries from the proposed pact, decided upon a personal visit to the major European capitals. He would take soundings generally on the powers' attitudes toward Baltic security and economic problems.[15]

Meierovics arrived in Berlin at the beginning of July, 1925, for

discussions with State Secretary von Schubert. The two men rang-
ed over general European issues, including the Locarno negotiations. Schubert emphasized that Poland's frontiers were not involved in the current pact talks. Meierovics, as if on cue, then
raised the question of a guarantee of Latvian and Estonian independence. Playing his only card, Meierovics "repeated several
times that Latvia had great apprehension about joining Poland
and France. . . . It seemed to him that an arrangement of the
border states with their great neighbors would be a good basis for
a guarantee."[16] Schubert, welcoming this opportunity to reinforce Meierovics's anti-Polish tendency, once more stressed that
Germany would use her influence upon Russia for definite guarantees for the Baltic states.

As if to underscore the German interest in Latvia, Schubert
arranged an interview for Meierovics with Stresemann and Reich
President von Hindenburg. Meierovics, whom the Germans considered "at least as vain as any of the foreign ministers of the new
Liliputstaaten," was highly impressed by the red carpet treatment.[17] The cordiality of his reception in Berlin and the
Wilhelmstrasse's definite intimation that it would be of service in
Moscow worked powerfully on the Latvian foreign minister. In
a burst of extravagant optimism, Meierovics told the German press
that relations with Russia had improved so much that a widen-
ing of the Latvian-Estonian defensive alliance was unnecessary
in the immediate future[18]

In this frame of mind Meierovics arrived in London. The
British assured the Latvian foreign minister of their continued
favorable view of a triple entente of Latvia, Estonia, and Lithuania. Indeed, some members of Parliament still urged the importance
of the independent Baltic states to Great Britain from an economic
point of view and also as a barrier to "the damnable communism
of Russia."[19] But while the Foreign Office wanted to curb
Franco-Polish ambitions in Eastern Europe, it would not underwrite a guarantee of the three Baltic states. Generally, Meierovics
was impressed with the growing British aversion toward conti-
nental commitments.[20] Neither did Meierovics find sympathy in
Paris for a policy of Latvian cooperation with Germany and Soviet Russia; instead, Aristide Briand urged closer relations with Poland.[21]

Before returning to Riga, Meierovics visited Rome, Prague, and Warsaw, and information which the Latvian minister obtained in these capitals made a close connection with Poland seem less attractive than ever. Mussolini informed Meierovics that he had offered to mediate the smoldering Soviet-Roumanian dispute over Bessarabia. But Roumania had resisted the settlement proposed by the Duce. Consequently, the Italian dictator expected a conflict between Roumania and the Soviets. The "impossible Bessarabian problem" was also a topic of conversation between Meierovics and Czech officials in Prague.[22]

The possibility of a Roumanian-Soviet conflict disturbed Meierovics; it could easily affect the Baltic as Poland was allied to Roumania. When Meierovics stopped off in Warsaw, he tried to obtain clear information on the Polish position. But the Poles tactlessly renewed pressure upon him for a Latvian commitment to Poland. Moscow, the Poles alleged, wanted an agreement with Warsaw. The northern border states must decide whether to conclude an agreement connecting them closely to Poland and confirming Poland in her anti-Soviet stance or "be prepared to accept the consequences of a Russo-Polish deal (*Ausgleich*)."[23] Meierovics rejected this rather crass attempt at blackmail.

Meierovics's *tour d'horizon* excited a Soviet press campaign of typical vituperation. He was accused of planning with British support a Baltic bloc as part of an anti-Soviet front; he was called an agent of Britain's interest in the Baltic. *Pravda* screeched that it was "fed up with the intrigues of the lackeys of the English and French bourgeoisie" and that the Soviets would deal with them accordingly.[24] The Soviet Union also angrily charged Estonia with negotiating the leasing of certain islands in the Gulf of Riga to the British navy.[25]

Action did not lag behind words. The Soviets dispatched a squadron of two battleships and six cruisers to drop anchor off the Danish island of Langeland at the south entrance to the Great and Little Belts. This "totally unheralded appearance" of a Soviet naval force at the southern entrance to the Baltic Sea created a deep impression on all Baltic countries. A Hamburg newspaper concluded: "The Russian fleet is therefore the most important factor in Baltic sea power today." According to press reports, six new cruisers, twelve destroyers, and eight submarines were in course of completion at Kronstadt in the summer of 1925.[26]

These heavy-handed threats and the naval demonstration under-scored once more the terrible isolation of the Baltic countries. Meierovics vainly denied any ambition to join an anti-Soviet coalition. Of course, as we know, he spoke the truth; there was no such coalition to join. None of the western powers seriously thought any longer about isolating the Soviet Union. No western power had given Latvia any commitment respecting her "security against an eventually aggressive Russia."[27] London had limited itself to a vague approval of the formation of a Baltic alliance; Paris had contented itself with its usual advice respecting Warsaw; Poland's ties with Roumania rendered her increasingly unattractive as a military ally.

In such circumstances, a German offer to facilitate Latvia's obtaining an understanding with Russia was highly welcome. It was admittedly a straw which the Germans extended to the drowning Latvians but no other great power would do as much. Meierovics asserted that a "kind of collaboration between German and Latvian interests" had developed.[28] His party press began to speak of Germany in friendly terms and to call for good relations with both Germany and Russia.[29]

In the relations of small states to great powers the only hope of the weaker is that one of the stronger will become its supporter. Meierovics was simply drawing the logical consequences of Latvia's situation *vis à vis* Germany and the Soviet Union. He may have erred by reading too much into Berlin's hints; he may have been overconfident of his ability to avoid becoming Berlin's catspaw in eastern Europe. But Meierovics thought the gamble worth taking. He therefore dramatically reversed the older Baltic bloc policy which had led to the 1922 Warsaw accord.

The Latvian foreign minister's new policy soon expressed itself in his relations with his neighbors. Meierovics dismissed as "unimportant" the usual conference of foreign ministers of Finland, Estonia, Latvia, and Poland scheduled to meet Tallinn on August 26, 1925. The quadruple arrangement was no longer necessary. Bringing Lithuania into an entente with Estonia and Latvia was more valuable than "the sterile repetition of these conferences of foreign ministers."[30] In a congratulatory passage a German journalist declared that "the more Meierovics matured as a clear and cool-headed statesman, the more he departed from the policy of close ties with Poland."[31]

The new line from Riga alarmed and angered the Estonian leader, Pusta. There was a strong element of personal rivalry between Pusta and Meierovics, and now the Estonian foreign minister threw cold water on Meierovics's efforts to bring Lithuania into a Baltic entente. As a counter to Meierovics's idea of such a combination endorsed by Soviet Russia and Germany, Pusta projected his old four-state alliance plan, or, at the least, an alliance of Estonia and Latvia with Poland. Pusta himself went to Paris, London, Warsaw, and Helsinki seeking backing for his plan.[32]

But Meierovics doggedly rejected Pusta's pleas. On August 21, 1925, Meierovics reported to the Saeima's foreign affairs commission on the Estonian-Polish attempts to draw Latvia into an alliance. He also noted that these attempts had strong French backing, but the foreign minister sketched for the commission the implications of the Bessarabian problem for Latvia if she were tied to Roumania's ally, Poland. After consideration of all these factors, the Latvians definitely decided against a connection with Poland. Meierovics was spared the necessity of publicizing this decision when Finland (as he had all along expected) rejected Pusta's quadruple alliance project and effectively scuttled the Tallinn conference.[33]

Meierovics rejected an alliance with Poland in favor of a gamble on an identity of interest between Germany and Latvia in Eastern Europe. He had obtained no German commitment in exchange for abandoning Poland—only her promise to be of assistance in Moscow. This reversal of his earlier policy was the last important political act of this most attractive of Baltic statesmen. On August 22, the day after his meeting with the foreign affairs commission of the Saeima, Meierovics left Riga for a brief vacation. On the road to Tukums in Kurzeme the chauffeur lost control of his automobile and it overturned, killing the Latvian foreign minister. He was thirty-eight years old.[34]

Except for a brief interruption in 1924, Zigfrids Anna Meierovics had been foreign minister of Latvia from the republic's founding. His death removed one of the key figures of postwar Baltic diplomacy and reduced the slender prospect for the successful establishment of German-Latvian-Soviet collaboration.[35] A veritable master of the art of improvisation and the soul of caution, Meierovics nevertheless had ended his career with a daring gamble on German goodwill. The alternatives to the gamble had been even more unattractive: submission to Polish hegemony or reduction to the status of Soviet satellite. Berlin offered a faint hope of escape.

5

The Gamble Interrupted, 1925-1926

Eastern Europe's general unease about the Locarno arrangements made in the West in the autumn of 1925 provided the conditions into which Meierovics's gamble was launched. Locarno, by implication at any rate, gave Germany a freer hand than heretofore in Eastern Europe. Poland in particular dreaded possible German revisionism while the Soviets feared the defection of their Rapallo partner. Both powers reacted with strong diplomatic initiatives which involved the Baltic states.

Meierovics's successor in the Latvian foreign office, Hermanis Albats, tried to fit his policy of linking Latvian security with one or more of the great powers into a Locarno-type scheme. Albats hailed Locarno as initiating a new epoch in European diplomacy. "We welcome the conclusion of the Locarno peace pact," Albats announced, but he stressed that "without the pacification of Eastern Europe a Western peace pact remains but an insignificant scrap of paper." Albats went on to propose an "East European Locarno" agreement. After undergoing several refinements, the Latvian project consisted of a guarantee and arbitration treaty between the Baltic states and Soviet Russia on the one side and between these states, the Scandinavian countries and Germany on the other.[1]

Albats's scheme thus incorporated the idea floated by Meierovics and Adolf Koester in the spring of 1925. This plan was an effort on Meierovics's part to identify Latvia's survival with the self-interest of at least one, but preferably both, of the great powers of the area. The only possible way Latvia could achieve such identity of interest was by adopting a frigid if not hostile stance with respect to Poland. But even while Berlin and Moscow welcomed this Latvian line, the basic question still remained: how far was it in the interests of Germany and Soviet Russia to support the security of Latvia and the other Baltic states? Meierovics, as we know, was willing to gamble on a positive answer to that question. How did the potential participants react to Albats's proposal?

Latvia's Eastern Locarno concept obtained a lively airing in the Baltic and Scandinavian press. It received the endorsement of a former Finnish foreign minister, Rafael Erich, who also suggested that the Baltic states, as especially endangered countries, be declared permanently neutral with their status guaranteed by the permanent members of the Council of the League of Nations.[2] But the foreign ministries of the Scandinavian countries maintained an official coolness toward the idea and rejected as dangerous any association with the Baltic republics.[3]

Of course, the attitudes of Germany and Russia were decisive for the fate of the Latvian Eastern Locarno plan. As usual, Moscow rejected any multilateral arrangement; the Kremlin condemned Albats's suggestion as a "proposal for an anti-Soviet league of border states." Chicherin made it clear Moscow would act to block such a scheme.[4] Berlin also viewed the plan in a negative light. The German press in general ruled out any German participation in an Eastern European security system by referring to the Memel question. Above all, *Ostlocarno* signified to German politicians a guarantee of Poland's western frontiers and was, therefore, anathema.[5] Beyond this immediate consideration, however, Germany refused to risk collision with the "vital interests " of Russia in the Baltic area. As one *Wilhelmstrasse* memorandum put it: "In any case, the geopolitical position of Latvia and Estonia is such that it is impossible for Germany to support their independence against Russia."[6] The two great powers of the area thus had little interest in a regional security system.

As the cause of an Eastern Locarno lagged for want of takers and as joint Baltic cooperation seemed as far away as ever, one Latvian newspaper editor dejectedly wrote, "*nolens volens*, we have to conclude that at the moment there is no Baltic policy."[7] Latvia was in a state of suspended animation subjected to the initiatives of other powers. No East European power was more active than security-conscious Poland.

In an effort to escape her own growing isolation Poland proposed to Sweden in December, 1925, that a guarantee pact be drawn up to include themselves, Finland, and, possibly at a later date, the Baltic states and Russia. This proposal, as had earlier Polish gambits, fell upon deaf Scandinavian ears.[8] When Warsaw approached Finland, Latvia, and Estonia directly the Poles got a similar reception. Finland refused to embark on an "adventurous policy under Polish hegemony." In Riga where the liabilities of associating with Poland were well understood, Hermanis Albats insisted that Latvia sought security through agreement with Germany and Soviet Russia.[9] Taking a leaf from Meierovics's book, Albats countered the Poles by demanding the inclusion of Lithuania in the proposed pact.[10]

But Poland was not easily dissuaded from her path. Her envoy in Riga nervously declared that if Latvia did not enter into agreement with Warsaw, Poland might find it necessary to deal with Moscow at Latvia's expense.[11] Faced with the threat of Polish blackmail, Latvia sought guidance from London.

The British refused to take a position on the Polish maneuver, although their envoy in Riga thought the Polish plans absurd and destined to failure.[12] But unknown to the Latvians, British indifference to their fate went much further. In the spring of 1926, the Foreign Office concluded that in the future, London should not object to any change in the status of the Baltic states including "their reabsorption by Russia."[13] This decision, so fateful for Latvia, was, of course, not publicized, but it guided British policy toward the Baltic states from that time forward. It completed the already obvious withdrawal of Britain from the Baltic region.

Both Britain and Germany had by 1926 disinterested themselves in the ultimate fates of Latvia and Estonia. But Poland could not be so indifferent. Warsaw attempted to speak to the Soviets in the name of the Baltic states, Finland and Roumania about mutual security arrangements.[14] The Latvians hastened to assure Moscow that Poland had no right to speak for them. Hermanis Albats stressed that Latvia did not forsee any kind of tie to Poland.[15]

Poland's diplomatic lunges caused Berlin once more to give momentary consideration to a pact including the three Baltic states, Germany, and Soviet Russia. Such a combination would produce "the desired collaboration with Russia in questions of Eastern policy and the isolation of Poland." But Stresemann, as before, concluded that such a pact wuld have to remain in abeyance. It was politically impossible for him to speak of guaranteeing Memel to Lithuania and the Corridor to Poland. Stresemann, therefore, limited himself to encouraging Moscow in its opposition to a treaty system which included Poland.[16]

German and Soviet interests dovetailed nicely. Chicherin assured Berlin that Soviet Russia would not participate in an Eastern Locarno. The Russian foreign affairs commissar personally stressed his opposition to such a pact to the Polish minister in Moscow.[17] The close collaboration of Berlin and the Kremlin cut the ground from under Poland's feet and her Locarno scheme collapsed completely.

The failure of these initial Eastern Locarno projects left the Baltic states vulnerable to renewed Soviet pressures. Throughout the remainder of 1926 and on into 1927, Moscow tried to draw the Baltic republics into a Soviet security and nonaggression treaty.[18] The object of the Soviet policy was naturally not to secure the territorial and political integrity of the border states, but, as Litvinov confided to Berlin, to separate the Baltic states from Poland and from each other.[19]

Moscow's diplomatic offensive began in March, 1926, when Alexei Chernikh, the Soviet representative in Riga, indicated that Soviet Russia wished to sign neutrality and nonaggression treaties with Latvia and Estonia similar to the Soviet-Turkish treaty of the preceding December. The suggested treaties would include mutual guarantees of frontiers as drawn by the peace treaties of 1920, pacts of nonaggression, and pledges of absolute neutrality and nonparticipation in hostile political, military, and economic coalitions.[20] On the surface, the Soviet proposals seemed to offer a certain amount of security to the states concerned. Why then were these proposals received with such foreboding and pessimism?

Baltic diplomats had several objections to the Soviet proposals. In the first place, the Baltic states wished a *joint* pact with Moscow. If *each* of the Baltic states was committed to a *separate* pledge of neutrality, Soviet Russia would have a free hand to deal with potential victims one by one. Latvia, for instance, could not come to the aid of Estonia as her treaty with that country required, if Riga were committed to absolute neutrality. Also, the League of Nations Covenant provided that no member state could appeal to its neutrality and refuse to participate in intervention and sanction procedures. If the League invoked sanctions against the Soviets, Latvia could not remain "neutral." Another problem was Latvia's desire for compulsory arbitration procedures. Latvia favored a court of arbitration with the presiding third member coming from a neutral country. But the Soviets claimed there could be no "impartial" judge selected from any of the "bourgeois" countries. The Russians demanded instead a conciliation commission composed only of the parties to a dispute.[21]

The Soviet proposal thus contained a number of traps and hardly constituted the "guarantee pact" which Albats had in mind. In order to counter the Russian ploy, Albats sought to bring the Estonians, Finns, and Lithuanians into common negotiation with Soviet Russia.[22] Albats enjoyed some success with the Finns and Estonians, but unfortunately, the ever-present Vilna issue prevented Lithuania's cooperation. Lithuania entered secret negotiations with the Soviets even as Latvia sought to build up a common position. Lithuania was willing to exchange Baltic solidarity for Soviet confirmation of her claims to Vilna.[23]

On May 5, 1926, the Latvian, Estonian, and Finnish governments submitted, in almost identical words, statements of position to the Soviet Government.[24] The replies all raised objections designed to slow down the Soviet drive to get the pacts signed. Latvia insisted that the proposed pact must not conflict with her obligations under the Covenant of the League of Nations, the convention on the Åland Islands, and the treaty of defensive alliance with Estonia. The Latvians also desired the compulsory arbitration of disputes and a prohibition of propaganda directed against the political and social order existing in the Baltic states.

As expected, the Soviets rejected the Latvian statement as unsatisfactory and alleged foreign influences on Riga. Moscow specifically threw out the Latvian arbitration proposal.[25] This exchange of views in May, 1926, set the pattern for several months of tedious negotiations in which the Soviets sought all possible advantages from an arrangement with the border states which was a guarantee treaty in name only.

Such was the unpalatable result of continuing Meierovics's policy of accommodation with Berlin and Moscow. This lack of success gave some weight to the arguments of those who had continued to trust in the possibility of an alliance with Poland as Latvia's only viable diplomatic option. A debate in the Saeima and in the press on the wisdom of "collaborating" with the Rapallo partners was probable when dramatic events in Warsaw made it inevitable.

On May 12, 1926, Pilsudski and his supporters seized control of the Polish government. Although himself occupying only the post of minister of war, Pilsudski was henceforth actually the dictator of Poland.[26]   Many Latvians gratefully remembered Pilsudski's military assistance in 1919 in clearing Latgale of Red Army elements. More recently, just before the Pilsudski coup, the Polish foreign ministry had proposed to Riga, Tallinn, and Helsinki, a treaty by which Poland would be obligated to aid them if they were attacked by Soviet Union but which would place them under no reciprocal obligation beyond benevolent neutrality should Poland be the victim of Soviet aggression.[27]

Pilsudski now made a slight but pointed refinement to this offer. If Poland were attacked by Soviet Russia, Latvia and Estonia would be obligated to assist Poland, but if Poland found it necessary to attack Soviet Russia first, then neither state would be under obligation to furnish assistance. Latvia and Estonia were asked to bring Finland and Lithuania into this agreement. Pilsudski also indicated he was ready to "solve" the Vilna question by means of a customs union and military alliance with Lithuania and by the establishment of a "condominium" over the Vilna territory.[28]   Pilsudski wanted to prevent Moscow from removing his only possible allies in Eastern Europe and his initiative made possible Latvia's return to an old diplomatic policy.

However, both Germany and Soviet Russia quickly moved to parry the latest Polish thrust. Germany chose this moment to bring to a close six years of weary and intermittent negotiations about a trade treaty with Latvia.[29]   The Soviets in the meanwhile raised a frenzy of propaganda against Pilsudski but directed at the Baltic audience. *Pravda* of Moscow warned Latvia and Estonia of the dangers to themselves of joining a Polish-led military alliance. The toiling masses of Russia would never allow enemy blocs on the western frontier. *Izvestiîa* predicted the subjugation of the border states to Poland and warned Russia "cannot suffer such intrigues against us." Moscow would not permit an anti-Soviet policy on the part of the Baltic states. Latvia, Estonia, and Finland must realize, the Soviet press advised, that "such small states as themselves could be secure only through absolute neutrality."[30]

The objects of this Bolshevik barrage quivered with anxiety. In a frantic peregrination the Latvian president, Jānis Čakste, and the Estonian foreign minister, Ants Piip, went to Helsinki in the middle of May; at the end of that month, Piip came to Riga, followed shortly by Finland's president, Lauri Kristian Relander. They discussed the diplomatic squeeze into which their states had fallen. In a burst of unusual Baltic zeal, Relander declared that the responsibility for the security of the "vital interests of our nations lies on each of us separately and on all of us together."[31] But how could this mutual responsibility be carried out?

The Latvian rightist press demanded the creation of a Baltic league tied to Poland as the best hope for mutual security.[32] This view was also shared by the leader of the Farmers' Union party, Karlis Ulmanis. As the dominant figure from the agrarian camp, Ulmanis had played a leading role in Latvian politics since before the republic's founding. Ulmanis had been Latvia's first prime minister (1918-1921) and had been a major factor in the Latvian constituent assembly. During the republic's early years, however, Ulmanis's party colleague, the universally respected Meierovics, seemed to outstrip him in parliamentary popularity. Meierovics was himself prime minister twice (June, 1921, to January, 1923, and from June, 1923, to January, 1924). But Meierovics's death removed him from the political scene in August, 1925. In December of that year Ulmanis once more became prime minister. On May 7, 1926, following a cabinet reshuffling, Ulmanis resigned as prime minister to accept the portfolio of foreign minister.[33] He was determined to call a halt to the recent policy of rapprochement with Berlin and Moscow and to reorient Latvia toward Poland.

The key to the whole diplomatic scramble lay in Lithuania. If she could be brought to compromise with Poland over Vilna the major obstacle to Baltic-Polish collaboration would be removed. Ulmanis's strategy was to delay and put off the insistent Soviets so that a Polish-Lithuanian compromise might be worked out. At the beginning of June, 1926, Ulmanis without difficulty convinced the Estonians and Finns of the correctness of this policy. They would each make dilatory replies to Moscow, offer counterproposals, and always respond to Moscow at the same time and in the same language. [34] As one official put it, Latvia would move from one difficulty to another in order to avoid a direct yes or no to Moscow on the nonaggression pact proposal. [35]

Moving to carry out this strategy, Ulmanis, Ants Piip of Estonia and Finnish foreign minister Setälä met in Tallin in mid-July and drafted identical notes to Moscow. The three statesmen proposed that the Soviets join them in setting up a preparatory commission to draft a treaty of neutrality, arbitration, and nonagression.[36] Having raised this cloud of dust for Moscow's benefit, Ulmanis and his staff left for Kaunas.

Ulmanis hoped that Lithuania could not resist the appeal of a solid Baltic front. He counted on being able to convince the Lithuanians that it was now possible to deal with Pilsudski on the Vilna issue. Then, having composed her differences with Poland, Lithuania could join the other states in common negotiations with Moscow.[37] But Kaunas coldly replied that it would join the other Baltic states only if it "received specific guarantees that Latvia sided with Lithuania and not with Poland on the Vilna question."[38]

Lithuania was secure in the knowledge that she could find support for her Vilna claims in Moscow. Both the Soviets and the Germans pressed the Lithuanians to sign the nonaggression pact alone "in order to prevent a coalition of the border states under Polish leadership."[39] Ulmanis's energetic attempt to bring Kaunas into a common Baltic-Polish bloc crumpled against Lithuanian obstinancy and Russo-German shrewdness. On September 28, 1926, Lithuania, in a fit of "Vilnoic passion," signed the Soviet pact alone.[40]

Once more Baltic solidarity had failed and basically for the same reasons we have previously encountered: the Vilna issue and clever diplomacy by Germany and Russia. The Baltic bloc concept had shattered against these hard realities between 1920 and 1925 and could not be put together again no matter how desperately Ulmanis and Pilsudski tried.

Lithuania's action received sharp criticism in Latvia and provoked a debate on the proper course for Riga to follow: to resume the Meierovics gamble on rapprochement with the two great neighbors or to seek safety with Poland. The rightist and agrarian press clamored for the Polish connection while the socialist organs urged a settlement with Moscow and friendship with Germany. The dead Meierovics's own party thus repudiated his foreign policy while the Social Democrats became its champions.

Ulmanis, of course, condemned Lithuania's action and rejected a similar move for Latvia.[41] But the chairman of the Saeima's foreign affairs commission, the Social Democrat, Felikss Cielēns, took the opposite view. Cielēns and his party, along with the small ethnic German party, approved what Kaunas had done and urged an anti-Polish stance for Latvia. Since these two parties dominated the foreign affairs commission, they forced a grudging assurance from Ulmanis that he would continue negotiations with Soviet Russia.[42]

In mid-October, 1926, the Soviets dispatched to Riga one of their best negotiators, Semen Ivanovich Aralov, chief of the Baltic states section of the Commissariat of Foreign Affairs. He held the status of special envoy to conclude a nonaggression pact with Latvia. However, Ulmanis stubbornly kept Aralov at bay by insisting on an arbitration clause. This action did not please those who had hoped for an early conclusion to the talks but Ulmanis counted on controlling the opposition in the Saeima by threatening to resign. Unfortunately for his purposes, his cabinet of agrarians began to lose control of the parliament. Cielēns attracted increasing support with his version of a conciliation arrangement with the Soviets rather than the arbitration court which Ulmanis insisted upon.[43]

As Ulmanis's support in the Saeima weakened, the Soviet negotiator adopted a hard line with the Latvian foreign minister. Aralov demanded that a clause be put into the treaty giving either party the option of denouncing the nonaggression pact if the other signed an objectionable treaty with a third power. When asked why this demand was put to Latvia and not to Turkey and Germany which had signed similar treaties, Aralov arrogantly answered that these powers were not expected to join an anti-Soviet coalition. The Kremlin's brutal demand amounted, of course, to a veto on Latvia's right to conclude treaties with other powers. Ulmanis rejected it out of hand and brought the talks to a screeching halt.[44]

But the breakdown of negotiations with the Soviets brought to a head the simmering revolt in the Saeima and resulted in the collapse of Ulmanis's cabinet. A coalition government now installed Ulmanis's rival, Felikss Cielēns, as foreign minister. If the Latvians would not follow Ulmanis into defiance of Moscow, could the interrupted Meierovics policy of rapprochement be resumed? Cielēns was certain that he could find a way to gain the confidence of Moscow and Berlin.

Sixteen months had passed since the death of Meierovics when Cielēns assumed the portfolio of foreign minister. As we saw earlier, Meierovics had maneuvered Latvia into an anti-Polish stance at just the moment the Eastern European powers began to react to the Locarno treaties. Albats's proposal in late 1925 for an Eastern Locarno got lost in the resulting diplomatic imbroglio. When Pilsudski sought to create a common front with Finland and the Baltic states, Karlis Ulmanis, reversing Meierovics's policy, worked energetically to bring the bloc to fruition. But Ulmanis himself was frustrated by Soviet offers to Lithuania and by growing leftist opposition at home. Perhaps at no time before 1939 was German and Soviet policy so successful and that of Latvia and the border states so dismal a failure.

6

The Gamble Played Out:

Felikss Cielēns As Foreign

Minister, 1926-1928

Felikss Cielēns, that redoubtable Social Democrat who assumed the portfolio of foreign minister in mid-December, 1926, proclaimed his return to the Meierovics policy in a public speech. Referring to his predecessor's work, he stated:

> The effort of the late Z. A. Meierovics to achieve . . . a political union between the Baltic states and Poland produced no results. The Warsaw treaty [of 1922] fell through and Mr. Meierovics realized the futility of the scheme. Our foreign policy was therefore directed towards an alliance with Estonia and Lithuania and the maintenance of cordial relations with Germany and Russia. Mr. Meierovics did not live to carry the plan into effect and it has fallen into my lot to do so.[1]

In drawing about his shoulders the mantle of the dead Meierovics, Cielēns gave notice to Poland, Germany and Russia that the Ulmanis interruption was over. Ulmanis had aligned Latvian policy with Poland and Estonia; Cielēns would try collaboration with Russia and Germany.

It will be useful to sketch the general outlines of Cielēns's foreign and domestic policies before we approach a detailed study of them. Put broadly, Cielēns wanted to settle the security question with Soviet Russia as a step toward a general international guarantee of the territorial status quo in the Baltic area. This latter project Cielēns called his "Eastern Locarno plan." German participation was vital, and Cielēns understood the necessity of accommodating German desires as much as possible. Indeed, as a Social Democrat, he believed himself well equipped to deal with both Weimar Germany and Bolshevik Russia. Also, Cielēns clearly understood that the situation of relative German and Soviet weakness was quite temporary. Latvia must move to obtain international support before the power conditions in Eastern Europe altered.

Cielēns's domestic political aims also impinged upon his conduct of foreign affairs. Stated briefly, Cielēns wanted to stimulate a Latvian industrial revival. For this he needed Russian orders; in addition, he wanted to make Latvia more attractive to the Soviets as their major transit area. A trade treaty with Moscow would help put Latvia's manufacturing and transit facilities to full use.[2]

Now all these domestic and foreign policy goals challenged the Latvian verities established by the nationalist-agrarian-bourgeois governments of the past. Cielēns's domestic policy objectives thus intensified the debate over Latvia's foreign policy options. The conflict sharpened differences between right and left in Latvian politics; Ulmanis and Cielēns became the champions of opposing alternatives.

Shortly after taking office Cielēns revealed his distrust of Poland and his readiness to seek a *modus vivendi* with Russia and Germany. He informed S. I. Aralov, the special Soviet envoy in Riga, that the arbitration question need no longer hinder negotiating a Latvian-Soviet nonaggression pact.[3] Cielēns knew, of course, that the Ulmanis camp would loudly object to a security pact with Moscow which did not contain the arbitration provision. He also expected objections from Poland, and from Estonia, Latvia's pro-Polish ally. Could Cielēns induce the Soviets to accept a formula on arbitration that would ease his domestic as well as his foreign political opposition? To this end the Latvian foreign minister solicited German aid.

Berlin viewed with satisfaction Cielēns's assumption of office. The Latvian's hostility toward Poland was appreciated in the *Wilhelmstrasse*. In Riga itself, Adolf Koester enjoyed a friendly relationship with Cielēns. Manifestations of German goodwill encouraged Cielēns to suggest that in return for German intercession with Moscow he could promise Latvian neutrality in the event of a Soviet-Polish or German-Polish conflict.[4]

Having just witnessed the reinforcement of Lithuania's hostility toward Poland through her nonaggression pact with Russia, Berlin was interested in Cielēns's request. Accomodatingly, Berlin relayed the Latvian's appeal to the German ambassador in Moscow, Brockdorff-Rantzau. While Germany did not assume the role of formal intermediary between Riga and Moscow, Brockdorff-Rantzau let Litvinov know of Germany's interest in the conclusion of a Latvian-Soviet treaty. Litvinov appreciated Berlin's concern but did not make any concessions designed to relieve Cielēns of his parliamentary difficulties.[5] The Germans thereupon informed Cielēns of their own approval of his intentions and suggested he go ahead and sign the nonaggression pact without Estonia.[6] In brief, Latvia must make all the concessions.

But the concessions already announced encountered serious challenges. Ulmanis attacked the government with such "blind hatred" that some observers speculated he considered "illegal means" of regaining power.[7] Indeed rumors of a coup against the Social Democratic government circulated throughout Riga. Even in Moscow, Litvinov told Brockdorff-Rantzau that he had "no doubt that a coup was being readied" in Riga; the "simple Kerensky-types" in the Latvian cabinet could not be expected to take decisive measures against the plotters.[8]

The Latvian government had reason to be concerned. In neighboring Lithuania, on December 17, 1926, a rightist-nationalist-agrarian *coup d'état* installed Antanas Smetona and Augustinas Voldemaras in power.[9] Cielēns and the Latvian Social Democrats feared similar developments in Latvia. The leading spokesman of the Latvian nationalist right was Arvēds Bergs, founder of the National Union, editor of *Latvis*, and Saeima deputy. Bergs, friendly with Ulmanis and his agrarian party, enjoyed a wide following among patriotic Latvian youth. He struck responsive chords with his advocacy of an end to the multiparty confusion in the Saeima and the installation of strong executive power.[10]

Moving to counter the angry opposition of the Latvian right, Cielēns introduced a bill to bring treason cases under the jurisdiction of courts-martial. Then concerned about the loyalty of the army, Cielēns persuaded the Latvian president to remove the chief of the Latvian general staff, General Aire, whose name was often connected with the coup rumors.[11] Finally, Cielēns convinced Karlis Ulmanis, Arvēds Bergs, and several military figures to join his prime minister in a declaration designed to cool down the public temper and curb the loose talk of coups.[12]

The measures Cielēns undertook did have a calming effect on the public, but the bitter divisions in Latvian domestic politics did not augur well for his foreign policy. The Farmers' Union continued its unrelenting attack on the government. *Brīvā Zeme* accused Cielēns of responding to the "friendly nudging" of German and Soviet spokesmen. These powers, the Farmers' Union paper warned, wished to drive a wedge between Poland and the Baltic states.[13] Ulmanis, speaking to a meeting of the Farmers' Union parliamentary group, denounced the break with Poland and the drift away from those powers, such as England, which had made Latvian independence possible. He called upon Cielēns to return to close relations with Poland and to traditional friendship with England.[14]

The agrarian leader did not mince words. He told the foreign affairs commission of the Saeima that Cielēns's policy of collaboration with Germany and Russia was foolish. He worked with Arvēds Bergs in an attempt to split one of the small center parties away from the government bloc and thus provoke a cabinet crisis. Rather underhandedly Ulmanis pressured foreign ministry officials appointed by him to sabotage Cielēns's policy by collaborating with the pro-Polish Estonians.[15]

Cielēns responded to this challenge by arguing before the Saeima that England merely wanted to use the Baltic states as pawns in her own disputes with Russia. The old World War Entente of the western powers was not really interested in the Baltic states now, he said. Germany was a much more important factor for Latvian policy than the western powers.[16] Cielēns's position coincided with the realities of Latvia's situation. Like Meierovics, he recognized that the withdrawal of the western powers from the Baltic made new arrangements necessary, arrangements which must include Germany and the Soviet Union. Consequently, Cielēns continued his close collaboration with Adolf Koester, Germany's envoy in Riga. The latter also directed his principal efforts toward furthering German-Latvian-Soviet cooperation.[17]

But Cielēns's persistence in his policy provoked continued opposition. Ulmanis and the Farmers' Union became so bitter they even tried to deny Cielēns the honor of concluding the long-touted customs union with Estonia.[18] The two states signed the Customs Union Treaty on February 5, 1927, after four years of talks.

Cielēns signed the treaty with hopes of drawing Estonia into agreement with his main policy objectives. But the Estonians dismayed him with their continued pro-Polish orientation. On February 21, without informing Riga beforehand, the Estonians concluded a commercial treaty with Poland. In a final protocol the two signatories agreed that neither would grant special favors to a neighboring state without first advising the other.[19] The action seemed a direct slap at Cielens.

The Estonian-Polish agreement had an immediate impact upon the Latvian Saeima. Cielēns alleged that Ulmanis had been secretly informed about the Estonian-Polish negotiations and accused the Farmers' Union of sabotaging his foreign policy. The weakness of his support in the Saeima had encouraged the Estonians to go their separate way. There now seemed no hope of getting Estonia's cooperation in the matter of nonaggression and trade talks with the Soviets. Only with the vote of the German minority party did Cielēns obtain the Saeima's authorization to continue these negotiations.[20]

Virtually abandoned by Estonia, and facing implacable opposition at home, Cielēns nevertheless moved steadily on with his talks with the Soviets. He had surrendered the arbitration principle in order to accept the Soviet "concession" of a conciliation commission. This commission would simply be a mixed negotiating team; it was, of course, no concession on the Soviet part. Now, when Cielēns requested a neutral chairman for the commission, Moscow refused a quid pro quo. In return for its "concession," Moscow demanded a neutrality formula which went beyond mere nonsupport of an aggressor. According to Hermanis Albats, secretary general of the Latvian foreign ministry, the Soviets still wanted a wording which would prevent Latvia from concluding treaties with any other powers.[21]

After a plea from Cielēns, Berlin told Litvinov it was hopeless to expect a greater concession from Latvia than had been obtained from Lithuania. In view of Latvia's difficulty in winning over

Estonia and Finland to a nonaggression pact, the Germans suggested that Moscow might be satisfied with a less rigorous neutrality formula.[22] It would be a small price to pay for confirming the isolation of the Baltic states from Poland.

After the representations from Berlin, the Soviets grudgingly
agreed to "acknowledge" a declaration from Latvia that the nonaggression treaty did not contravene Latvia's obligations under
the Estonian-Latvian treaty of defense. And the Soviet negotiator
held out hope of important economic concessions benefiting
Riga's languishing industry if Cielēns signed the nonaggression
pact. Cielēns rose to the bait. He would sign, even if Estonia did
not.[23]

On March 9, 1927, Cielēns and Aralov initialed certain para-
graphs of a nonaggression pact. These preliminary sections called for neutrality in case of attack by a third party, and abstention
from coalitions aiming at the economic or financial boycott of
the other. Revealing a basic duplicity, the Soviets did not offer
for initialing their "concession" on settlement of disputes by a
conciliation commission.

Cielēns told the press that Latvia's policy of signing "concrete
security treaties" was a necessity in view of her geographical position. Her location required "special peace arrangements with
her neighbors who had not yet joined the League of Nations."[24]
At the same time, Cielēns admitted he had no illusions that he
had "guaranteed the security and peace of the Baltic." This required the participation of the great powers in a general security
system.[25]

The Latvian socialist press naturally praised Cielēns's action in
initialing parts of a nonaggression pact with Moscow, and the
leading spokesman of the Baltic-German community, Paul Schiemann, also supported the socialist foreign minister.[26] But the
rest of the Latvian press unanimously denounced Cielēns. Arvēds
Bergs's organ and the Farmers' Union paper accused him of making Latvia a Soviet vassal state. Latvia's interests in Western Europe were prejudiced, relations with Estonia were disturbed, and
Latvia's loyalty to the League of Nations had been called into
question, according to Cielēns's opponents.[27] The inflamatory
opposition again gave Litvinov in Moscow visions of an im-
pending coup against Cielēns.[28] Cielēns himself admitted to

fears that the "Fat One" (Ulmanis) would try to come to power, toss the socialist foreign policy overboard, and place Latvia in "Poland's wake."[29]

Indeed, an American observer termed Cielēns's actions a "severe blow to Polish diplomacy" in the Baltic area.[30] The Polish response was accordingly very hostile. The Polish press condemned Cielēns as a "tool in the hands of German and Soviet Russian diplomatists."[31] Polish journalists accused Latvia of "disloyalty" in making agreements with Russia behind Poland's back.[32] The Estonian press echoing these charges pictured Cielēns as being under the influence of Germany's minister in Riga. Equally embittered, the Estonian government refused to send an official deputation to the state funeral of Latvian President Jānis Čakste who died on March 14, 1927.[33]

The angry reaction of Cielēns's neighbors found support in London. Latvia's attempted rapprochement with Russia came at a moment of extreme tension between Britain and the Soviet Union. Consequently, the British viewed the projected Latvian-Soviet nonaggression pact as part of a general Soviet campaign against themselves.[34] Indeed, Soviet spokesmen loudly proclaimed their "diplomatic victory at Riga over England", and boasted of having snatched Latvia from "England's embrace."[35] The British minister in Riga, accompanied by his French colleague, called on Cielēns to express official concern about the Latvian-Russian agreement on the very day Cielēns and Aralov initialed certain sections of that document.

Cielēns rather pointedly reminded his callers that in view of the western attitudes at the time of the attempted communist coup in Tallinn, Latvia could scarcely depend on assistance from them. Latvia needed other security measures and the nonaggression treaty with Soviet Russia was one such device. Cielēns suggested that if the western powers were really concerned about saving Latvia and the other Baltic states from subjugation by Soviet Russia, they should consider entering a joint pact with Germany and Russia to guarantee them.[36] As we know, neither Britain nor France was prepared for such action.

Among all the powers, Germany viewed the Latvian developments with the greatest satisfaction. The coolness between Riga and Warsaw was Germany's reward for encouraging the Latvian-

Russian nonaggression treaty. Adolf Koester had certainly done "his part in strengthening Cielēns in his orientation" toward Berlin and Moscow.[37] Naturally, the British suspected a German role in "expediting" the Latvian-Soviet negotiations. A British-inspired article in Bergs's paper, *Latvis*, accused Stresemann of urging the Latvians to adopt the German concept of political rapprochement with Moscow.[38] The British embassy in Berlin inquired as to the German position on the Latvian-Russian talks and hinted that German diplomats were actively supporting the negotiations. The *Wilhelmstrasse*, of course, denied having played a mediatory role between Riga and Moscow.[39] This was the official truth; Germany had not been a formal intermediary between Latvia and Russia. Berlin had achieved her objectives through the nuances of personal relationships between Brockdorff-Rantzau and Litvinov in Moscow and between Koester and Cielēns in Riga.[40]

Cielēns's policy of seeking security through collaboration with Berlin and Moscow alienated Estonia, Poland, and Britain. How did his economic initiatives fare? In the hope of industrial development and in order to consolidate Riga's position in the transit trade, Cielēns sought a commercial treaty with Moscow.[41] Following some encouraging hints, a Latvian negotiating team went to Moscow and, on June 2, 1927, one week after London and Moscow had broken diplomatic relations, signed a trade treaty.[42] The treaty granted reductions in tariff charges on goods in transit far below those contemplated even in the Latvian-Estonian customs union. It also bestowed diplomatic immunity upon the Russian trade mission in Riga. Latvia received no reciprocal privileges in Moscow, but, more important in Cielēns's view, the Soviets agreed to place industrial orders in the amount of 40 million lats annually.[43]

Once more Cielēns pleased the Germans, who concluded they were the ones who benefited in the final analysis.[44] But the Estonian press and public raised a hue and cry against the Latvian-Soviet commercial agreement. In view of the Estonian-Polish trade agreement, the Estonian reaction seems rather gratuitous. The Estonians accused Latvia of destroying all hope of close relations between their two countries.[45] Estonian journalists mercilessly flailed Cielēns as "Moscow's flunkey," and one even called for an "armed occupation" of Latvia by Estonia to prevent "communist infiltration."[46]

One of Cielēns's more perceptive Estonian critics wrote:

> The aim of the Latvian socialists' Russian policy is the rejuvenation of Latvian industry through Russian orders, thereby increasing the number of the proletariat and thus strengthening the influence of the Social Democratic Party in Latvia.[47]

This accusation came fairly close to the truth. As a good socialist Cielēns wanted to solve the economic problems of Riga and other cities. The empty factories and dead smokestacks of Riga were like goads driving him to a commercial treaty with the Soviets. "Latvia cannot and will not remain simply an agrarian state," proclaimed the socialist news organ.[48]

But this position alarmed Latvia's agrarian interests. In the eyes of the Farmers' Union, Cielēns threatened to divert the economic orientation of the country in "an undesirable direction" by eclipsing the importance of agriculture. This portending change in "the base of the national edifice" aroused Karlis Ulmanis to renewed opposition.[49]

The Farmers' Union's economic program emphasized increased dairy exports to Western Europe. Ulmanis and the Latvian right were prepared to "sacrifice industrial Riga to the cause of Latvian independence and Baltic solidarity." The rhetorical question raised in a British journal neatly defined the Latvian economic alternatives: "Toward dairy-farming and the West or toward industry and the U.S.S.R.?"[50]

The Cielēns commercial treaty with Moscow thus went to the heart of Latvian political issues and involved the national identity and destiny. Latvian agrarians, nationalists, and supporters of a Baltic league united in opposition to Cielēns's industrial program, his socialism, and his foreign policy of rapprochement with Soviet Russia.

Farmers' Union opposition to the commercial treaty with Soviet Russia was based in actuality, then, on opposition to the policy of collaboration with Germany and Russia.[51] Ulmanis quite naturally looked back to his British benefactors of the 1918-1920 period. Now, at the moment when England had broken relations with the Soviets and, according to some accounts, was calling for a new anti-Bolshevik front,[52] Ulmanis urged a pro-English course for Latvia. Arvēds Bergs claimed it was infantile to speak of being neutral in a struggle between England and Soviet Russia. England, said Bergs, would never accept the "bridge" policy of Cielēns.[53]

But Cielēns, rather more realistic than his rightist critics, determined to fight for ratification of his trade treaty. Distant Britain could not dictate Latvia's policy. According to one Latvian official, "We have got to act in the same way as we did with the peace treaty in 1920, when the situation was as now."[54] What the official meant of course was that Latvia should not be Britain's catspaw in a conflict with Russia when Britain would offer no support to Latvia.

Cielēns's determination to reach an understanding with Moscow in security and economic questions, as we have seen, produced a domestic uproar, sharpened differences with Estonia and Poland, and irritated Great Britain. As a consequence, Cielēns needed an appealing instrument with which to disarm his vociferous foreign and domestic critics and rescue his whole program. The Eastern Locarno concept suited his purposes exactly. Not only would his domestic opponents be silenced but, if the great powers proved amenable, Latvia's security problem would be solved. A public statement by Lithuania's strongman provided Cielēns with an opening.

Latvian Social Democrats viewed with distaste the regime of Augustinas Voldemaras in Lithuania. But on February 25, 1927, Voldemaras issued a foreign policy declaration calling for an "Eastern Locarno" which would settle such questions as Vilna. He called for the permanent neutralization of Finland, Estonia, Latvia, and Lithuania under international guarantees of the great powers.[55] Cielēns visited Voldemaras early in March hoping to pursue the Eastern Locarno concept, but when the wily Lithuanian offered to accept Latvia as an ally against Poland, Cielēns declined involvement in the Vilna dispute.[56]

In any case, shortly after seeing Voldemaras for the first time, Cielēns answered the criticism of the British and French ministers in Riga by proposing a security pact in which England, France,

Germany, and Soviet Russia would guarantee the neutrality and integrity of the Baltic states.[57] In a speech on March 10, 1927, Cielēns called for an "Eastern Locarno" to preserve the status quo in the Baltic region. Such a guarantee arrangement should include Finland, Estonia, Latvia, and "if possible," Lithuania on the one side, and Germany, Soviet Russia, Britain, and France on the other. An Eastern Locarno, Cielēns stated, "has to be the great goal toward which eastern policy moves."[58]

Cielēns's domestic political ally, Paul Schiemann, editor of the *Rigasche Rundschau*, warmly endorsed the Eastern Locarno plan. According to Schiemann, the central question in the matter of an Eastern Locarno was whether the continued existence of the Baltic states furthered Russo-German collaboration. Schiemann argued that both Soviet Russia and Germany enjoyed benefits from the existence of the Baltic states. Guaranteed by a Locarno of the East, these states could fulfil their "fateful role as bridges" between Germany and Russia.[59]

But Germany's long range desire to revise her frontier with Poland kept her in opposition to an Eastern Locarno.[60]

Stresemann outlined his position on the proposal in a secret communication on March 21, 1927, to all major diplomatic posts. Countries with "firmly settled" borders such as Latvia, Finland, and Estonia, could certainly seek international commitments, but Germany would not entertain any idea of a guarantee for Lithuania and Poland. However, any Eastern Locarno worthy of the name must contain Poland; the western powers would insist upon that. But Germany had no interest in bringing in the western powers as arbitors and guarantors of Eastern Europe, where "only Russia and ourselves are immediately concerned." Stresemann therefore concluded that, as long as there was no hope for a favorable revision of Germany's eastern frontier, "an Eastern Locarno conference could only produce political embarassment for us." He instructed all German diplomats to exhibit a cautious reserve toward any Eastern Europe security proposals.[61]

Despite Germany's negative attitude, Cielēns continued his campaign for an Eastern Locarno arrangement throughout the summer and fall of 1927. The concept had been discussed off and on since 1925 and was familiar to Baltic and other diplomats. There were even historical precedents for such an arrangement. In 1907

Britain, France, Germany, and Russia had signed a treaty concerning the territorial integrity of Norway. The following year, Russia, Germany, Denmark, and Sweden had signed the Convention of St. Petersburg in order to preserve peace and "maintain the territorial status quo" in the Baltic.[62] This appeal was interesting but not persuasive to the great powers. The conditions which had made possible the earlier agreements no longer obtained.

In a tone of desperation Cielēns argued that Germany and Soviet Russia could hardly oppose an Eastern Locarno pact because to do so would expose the "casual and temporary" nature of their recognition of the Baltic states. Cielēns, seeking to anticipate German objections, omitted Lithuania from his proposed scheme, alleging that as she did not yet possess all the territory she claimed, she could not be interested in preserving the status quo. As for Poland, she could not be included because to do so would give rise to "interminable discussion."[63] Perhaps fortified by such sophistry, Cielēns went to Geneva in September, 1927, in a final effort to convince the great powers of his plan.

Never was there such a "babel of tongues or such conflicting opinions at Geneva" about security problems as when the Eighth Session of the Assembly of the League of Nations met.[64] Cielēns added a somber note to the proceedings when he arose to deliver his address on September 7.

Rivalry in armaments and military spending, he said, was nearly equal to that obtaining in 1913. The present situation was almost identical with that preceding the last war. "We may even have come down already to the level of those celebrated conferences held at The Hague before the war." The major burden of his remarks concerned security. The Locarno agreements, he pointed out, had

> benefited the countries of Western Europe . . . [but] Western Europe is not the whole of Europe, still less the whole of the world. . . . We have in mind a "Locarno Agreement of the East." Such an agreement would guarantee the status quo on the eastern shores of the Baltic. . . . Our own political efforts to achieve a stable peace and an increase of security cannot lead to decisive results. The problem is more far-reaching and must be solved by international agreements.[65]

In search of those "international agreements," Cielēns called on the representatives of the major powers and on League officials. He first saw French foreign minister, Aristide Briand, upon whom he urged that France must take an interest now in the status quo. Later, Germany and Soviet Russia would be strong enough to change the face of Eastern Europe; now was the time to guarantee the Baltic states. But Briand evaded commitment. He agreed with the Latvian foreign minister in principle but stipulated that Poland must be invited to join any guarantee scheme and that Britain and Germany must also sign the instrument.[66]

Poland was the albatross around Cielēns's neck. When he called on Stresemann, the German foreign minister at once pointed out that because of the Memel issue and Polish border problems Germany could not participate in an Eastern security scheme. Cielēns repeated that Lithuania could be omitted from the pact; he had not included Poland at any time. If England and France refused to participate, Cielēns would be satisfied with a commitment from Germany and Russia alone. But Stresemann remained politely evasive.[67] Germany steadily refused to take up the question of an eastern security pact.[68]

Cielēns encountered a frigid atmosphere when he called upon Sir Austen Chamberlain. The British had already made clear their irritation with Latvia, and Cielēns saw at once that his arguments about the importance of the Baltic for Britain's naval interests would not sway Chamberlain. Chamberlain told Cielēns that England's policy was not to commit herself to hypothetical cases; the Western Locarno agreement was the only great exception. The Rhine was the limit of British involvement on the continent; the dominions would not support a British commitment in Eastern Europe. Although Chamberlain admitted that regional pacts might be beneficial, he emphasized that England could "in no circumstances enter into any further treaties of guarantee."[69] England would not assume new security obligations. As regards the Baltic states, as we now know, she had no plans for objecting to their reabsorption by Russia. Cielēns experienced to the full the legendary perfidy of Albion. Further talk with London was pointless.

All the great powers found reasons not to burden themselves with responsibility for Baltic security. Chamberlain's flat refusal was based on a policy of noninvolvement beyond the Rhine to which Britain adhered until 1939. Briand insisted on the inclusion of Poland in the arrangement, to which Germany, of course, would not agree. On his part, Stresemann told Briand that if Russia supported the Cielēns plan then he would give the matter "prompt and careful consideration."[70] Stresemann knew that Russia had no interest in an Eastern Locarno.

In the face of this great power indifference, Cielēns ended his search for an eastern security pact. He made a last plea with League of Nations officials. In the event Soviet Russia made war on Latvia, could Riga expect "immediate and adequate help" from its fellow members in the League? The answer came with devastating clarity: the nature and the amount of support to be rendered in such a case was a "matter for each state to determine."[71] International guarantees for the Baltic could not be had.

Empty handed, his security policy in ruins, Cielēns returned to Riga to face a bitter parliamentary fight over ratification of his trade treaty with Soviet Russia. Could he salvage his economic policy? Having gained no victories in Geneva, Cielēns began the struggle with his prestige diminished. His opposition in the meanwhile had increased in numbers and in noise-level.

Latvian economic organizations and business circles objected to the freedom which the treaty gave Soviet agencies in Latvia while Latvian firms got no similar privileges in Russia. Several spokesmen criticized Cielēns's concession of diplomatic immunity to Soviet trade personnel and extraterritoriality for the premises of the Soviet trade mission. Communist agitation and subversion in Latvia could be expected, especially in view of England's experience with Soviet trade missions in 1927.[72] Bergs argued that it was in any event unwise to construct industrial and transit facilities for the unpredictable and uncontrollable Soviet market.[73]

Cielēns defended the treaty by pointing to Latvia's unfavorable balance of trade, the continuation of which threatened an economic and monetary crisis. Industrial development and export of finished goods were necessary, and for that Latvia needed the Russian market. The export of dairy products, the Farmers' Union solution, would not, according to Cielēns, bring enough return.[74] Cielēns's rational arguments had validity as long as Soviet Russia continued along the lines of the New Economic Policy; but Stalin was shortly to launch the Five-Year Plan, rendering superfluous such devices as the Latvian-Soviet trade treaty of 1927.

The Latvian foreign minister's arguments came under attack, a few days before the scheduled vote on ratification, from the British minister in Riga, Sir Tudor Vaughan. Taking a step he would have hardly dared in a more powerful capital, the British envoy, in an interview in *Jaunākās Zinas*, made clear Britain's opposition to the treaty.[75] To the embarrassment of Cielēns the Latvian press gave the story prominent coverage.

The Saeima debate concluded in fury on October 27, 1927. At one point in the proceedings, the Social Democrats were so angered by the hostile remarks of the Orthodox Archbishop of Riga (a member of the Saeima) that "they rushed towards him threatening personal violence. The other members rallied to the prelate's support and after a noisy scene the archbishop concluded his speech against ratification."[76] At midnight the Saeima narrowly ratified the treaty by a vote of fifty-two to forty-five (two abstentions, one member not present). Four votes from the German party tipped the scales in favor of the treaty. The treaty ratification came after a struggle which "convulsed all Latvia for five months" and left unsettled many basic issues.[77]

As the political debate descended to demagogic levels, the Farmers' Union and the rightist parties attempted to smear Cielēns with communist tar. The slogan, "For or Against the Bolshevist Regime?" (i.e., the Cielēns cabinet), expressed the Latvian right's animosity toward the foreign minister. The growing strength of the anti-leftist sentiment fed on the sensational revelations of espionage trials which occurred in October and December.[78]

Inevitably and in typical Latvian style the agitation culminated in a government crisis. A concert of agrarians and rightists sought to regain control of the government.[79] On December 13, 1927, Cielēns and his cabinet lost control of the Saeima and resigned. Five weeks later a coalition cabinet mustered 51 votes in the 100-seat Saeima. The end of the Cielēns era left the Latvian nation deeply and bitterly divided.

The drift of Latvian domestic politics; Estonia's refusal to cooperate in Cielēns's security and trade policies; Lithuania's devotion to recovery of Vilna; the policies and objectives of the larger powers; all interacted to frustrate Cielēns. He could realize neither a rapprochement with the U.S.S.R. nor his Eastern Locarno project.

The conflict over Latvian foreign policy from the death of Meierovics in August, 1925, to the departure of Cielēns from office in December, 1927, revealed the inability of Latvian politicians and people to choose between alternatives. Yet, as we now know, the Ulmanis option of close ties with Poland and reliance upon British support was an illusion. Cielēns's version of Meierovics's policy of rapprochement with Berlin and Moscow was a rational, albeit, despairing gamble. It rested upon the assumption that Latvia's great neighbors were content with the territorial status quo in the Baltic.

But the long-range territorial ambitions of Germany, Soviet Russia, and to a minor extent, Poland, were opposed to the status quo. At the same time, the western powers perceived no vital interests of their own at stake in the Baltic. Consequently, the western powers refused to become involved in the Baltic security problem. The British would not object to the annexation of the Baltic states by Russia while the French merely sought to connect them to a Polish alliance. Weimar Germany was interested in revision of her Polish frontier, and for that Germany needed Soviet as well as western goodwill. Berlin, therefore, was willing to write off the *Baltikum* and refused to cross Soviet ambition in that area.

It is clear Cielēns presided over the closing out of all the options for Latvian security. The fate of the Baltic states was settled, not in the fall of 1939, but in the fall of 1927. Although not aware of it in 1927, Latvia and her sister republics had already entered upon their *via dolorosa*.

7

Latvia Adrift, 1928-1933

After the excitement and stress of the Cielēns year, Baltic affairs subsided into a temporary stagnation. There was a momentary hiatus between the closing of the postwar era and the opening of another prewar period. During this interlude the failure of the security initiatives previously undertaken did not seem particularly alarming. As an American observer noted in 1929, "There is nothing on the horizon, unless it comes suddenly over the eastern, that is likely to disturb the slow but steady progress and development of the Baltic states."[1] This period of calm ended with the revival of German power and the onset of the great depression.

A policy of drift became apparent when forty-eight year old Antons Balodis assumed the foreign ministry. Balodis served in this position in two cabinets from January, 1928, until March, 1931.[2] The new foreign minister did not follow up any of Cielēns's policies. He dryly commented: "Although the plan of a Baltic Locarno may be commendable in itself, I am not aware of any particular interest having been shown in the same by either the Western Powers or Soviet Russia."[3] Balodis proclaimed a restoration of the "western orientation" in Latvian foreign policy and called for formation of a Baltic alliance as a "bridge of peace" between the West and Soviet Russia.[4] No enthusiasm greeted the Latvian's announcement of this policy.

The impetus for Baltic cooperation had long since withered. Tedious and petty quarrels and jealousy continued as hallmarks

74

of Baltic relations. An Estonian diplomat remarked in 1929 that the idea of a Baltic league had fallen into such oblivion it was embarrassing to talk about it.[5] Progress was minimal even in economic matters. The Latvian-Estonian customs union treaty remained a dead letter.[6]

Even on the substantive matter of military cooperation little was achieved between the two allies. Latvian and Estonian land and naval forces held joint maneuvers in August, 1931, but this proved to be the last such operation.[7] General Johann Laidoner of the Estonian army noted that political relations between Latvia and Estonia were so poor that if the two were attacked by a common enemy, it would be "extremely hard to induce Estonian and Latvian soldiers to fight side by side."[8] A more telling comment on the status of Baltic relations can hardly be found.

Latvian relations with Lithuania underwent no improvement during these years. Antons Balodis had several clashes with Lithuania's fiery strong man, Voldemaras, whom Balodis described as "conceited and stubborn."[9] An excellent example of Lithuanian stubbornness occurred in 1928 when Balodis called for the opening of the Liepāja-Romny railroad.[10] The railroad had been closed when Lithuania sealed her borders to all communication with Poland. This line, which ran through Vilna and Minsk, connected Liepāja on the Latvian coast with Romny, 1,153 kilometers away in the Ukraine. Before World War I, the annual traffic on this line was about three million passengers and 6,660,000 tons of freight. The Latvians had long maintained that blocking this railroad deprived Liepāja of its natural hinterland and had produced unemployment and loss of revenue.[11]

Now given the state of Soviet agriculture and industry, under both N.E.P. and the Five-Year Plans, it is extremely doubtful that Liepāja would have benefited had the line been open, but the Latvians thought so. When Balodis brought up the issue, the Lithuanians' ire knew no bounds. They accused Balodis of trying to be "another Meierovics" under Polish influence.[12] The two states could not be friendly. After signing a trade treaty with Latvia in November, 1930, the Lithuanians denounced it the following April. Kaunas harbored a suspicion that Riga had a secret understanding with Poland recognizing the permanent incorporation of Vilna into Poland.[13] On that issue Lithuania was unmovable.

Despite Lithuanian accusations, relations between Poland and Latvia were not especially intimate. Press articles, doubtless inspired by the Polish legation in Riga, spoke of Poland's interest in the independence of the Baltic states. According to one such report in the *Jaunākās Zinas,* Poland was willing to consider a guarantee treaty for Latvian independence and still supported the notion of a Baltic league.[14]

But official Latvia remained skeptical of Polish benevolence. A functionary in the foreign ministry remarked in April, 1928, that "Poland and Polish policy were absolutely unreliable."[15] Some segments of the Latvian press still suspected a Polish urge to restore the boundaries of 1772, thus incorporating Lithuania, Courland and Latgale into Poland.[16]

Nevertheless, strong support for a Polish orientation did exist in Latvia. This support was concentrated in agrarian and conservative circles. Arvēds Bergs wrote in 1929 that "Poland is not only a desirable participant [in defensive arrangements], but is also a completely reliable ally."[17] The cleavage which had appeared in Latvian political thinking and which had been fought out between 1925 and 1927 still existed. Latvian conservatives and some of the army leadership favored a Polish orientation but the foreign ministry opposed it. Balodis rejected the concept of a Baltic alliance under Polish leadership.[18]

In any case, Polish-Latvian relations were marred by a number of dreary squabbles concerning Latvia's Polish minority. The number of Poles in Latvia in 1930 was 59,374, or about 1.4 percent of the total population.[19] A special investigation committee of the Saeima found that Polish cultural organizations were using the schools of the Polish minority in the Illūkste district and in Latgale to "polonize" the pupils. A Latvian court subsequently ordered the dissolution of the Association of Latvian Poles and of the Society of Catholic Youth. When the Polish envoy in Riga protested and demanded that the organizations be permitted to function, the Latvian government rejected his demands as an interference in domestic affairs.[20] The press of both countries had a field day. In Warsaw and in Vilna, anti-Latvian demonstrations took place.[21]

Thus Baltic cooperation remained the elusive fugitive it had been since the beginning of the independence era. The Latvian newspaper, *Jaunākās Zinas,* took a sampling of public opinion in all three Baltic states in October, 1931, and found wide sentiment for Baltic collaboration.[22] Nothing could be accomplished. But narrow nationalism and sterile, unimaginative policies were luxuries the Baltic states could ill afford. Slowly the painful fact of a German power revival pressed itself into the Latvian public consciousness.

That indefatigable Latvian rightist, Arvēds Bergs, once remarked that a "weak Russia and a weak Central Europe" were necessary for the security of the Baltic states.[23] This circumstance began to change as the decade of the 1920s drew to a close. Felikss Cielens had already urged in 1927 that Germany could no longer be taken lightly. As if to fulfill his contention, the budget committee of the German Reichstag in March, 1928, approved the construction of four pocket battleships.[24] That same year the Germans launched four new destroyers at Wilhelmshaven. Between 1925 and 1931 five new German cruisers made their appearance.[25] Germany's neighbors took notice.

Already by 1928 a Swedish paper, *Svenska Dagbladet,* noted that the German fleet could effectively bar entry to the Baltic Sea, given the geography of the Sound and the Belts. The same paper concluded that "one must not underestimate the capacity of Germany nor its will to affirm its naval power."[26] The German naval command seemed to make such an affirmation in January, 1930, by moving its headquarters from Wilhelmshaven on the North Sea to Kiel on the Baltic Sea. The future field of operations of the German navy was the Baltic; according to one commentator, Germany's future enemy was "possibly Russia, but more probably Poland."[27]

A revival of German naval power on the Baltic sea was unsettling enough to Latvia, but the public remarks of German officials did nothing to quiet such apprehensions. Gottfried Treviranus, the thirty-nine year old former naval officer, now Minister for Occupied Territories, in a speech in Berlin on August 10, 1930, remarked that as the Rhineland chapter of German foreign policy closed a new one opened. The settlement of the "Eastern Question" was the next item on the agenda of Germany's foreign policy.[28]

The Treviranus speech attracted immediate attention in the Baltic states. The Farmers' Union adopted a strong anti-German tone. *Brīvā Zeme*, organ of the Farmers' Union, compared Treviranus's statements to some remarks made by Hitler extremists. They required careful attention in Western and Eastern European capitals, the paper warned.[29] The German minister in Riga reported that the pro-Polish ranks of the agrarian party viewed a German demand for alteration of her eastern boundaries as threatening Latvia as well as Poland.[30]

But it was the striking gains of the National Socialists in the German parlimentary elections in the fall of 1930 which intensified concern in the Baltic over Germany's future course of action. The National Socialists made an interpellation in the Reichstag in December, 1930, concerning a treaty obligating the Latvian government to award land to German soldiers who had fought in *Baltikum* in 1919. It produced a sensation in Latvia.[31]

The treaty to which the National Socialists referred was a Latvian-German agreement signed December 29, 1918, about conferring Latvian citizenship on German volunteers who fought the Reds. Latvian citizenship would of course be *one* necessary precondition to acquiring land in Latvia. This subtle distinction was not made by recruiters in Germany in the winter of 1918/1919. The deceived Baltic fighters had at last found spokesmen in the National Socialist Party.[32]

Karlis Ulmanis, one of the signatories of the treaty in question, correctly denied that an agreement on land awards had been made. The Latvian government warned the German legation in Riga that pursuing the matter would only provoke a renewal of the bitter resentment against Germany in Latvia. The minister assured the Latvian government that the interpellation served only the agitation purposes of the National Socialist Party and did not express official policy.[33]

Nevertheless, Latvian fears respecting the territorial ambitions of German National Socialism, once aroused, did not subside. The question of land in the Baltic cropped up in several places. Adolf Hitler, in *Mein Kampf*, spoke of resuming the German push to the East which had stopped six hundred years earlier. As Hitler put it, "if we talk about new soil and territory in Europe today, we can think primarily only of Russia and its vassal border states."[34]

Hitler restated his basic position in an interview which he granted to the London *Times* in June, 1931. He remarked that the recovery of Germany's lost overseas colonies was not essential; he contemplated "colonization of an unlimited eastern area." One of Hitler's associates stated in the same interview that Germany might in time demand compensation for her lost colonies by seeking to extend to the East "in order to colonize the land there. Here we find ourselves at once in the center of the Eastern Idea."[35]

In view of the unmistakable ambition on the part of Germany's fastest growing political party, it was no wonder that travelers in the Baltic states in 1932 reported that uneasiness about Germany had replaced fear of the Soviet Union.[36] The great question dominating Latvian foreign policy during the first half of the 1930s was how best to meet the German danger. As we well know, most security options had already been explored to no avail. What remained to be done?

Felikss Cielēns, in a published article—"Is a New World War to be Expected?"—advised Latvia to steer clear of all commitments and retreat into strict neutrality.[37] But this was a counsel of despair and Cielēns himself later advocated alliances for Latvia. But was there any hope of Latvia's getting an alliance with other powers who might be disturbed at a German resurgence? That meant Soviet Russia, Poland, France. Perhaps Latvian participation in a French-sponsored collective security pact was a possibility. Or, could Latvia and Estonia associate themselves with Sweden and Finland in a bloc of neutrals? Was there even an outside chance of coming to terms with the new Germany? These were the questions hounding Latvia's diplomats as relentlessly as the legendary Furies.

In a major foreign policy statement in December, 1930, under the heading, "How is Peace to be Secured?" the Latvian Farmers' Union went back to the policies of the earliest days of the Republic. The Latvian agrarians noted that the post-Locarno optimism had evaporated in France where demands were being made for an increase in the French army. A "new doctrine," in essence a return to the old Clemenceau system, called for creating a solid barrier of states between Germany and Russia. Joseph Paul-Boncour, chairmen of the French parliament's foreign affairs commission, had proposed a great coalition of states within the League of Nations to include France, Poland, the Little En-

tente, the Baltic states, and Finland. The purpose of such a coalition was to defend the peace against the revisionist powers. The
Farmers' Union endorsed Paul-Boncour's concept of collective
security.[38]

The notion of collective security pacts (an echo of earlier
"Eastern Locarno" projects) was a bit premature in 1930. It required about four years for the idea to reach fruition in Louis
Barthou's Eastern Security Pact proposal of 1934. In any event,
one could not talk about eastern security without considering the
role of the Soviet Union.

The Soviet Union shared the general anxiety about a powerful
Germany. In 1931 and 1932 the Russians made overtures to the
Baltic states and other countries. These diplomatic maneuvers
may have stemmed originally from Soviet concern about Japanese
activities in Manchuria.[39] But Litvinov's renewal of nonaggression pact offers also coincided with the growing unease respecting Germany.

In August, 1931, France and Soviet Russia initialed a draft
pact of friendship and nonaggression. At this time the French
negotiators insisted that Moscow also conclude such pacts with
Poland and Roumania.[40] Rumors circulated in Riga to the
effect that a Franco-Russian pact would be followed by a Russo-
Polish agreement and this by a Finnish-Baltic-Russian pact.[41]
Late in 1931, Litvinov did indeed make an offer to Warsaw.[42]
Then early in 1932, Boris S. Stomoniakov, member of the Collegium of the Commissariat for Foreign Affairs, arrived in Riga to
conduct negotiations with Latvia.

In the Latvian capital concern about the potential German danger overrode the objections which had prevented Cielēns from concluding a similar agreement in 1927. The Soviet offer now had the
backing of Poland and France. Consequently Latvia signed the
document on February 5, 1932. The pact reaffirmed the peace
treaty of 1920 as the invariable and permanent foundation of the
relations of the two powers. Respect for sovereignty, political independence, territorial integrity, and inviolability was enjoined.
Each party pledged to refrain from any act of aggression against
the other; to refrain from military or political agreements directed against the independence, territorial integrity, or "political

security" of the other; and to abstain from any agreement aimed at an economic or financial boycott of the other.

The two signatories agreed that Latvia was to issue a unilateral declaration to the effect that the new pact did not conflict with Latvia's membership in the League of Nations. The pact also provided for a conciliation commission, composed equally of Latvians and Russians, to handle disputes. This is the position Cielēns accepted in 1927 but which the Latvian Saeima rejected at that time. The pact was to last for three years, continuing thereafter automatically, unless denounced, in two-year periods.[43] In April, 1934, a protocol extended the treaty to December 31, 1945.

In so far as written commitments go, the nonaggression pact seemed to bestow considerable security upon the signatories. The Soviets were careful, however, not to sign collectively or concurrently with the other border states.[44]

This written affirmation of the Kremlin's renunciation of territorial ambitions along with Litvinov's "bewitching eloquence" succeeded in lulling Baltic fears of Russia. The apparent reconciliation of the Kremlin with the border states and the Franco-Soviet pact of November, 1932, marked an historic shift in interwar diplomacy.

The turn of events led Felikss Cielēns to proclaim the end of the Rapallo era in European diplomacy. The old Berlin-Moscow axis around which East European diplomacy moved was collapsing. The Latvian Social Democrat noted that France and Poland had been compelled to a rapprochement with Soviet Russia by the collapse of democracy in Germany and by the drift toward a National Socialist dictatorship.[45]

Because of the changed international situation, Cielēns, chairman of the Saeima's foreign affairs commission, dramatically altered his own foreign policy position. According to his analysis, when the National Socialists came to power in Germany, they would follow an aggressive course. In the long run this course would be directed against France, necessitating a German-Italian alliance. In the short run, however, Germany would follow the line of least resistance and move against Poland. Afterwards, Germany could be expected to occupy Lithuania and Latvia in order to have a more advantageous position from which to launch a war against Red Russia. Confronted with this new international situation, Cielēns called for an alliance of Latvia with Poland, Estonia, Lithuania and Russia.[46]

The reversal of position by Poland's staunchest opponent in Latvian politics astounded the Social Democrats. Cielēns could not carry many socialists into his new line of thinking; he lost control of the party to Fircis Menders, who rejected any hint of alliance with "fascistic" Poland.[47] Nevertheless Cielēns's dramatic switch of position is an individual testimony to the impact of the German revival on the Baltic area.

The startling shifts in Eastern European diplomacy were also influenced by the world economic crisis. The total value of Latvia's agricultural and timber exports had averaged 261.0 million lats annually in the period 1928-1930. But by 1932, the value of Latvia's principal exports had dropped to 96.5 million lats, a decline in value of 63 percent. The depression damaged the ability of Great Britain and Germany to buy Latvian products; between 1930 and 1931, the value of the annual export to Britain declined by 42 percent while the value of the annual export to Germany fell by 36 percent.[48]

The catastrophic drop in agricultural prices brought great suffering to the Latvian population, over 60 percent of whom were engaged in farming.[49] Parties and spokesmen of the agrarian interests demanded that new policies, domestic and foreign, be adopted to meet the economic emergency. Agrarians in particular and conservatives generally grew impatient with the faction-ridden Saeima and the weak executive authority. They launched demands for constitutional reform.

The general sense of unease and disorientation in Latvian politics was revealed in the elections to the fourth Saeima in October, 1931. Some 46 parties competed for the 100 seats in the Latvian parliament. Leftist strength (mainly the Social Democrats) fell from thirty-six to twenty-eight seats; the Farmers' Union declined from sixteen to fourteen seats although the agrarian bloc climbed from twenty-nine to thirty-four seats; the center bloc rose strikingly from nine to nineteen members; the older rightist bloc of parties declined from eight to five seats, while several new groups made an appearance.[50] The tone of Latvian politics became suspicious, sour, and marked by outbursts of chauvinism.

The cabinet installed in December, 1931, launched a campaign against the School Autonomy Law of 1919, provoking accusations of attempted "Latvianization" from the alarmed minorities. In January, 1933, the cabinet asked the Saeima to confirm an emergency decree withdrawing state support from the schools of the minorities and authorizing the transfer of their students to public schools where instruction would be in the Latvian language. The agrarian bloc, seeing an opportunity to come to power, voted with the socialists and the minority parties against confirmation; the cabinet had to resign.[51]

Negotiations for the formation of a new government lasted six weeks, something of a record even for Latvian parliaments. A combination of agrarians, centrists, and rightists composed the new cabinet headed by Adolfs Blodnieks of the New Farmers and Smallholders Party.[52] The foreign minister in the new government, Voldemars Salnais, came from the centrist Progressive Union.

Salnais, born in 1886 into a peasant family, had fought in the revolutionary outbreak of 1905 and had suffered exile to Siberia. In 1917, at Vladisvostok, he had formed a council of his compatriots to seek autonomy for Latvia. He had been briefly vice-minister for foreign affairs in 1921. The Germans considered Salnais rather pro-Polish in his orientation.[53]

By the time Salnais took up his duties on March 24, 1933, the feeling of insecurity in Latvia was greater than at any period since World War I.[54] Germany was the source of that insecurity. The National Socialist regime's treatment of German socialists and Jews in particular alarmed these groups in the Baltic.

Latvia's Social Democrats and Jews instituted a propaganda campaign against the new Germany. *Sociāldemokrats* featured atrocity stories from Germany and proclaimed that "the entire world knows without a doubt that today raving sadists and beasts in human form rule Germany."[55] The Latvian socialists, not content with words, organized an effective boycott of German goods. The German government retaliated in June, 1933, with an embargo on importation of Latvian butter.[56]

The German action dismayed the agrarian element in the Saeima who promptly directed their hostility toward those whose activities had cost the Latvian farmer the German market. The cabinet authorized the interior minister to prosecute all "illegal actions by specific organizations." Salnais, who considered the butter dispute "quite serious and of far-reaching consequence," directed some conciliatory words toward Germany and condemned attacks against the party and person of the new German chancellor. Salnais conferred with German foreign minister Neurath at the World Economic Conference in London and pledged to stop the boycott. Upon receiving these assurances, Neurath agreed to lift the embargo and end the "butter war."[57]

Economic necessity thus produced in Latvia's agrarian and rightist politicians a willingness to deal with their fearful neighbor to the west. The man who emerged as the spokesman of these economic and political interests in the foreign ministry was Vilhelms Munters. The Latvian cabinet, on May 30, 1933, directed the appointment of Munters as secretary general of the foreign ministry.[58]

Munters was one of the most enigmatic characters in a region which produced them bountifully. Many considered him a Baltic-German. His maternal ancestors were purely German and his paternal background was one of Latvians who had adopted the German language and culture. Born in 1898, Munters attended German schools in Riga. His marriage to a Russian seemed to complete his alienation from his Latvian associates. However, shortly after Latvian independence, he joined the Farmers' Union and entered the foreign ministry under Meierovics. Munters's first job in the ministry was in the press department. He accompanied Meierovics on the latter's trips abroad in 1921 and 1925. From 1925-1931, Munters headed the Baltic States section, but after the death of Meierovics, who liked the young Munters, he could not influence major foreign policy decisions. He never held a post outside Latvia. Karlis Ulmanis took an interest in Munters and secured his appointment as secretary general of the foreign ministry in 1933. Munters subsequently (in 1936) became foreign minister. After the Soviet occupation, he was deported to the Soviet Union, only to reappear in 1959 in Riga, as apologist for the Moscow political line.[59]

The German minister in Riga regarded Munters as a political neutral. But, because of his connection with Karlis Ulmanis, "the coming personality" in Latvian politics, Munters obtained a friendly hearing at the German legation.[60] Was there a possibility for Latvia to escape her isolation and reach an understanding with the new Germany? Had a new option opened in Latvia's quest for security?

Munters thought so for a time during 1933. He told Georg Martius, German minister in Riga, that important political circles in Latvia viewed with sympathy the new Germany's "campaign against communism and *Judentum.*" This sympathy could be strengthened, Munters hinted, by increased German imports of Latvian agricultural products. This would also help prevent a Latvian political orientation toward Poland.

Martius was convinced that the sympathy of Ulmanis's Farmers' Union could be of both political and economic value to Germany. A few timely concessions on the matter of imports would enhance the party's position, thereby securing a German industrial market in Latvia and insuring continued cultural privileges for the German minority and favorable treatment of Reich German interests.[61]

Munters pressed his efforts for a rapprochement with Germany. At the end of November, 1933, Munters suggested that the increasingly favorable Latvian opinion of the new Germany could be strengthened if the Reich Chancellor would receive the Latvian minister in Berlin and afterwards issue a statement on the peaceful aims of German policy toward Latvia.[62] Martius seemed to support this idea as a way to boost the political clout of Ulmanis and his Farmers' Union. Surprisingly enough, Reich German National Socialists in Latvia urged the German foreign ministry and the Reichsbank to extend financial support to the Farmers' Union.[63]

But National Socialist Berlin remained indifferent to these suggestive possibilities coming from Riga. Martius's view of a collaboration with the Latvian Farmers' Union seemed tame and old fashioned to Germany's new rulers who in any case sought a stronger partner in Eastern Europe than Latvia. Upon receiving one report of a conversation between Munters and Martius, State Secretary von Bülow wrote in the margin: "The Latvians have illusions of grandeur. . . . Martius ought to have toned down

Munters at once."[64] Although even Neurath once reflected that preservation of the Baltic states' independence was in Germany's interests,[65] a Latvian "understanding" with the new Germany was impossible.

A rapprochement was impossible because of the persistent territorial aims of the German National Socialists. At the end of April, 1933, Alfred Rosenberg spoke of Germany's future as "lying in the European East." It was a dream of his, he indicated, to create a group of "pliant German States along the Baltic coast of Russia's western frontier."[66] Munters told Martius the most serious obstacle to their relations were expressions of expansionist plans at the highest level of the German government.[67]

Possible German designs on Eastern Europe also aroused apprehension in Moscow. At the London Economic Conference, Litvinov invited the representatives of the border states to sign a protocol defining aggression. On July 3, 1933, in the Soviet Embassy, Salnais, along with representatives from Estonia, Poland, Roumania, Turkey, Afghanistan, and Persia, put his signature to the protocol. According to this document, "no political, military, economic, or other considerations" could serve as justification for aggression.[68]

Salnais concluded that fear of Hitler's imperialism had moved Soviet Russia to seek detente with the states on her border. For the immediate future, therefore, Salnais saw no danger from Moscow. It was Germany who now threatened the status quo and Latvia had to seek security against her.[69]

By the end of summer, 1933, Latvia's general situation looked grim. Salnais had small grounds for optimism. The domestic economic and political scene was a confused jumble. Unable to come to terms with a suddenly menacing Germany, Salnais thrashed about in search of an alternative foreign policy. At the Assembly of the League of Nations he referred to a growing disillusion with the world organization. It too had failed to cope with economic problems and with the armaments race.

The whole edifice of European cooperation seemed on the verge of collapse. Salnais concluded:

Failures of important initiatives, political and economic, growing chaos in world economy, growing uncertainty and tension in the political situation, dwindling confidence and tumbling ideas and ideals—such is without exaggeration the present state of affairs.[70]

Only the combined efforts of the great powers could reverse the trend. Such efforts were not forthcoming. On October 14, 1933, Germany withdrew from the League of Nations, raising to new heights the fever of anxiety in Latvia.

8

Out of the Maelstrom
of European Diplomacy:
The Baltic Entente of 1934

Salnais's doleful words to the League of Nations in September, 1933, were not contradicted in the following months. General Aleksanders Kalejs, Chief of Staff of the Latvian army, asserted in October that "storms" were brewing in both Germany and Russia, although he personally regarded the Soviets as the greater threat to Latvia.[1] But the revival of German power was the chief cause of fear and the major catalyst of diplomatic action in Eastern Europe. "Something solid began to emerge out of the political fluidity in which the Baltic states had so far existed."[2]

Rumors began circulating in Riga in late 1933 of a Polish-German rapprochement. According to one of them, Poland was prepared to give Germany a free hand in the *Baltikum* in exchange for similar privileges for herself in Lithuania and Latgale.[3] Then on January 26, 1934, the Germans and Poles signed a non-aggression pact.[4] It marked a general reversal of the established diplomatic pattern in Eastern Europe and plunged the Baltic states into a diplomatic maelstrom.

A German-Polish understanding particularly alarmed the Latvians. Rumor-haunted Riga feared the Poles had agreed to abandon the Corridor in exchange for Courland and Liepāja. The Latvian Chief of Staff, General Kalejs, refused to believe that Chancellor Hitler had suddenly become more friendly toward Poland than his liberal and conservative predecessors. Kalejs was convinced Poland had given Germany "considerable *quid pro quo*." The Polish-German pact also increased the danger of a Soviet threat to the Baltic states in General Kalejs' opinion. The Russians might decide to anticipate a German move toward the *Baltikum* with a *fait accompli* of their own.[5] Initially, the Latvian reaction was one of astonishment and suspicion of Poland.

The Latvians had hardly time to digest the fact of a German-Polish rapprochement when they were confronted with a Soviet maneuver designed to frustrate it. The Soviets proposed to Poland on December 14, 1933, that the two jointly declare that the preservation of the independence of the Baltic states was necessary to the peace of Eastern Europe. Should the independence of these states be threatened, Warsaw and Moscow would consult on a course of action. On December 19, the Polish government accepted the Soviet proposal. Two days later, Stefan Brodowski, Soviet minister in Riga, presented the proposition to Latvian foreign minister Salnais.[6]

Brodowski asked Salnais whether he would be prepared to consult with the Soviet Union on common measures "in case of attack by a large neighboring State." Salnais limited himself to a cautious acknowledgement of this proposal. He privately held that the proposed declaration was meant as a demonstration against Germany and that Latvia must reject it.[7]

The Soviets sounded out Tallinn, Kaunas, and Helsinki at the same time. Finland rejected the offer on December 27; Estonia and Latvia followed suit in mid-January.[8] The Finns leaked news of the proposal to the press in order to "torpedo the entire proposition." Poland and Soviet Russia issued embarrassed and indignant denials to press and diplomatic inquiries.[9]

The fact that Poland did not inform the Baltic states about the proposed joint declaration until December 28, 1933, a week after the Soviets had done so, increased Latvian suspicion of Polish intentions.[10] The Latvians recalled a remark once made by Polish foreign minister August Zaleski that "Poland would only need to talk five minutes with the Bolsheviks" in order to obtain her territorial demands on Latvia. "Have these five minutes occurred?" the Latvian foreign ministry wondered. A Latvian memorandum argued that only in pursuit of her wider ambitions had Poland agreed to make the declaration with Soviet Russia.[11] Evidently Poland and Soviet Russia sought

to use the German threat as an excuse to reduce the independence
of the Baltic states.

In January, 1934, the Finns revealed evidence to Salnais dem-
onstrating that if the Russian-Polish declaration had been accepted, it "would have meant the immediate occupation of the
country by Poland in the south, the remainder being drawn in by
Moscow. Not only was the occupation planned, but a complete
program was already drawn up for reconstructing Latvia along
Bolshevist lines."[12] Salnais despondently concluded that Latvia was sitting on a volcano that could blow up any day; counter-
measures could only delay, not prevent, the catastrophe.

The Soviet maneuver with Warsaw was clearly an effort to
forestall any German move toward the Baltic states and to frustrate the Berlin-Warsaw rapprochement.[13] Another, but related,
motive for Litvinov's action appeared on January 5, 1934, when
he expressed his dissatisfaction about the domestic inclina-
tion of Latvia and Estonia toward German fascism.[14]

The allegation was not altogether new. In July, 1930, Litvinov
had complained of "aggressive and chauvinist movements" in
Soviet Russia's closest neighbors, while in mid-December, 1933,
Karl Radek had written in *Izvestiiâ* that the economic crisis was
driving the Latvian "kulaks and petty bourgeoisie" toward fascism: ". . . the powerful Farmers' Union, led by Ulmanis, is
now for a strong government which will not be hampered by
petty party politics and which will maintain the export of Latvian butter to Germany."[15] Radek concluded that Germany
hoped to make the Baltic states a jumping-off place for a campaign
against the Soviet Union. Litvinov stressed this theme on December 29, 1933, in a speech to the Soviet Central Executive Committee when he referred to internal developments which threatened
the independence of the Baltic countries.[16]

The Soviet propaganda line as well as official statements left
no doubt in Latvian minds, long accustomed to Muscovite soph-
istries, that the Kremlin equated the movement in Latvia for a
strong, centralized executive authority with fascism. Salnais indicated that the offer of a Soviet-Polish declaration revealed a
Soviet desire to counteract the shift to the right in Latvian and
Estonian politics. The Kremlin was particularly suspicious of
Karlis Ulmanis's drive to reduce parliamentary power and increase
executive authority.[17]

In brief, Moscow alleged that the political movement for a strong executive could lead to collaboration with National Socialist Germany. Therefore, the reform movement threatened Latvian independence; in order to safeguard Latvian independence, a Soviet intervention might be necessary. Salnais was convinced that if the Polish-Soviet declaration had been accepted, an intervention would have taken place.[18] The Estonian press also maintained that such was the "concealed intent of the Litvinov plans."[19]

Litvinov's charge of a connection between Latvian political groups and German National Socialism collapses upon examination of the actual situation.[20] The specter of German control of anti-Soviet fascist movements in the Baltic may well have frightened Litvinov. But it was only a specter. It provided the Kremlin with a convenient excuse for putting pressure on the Baltic States.

Latvia was now caught between two hostile forces: National Socialist Germany and Communist Russia. In the view of Fircis Menders, spokesman of the Latvian Social Democrats, there was "no third way between association with Hitlerian Germany and coordination of our foreign policy with Soviet Russia."[21] Menders chose the latter. Other Latvians, such as General Aleksanders Kalejs of the General Staff, called for alliances to insure Latvia's survival.[22] Could, at this late hour, such allies be found? Were there any remaining alternatives to dominance by either Germany or Russia?

The menacing currents in international relations during 1933 and 1934 revived interest in Baltic collaboration as a security measure. A former Lord Mayor of Stockholm, Carl Lindhagen, in March, 1933, submitted to the Swedish Riksdag a proposal for a Scandinavian-Baltic-Polish Confederation.[23] Needless to say, Lindhagen's idea never picked up much support in Sweden but it found a responsive echo across the Baltic Sea. That same month a group of prominent Latvians formed an association called the "Baltic Union" to promote the concept of collective security. However, a combined meeting with similar societies from Estonia and Lithuania later in the spring was a dismal failure; when her neighbors refused to endorse a resolution calling for the restoration of Vilna to Lithuania, the Kaunas delegation angrily departed.[24]

Politicians like Felikss Cielēns lamented the Vilna issue as still the greatest barrier to Baltic collaboration. Cielēns called for a "complete federation" of Latvia, Estonia, and Lithuania in order to meet the threat of an annexationist Germany. The Lithuanian hope of recovering Vilna in the event of a German-Polish war was a vain one. Hitler would probably occupy Lithuania as well as Poland if he defeated that power. Lithuania must choose the Baltic alliance, Cielēns warned, or "go with closed eyes to her destruction."[25]

But Lithuanian eyes remained fastened upon Vilna. In April, 1933, the Lithuanian president, Antanas Smetona, publicly declared his opposition to a Baltic alliance. The founding of a Baltic league before Vilna had been settled was a "primitive idea." So long as Latvia and Estonia were friendly to Poland, there could be no talk of an entente.[26] Smetona's sentiments were widely shared in Lithuania; one newspaper held that until Latvia and Estonia adopted Lithuania's view on Vilna, it was not possible "even to discuss" a Baltic alliance.[27]   On the matter of Vilna, Lithuania could not be moved.

Meanwhile, the German-Polish pact and the proposed Soviet-Polish declaration on the Baltic states stimulated action at the official level. Latvian foreign minister Salnais and his Finnish counterpart, Hackzell, signed a secret Protocol of Agreement in Riga in December, 1933. The two foreign ministers agreed to make no treaty with a third power without informing the other and to provide for the "closest possible collaboration in all military matters." The general staffs of both countries were to be in "uninterrupted communication" and to elaborate common defensive plans. More importantly, the protocol called for joint efforts to form an alliance between the Baltic and Scandinavian states.[28]

Salnais was resolved that this protocol should not become just another "agreement to agree." In an atmosphere of urgency, Salnais prepared in January, 1934, for a trip to Stockholm, Helsinki, and Tallinn.   He would seek the Baltic-Scandinavian alliance. On the eve of his departure, Salnais stated that everything must be done to bring the Baltic and Scandinavian states closer together.[29] In his opinion, Latvia had two basic choices: to help unify the Baltic countries and develop ties with Western Europe, or to submit to the Red International and merge with the "Asian chaos."[30]

But Sweden had maintained a consistantly detached attitude toward her postwar neighbor across the Baltic Sea. The Swedes gave Salnais a cordial reception in Stockholm but were careful to avoid giving his visit an "official" character. Sweden, despite some sentimental and commercial interests, was not at all willing to become politically involved with the Baltic states.[31] She would not play Britain to Latvia's Belgium.

Salnais's welcome in Helsinki was, of course, much friendlier. He was a personal acquaintance of Finnish President Svinhufvud; the two men had suffered exile together after the Revolution of 1905. Foreign minister Hackzell seconded Salnais's efforts for pulling together the states bordering the Baltic Sea. The Latvian and Finnish partners agreed to resume regular meetings with the Estonian foreign minister, a habit interrupted since the middle 1920s.[32] But this was about all Salnais could show for his laborious spadework in behalf of Baltic solidarity. Salnais's hope of a bloc of states including Sweden and Finland collapsed; only Estonia and Lithuania remained as possible allies.

The retiring Chief of the Latvian General Staff, General Aleksanders Kalejs, called it a "necessity of life" for the three Baltic states to "unite politically, economically, and militarily."[33] Early in February, 1934, the Latvian and Estonian General Staffs agreed on the need to include Lithuania in a common alliance.[34] Lithuania, however, still hesitated to join a combination that might be exposed to Polish influence. Dovas Zaunius, Lithuanian foreign minister, in a public speech on February 24, 1934, threw cold water on the idea of a Baltic alliance.[35]

The threats, real and implied, coming from west and east in 1933 and early 1934 could not yet bring the Baltic states together. Sweden maintained her indifference while Finland's government refused to support Hackzel's and Salnais's enthusiastic efforts for a Baltic-Scandinavian bloc. Even the narrower union of the three Baltic republics encountered the usual Vilna obstacle. However, one formidable barrier to a Baltic alliance began to give way in 1934: the opposition of Moscow.

The Kremlin's attitude toward the close collaboration of the three Baltic states underwent a change during 1933-1934. As late as March, 1933, Litvinov had stressed the identity of Soviet and German interest in preventing an alliance among the Baltic countries.[36] But, toward the end of September, 1933, Estonia gained the impression that Litvinov would not hinder a political alliance among the three states.[37]

By the beginning of 1934, Soviet mistrust of Germany had reached such a point that Moscow completely abandoned the old policy toward the Baltic states: ". . . this group of States has assumed in Russian eyes a great political significance—that of a defensive wall against aggressive national socialism, of a perimeter which must be defended and consolidated."[38] In February, 1934, the Latvian foreign ministry received definite reports that no further opposition existed in Moscow to a union of the three Baltic states. "Litvinov wished rather to promote the founding of this union since the Baltic states would form a strong barrier against Germany."[39]

Assured of Moscow's favorable attitude, Salnais and Julius Seljamaa of Estonia signed a "Treaty for the Organization of an Alliance" on February 17, 1934. The treaty "organized" the defensive alliance of February, 1923; it was patterned after the organization pact of the Little Entente (February 16, 1933) and paralleled the Balkan Pact of February 9, 1934. The new agreement provided for biennial foreign ministers' conferences, established a council for legislative coordination, and provided for joint action at international conferences. The treaty was open for the adherence of third parties. Seljamaa optimistically described the agreement as the nucleus for the "future Union of the Baltic States."[40]

Before Salnais could bring to completion the projected triple Baltic alliance, Latvia's domestic political crisis exploded. The Farmers' Union and Ulmanis were determined to solve Latvia's economic and political problems through a constitutional reform of an authoritarian nature. Accordingly, at the beginning of March, 1934, the Farmers' Union withdrew its support of the Blodnieks cabinet and forced its collapse.[41] Ulmanis needed fifteen days to construct a new government in which he served as both prime minister and foreign minister. There was no real change in foreign policy, but the Farmers' Union was favorably disposed toward Poland. In his "program speech" to the Saeima, Ulmanis also called for the formation of a Baltic union. Latvia must "reckon with the new opportunities of the hour," he said.[42]

The new Ulmanis government had to reckon with another Soviet maneuver instead. On March 28, 1934, Litvinov suggested to Rudolf Nadolny, German ambassador in Moscow, a joint declaration on the necessity of preserving the independence of the Baltic states which were "previously a part of the former Russian Empire." Germany and Russia were to abstain from any action which might directly or indirectly damage the independence of the Baltic states. Litvinov indicated that the Baltic states need not "officially" be told of the planned action.[43] Nadolny, convinced that Moscow was really concerned about German intentions in the Baltic area, and wishing to preserve the traditional friendship with Moscow, suggested Berlin make some gesture to put Soviet fears to rest.[44]

But Germany could not accept Litvinov's proposal. To do so would be tantamount to admitting that German National Socialism threatened either the Baltic states or Soviet Russia. In any case, such a pact would impose obligations respecting the border states that would deprive German eastern policy of freedom of movement. Nadolny had to inform Litvinov that since, in the opinion of the German government, neither Moscow nor Berlin, nor any other power threatened the independence of the Baltic states, there was no need for the proposed declaration.[45]

Litvinov angrily charged Berlin with ignoring the international realities. The Soviet Union had to be concerned with the security of the Baltic area; the Baltic states themselves were alarmed about their independence. "Violation of the peace in this part of Europe may and in all probability will prove to be a prelude to the outbreak of a new world war," Litvinov warned.[46]

To put a stop to rumors and to prevent any undue publicity, the Germans informed Riga about the Soviet offer and the reasons for Germany's rejection. When Munters received this information, on April 23, 1934, he rather lamely agreed with Martius on the inappropriateness of the Soviet proposal. Nevertheless, Munters and Ulmanis both anxiously inquired if Germany might explore other ways to achieve some general security agreement for Eastern Europe. Berlin curtly refused to discuss the matter further. Neurath instructed Martius to be "absolutely sure to avoid giving M. Ulmanis any ground for discussion of other possibilities in this field."[47]

Thus rebuffed, the Latvians decided to publish Litvinov's proposal and Neurath's rejection despite a German request not to do so. While Riga was not pleased at being the uninformed object of a Soviet proposal, the Latvians were even less satisfied with the German reply, which they found "decidedly unconvincing."[48] A public exposure would at least keep the record straight.

The conservative Latvian press (*Latvis, Brīvā Zeme, Latvijas Kŭreivis*) denounced the efforts of "solicitous uncles" to guarantee Latvia's security by secret deals without Latvia's participation. The more inflammatory *Pēdējā Brīdī* headlined, "And Now the Dagger behind the Back!" It dismissed Germany's reasons for not joining a guarantee declaration as "laughable."

> Is there any one who believes this childish subterfuge? Germany can hurt neither itself nor others by signing this protocol; on the contrary it could help clear up the atmosphere of distrust produced by Rosenberg and others. The pen in one hand is stayed because in the other hand, behind the back, the dagger is readied for the blow.[49]

Other newspapers, including *Sociāldemokrats*, congratulated Moscow on thus exposing Germany's aggressive intentions toward Eastern Europe.[50] Moscow had scored a propaganda victory. Soviet Russia seemed the very angel of peace while National Socialist Germany appeared a sinister and cynical threat to the security of Eastern Europe.

Lithuania, now realizing that the old Berlin-Moscow friendship upon which she had depended to keep Poland at bay no longer existed, became conscious of her utter isolation. On April 25, 1934, just two days after Germany notified the Baltic states of the Soviet proposal and her rejection of it, Lithuania proposed a Baltic triple alliance.[51]

The Lithuanian *aide-mémoire* of April 25, 1934, called for negotiations among the three states to establish the closest possible entente. A list of vaguely worded general principles was offered as a basis for Baltic solidarity.

Riga reacted with surprising caution to the Lithuanian overture. Three weeks passed before Munters and his Estonian opposite, Hans Laretei, agreed to request concrete proposals from Lithuania regarding her entrance into the Latvian-Estonian alliance.[52] The caution was due to Poland.

Poland's foreign minister Jozef Beck admonished both Riga and Tallinn that if the Vilna question was not settled before Lithuania entered a Baltic alliance, Poland would consider such a bloc directed against herself.[53] The Estonians, always partial to Poland, sent foreign minister Seljamaa to Warsaw on May 22 for an official two-day visit with Pilsudski and Beck. Seljamaa made it clear that Estonia and Latvia would not be involved in Lithuania's quarrels with Poland.[54]

When Munters inquired as to Germany's attitude toward a Baltic entente, Martius gave him a negative answer. German and Polish opposition to a Baltic rapprochement "had the effect of a cold douche" on Lithuania's chances of joining the Estonian-Latvian alliance.[55] It seemed that only Soviet Russia, and, perhaps, France supported the concept of collective security.

But Lithuania pressed her suit for a Baltic agreement on May 29, with a request for negotiations in Kaunas among the foreign ministers of the three states. Latvia finally agreed to a meeting of "responsible officials" of the foreign offices.[56]

Vilhelms Munters and Hans Laretei still hesitated to extend the Latvian-Estonian defensive treaty to Lithuania. Instead, at the meeting in Kaunas with the new Lithuanian foreign minister, Stasys Lozoraitis, on July 7-9, 1934, the possibility of a new kind of treaty was taken up. There was "no discussion of military cooperation" because Lithuania demanded a free hand respecting Vilna; the other two states naturally would not underwrite a campaign to obtain that city for Lithuania.[57]

Nevertheless a "gentleman's agreement" was worked out regarding Vilna. Latvia would do nothing likely to prejudice the Lithuanian position while Lithuania would not embarrass Latvia and Estonia by pushing her claims on Vilna too actively.[58] Whether this formula could be worked into a formal treaty was another question.

Munters gave a pessimistic report of the Kaunas meeting to the press. He emphasized the difficulty of making an agreement with Lithuania.[59] It is obvious that Polish pressure was at the root of this Latvian caution respecting Lithuania. Poland also played a role in dampening Baltic enthusiasm for the Franco-Soviet Eastern Locarno project of 1934.

The Franco-Soviet attempt to negotiate a general Eastern European security pact interrupted the halting progress toward a Baltic entente. The concept of an Eastern security pact was an old one by 1934, having been pursued rather strongly by Cielēns in 1926-27. In November, 1927, Litvinov and Briand had briefly discussed a guarantee of the status quo in Eastern Europe.[60] But only with the signing of the Franco-Soviet nonaggression agreement in November, 1932, did an Eastern pact enter the realm of practical politics.

Joseph Paul-Boncour, French foreign minister, suggested in October, 1933, a regional pact including France, Germany, Soviet Russia, and the Little Entente and Poland. The Soviets countered by insisting that the Baltic states be included; it was through this region that the Soviets expected a German attack might come. Felikss Cielēns, now Latvian minister in Paris, urged Paul-Boncour and other officials to bring the Baltic states into the collective security pact.[61]

By early June, 1934, Litvinov and Louis Barthou (who had become French foreign minister in February) reached a firm agreement. Two treaties would be proposed. One, called "An Eastern Pact of Mutual Assistance," would include the Soviet Union, Germany, Poland, Czechoslovakia, Lithuania, Latvia, Estonia, and Finland. The second treaty would be between France and Soviet Russia; the Soviets would accept the obligations of the treaty of Locarno toward France, while France would assume the obligations of the Eastern Pact toward Soviet Russia—but *not* toward the other countries.[62]

France presented the plan for Eastern security to Berlin and London on June 7, 1934. The British agreed to "recommend" the plan to Germany and Poland. But Germany reacted negatively, condemning the pact as an encirclement attempt.[63]

The Latvians, Estonians, and Lithuanians were informed about the plan and invited to adhere. Why did Munters react so slowly to a plan which the Latvians had once advocated so vigorously? For its effectiveness in Eastern Europe, the proposed pact would depend upon the Soviet Union and Germany, if Berlin adhered to it. Under this pact France had undertaken no obligations toward any East European state except the Soviet Union. These factors left Latvia and the Baltic states at the mercy of Soviet Russia's interpretation of the treaty. "Mutual assistance" might call for Soviet troops to be stationed in the Baltic

states and for Soviet intervention in domestic politics. Latvia hesitated to join and urgently desired the participation of Germany
in order to balance the Soviet presence and also to blunt Germany's
own ambitions. Estonia and Finland shared Latvia's lukewarm
attitude toward the proposed pact; Lithuania supported it.[64]

Poland also reacted negatively to the pact idea. In fact,
during June and July, 1934, the Baltic states became the scene of
a diplomatic contest between Poland and France over the adherence of these states to the Eastern Locarno project. Poland objected to Lithuania's presence in the proposed pact; Warsaw was
convinced that the pact would only reinforce Lithuanian intran-
sigence about Vilna and about restoring normal relations with
Poland. But Warsaw also objected to the pact since it threatened to prejudice her new nonaggression treaty with Germany.[65]
Poland therefore sought to align the Baltic states—including
Lithuania—with Warsaw and Berlin instead of with Paris and
Moscow. What were the prospects of such a plan?

The new Lithuanian foreign minister, Stasys Lozoraitis, was
not disinclined to compose difficulties with Poland. An intimate
of Marshal Pilsudski's, Colonel Aleksander Prystor, arrived in
Kaunas on June 20 for unofficial conversations with Lozoraitis and
Antanas Smetona. The outline of an agreement emerged from
these talks; Poland would grant autonomy to the Vilna territory and would give Lithuania a guarantee of help in the defense
of Memel. The Lithuanians would establish diplomatic relations with Poland, open the frontier between their two countries,
and cooperate with Poland in case of war.[66]

The French moved quickly to counteract the threatened defection of Lithuania from the Eastern pact. The French dispatched
one Pfeiffer, a newspaperman and vice-chairman of Herriot's
party, on an unofficial mission to Kaunas in July, 1934. When
Pfeiffer assured the Lithuanians that France would stand by
them on Vilna against Poland, the Lithuanians broke off the in-
formal discussions with the Poles.[67]

The French, perhaps acting at Soviet request, may have interrupted more than they realized. A settlement of the Polish-Lithuanian dispute was the first requirement for any revival of a Baltic
bloc with Polish participation. Such a settlement, combined with
Poland's good relations with Estonian and Latvian military and

agrarian circles, certainly opened up the prospect of an alignment of the Baltic states with Poland or of their inclusion in the German-Polish friendship and nonaggression arrangement.[68] But the French, determined to satisfy the Soviet demand for the inclusion of the Baltic states in the Eastern pact, killed such a development.

Poland did not let her defeat by Paris go unchallenged. When news leaked that Litvinov had invited Estonian foreign minister Seljamaa and Lithuanian foreign minister Lozoraitis to visit Moscow, Polish foreign minister Beck travelled to Tallinn and Riga, seeking to deflect these states from the Eastern pact and toward a common front with Poland. A German newspaper reported that Poland fought the Eastern pact because it would frustrate her plans for a Baltic bloc. "Thus Poland is now carrying on a struggle in the Baltic against the Soviet Union on the one hand and against France on the other."[69]

The two Baltic capitals gave Beck a cordial reception. Seljamaa of Estonia and Munters of Latvia dutifully expressed reservations about the projected Eastern security pact and Beck returned to Warsaw reporting that "on the whole" Riga and Tallinn shared the Polish view.[70]

Poland's success, however, was short-lived. Great Britain now joined France and Russia in putting strong pressure on the Baltic governments. According to Walter Duranty, *New York Times* correspondent, British and Soviet diplomats cooperated in pressuring the two northern Baltic states: "It was British influence that swung Estonia and Latvia away from Poland to support the Franco-Russian pact project."[71]

Baltic resistance to such combined arm-twisting proved slight. Riga and Tallinn found it impossible to align with Warsaw and Berlin. Accordingly, Seljamaa went to Moscow where he joined the Latvian envoy there, Roberts Bilmanis, in signing on July 29, 1934, a declaration agreeing to enter the Eastern pact. Lithuania's Lozoraitis came to Moscow and on August 2, 1934, issued a similar statement. Litvinov "was in a state of triumphant delight" at the diplomatic defeat of Poland.[72]

Litvinov's triumph was brief. The Eastern Locarno plan was dead without German and Polish participation. Despite the urging of Britain and France and the anxious pleas of Baltic diplomats Germany officially rejected the pact on September 8, 1934; Poland followed suit on September 27.[73] The death by assassination of Louis Barthou in October removed the chief French advocate of the plan.

The Baltic states, Latvia and Estonia in particular, were the real losers. Both alternatives—the possibility of alignment with Warsaw and Berlin and the prospect of an Eastern Locarno—were now destroyed. Both alternatives had held danger as well as hope for security. Association with Warsaw might have quickly reduced Riga and Tallinn to Berlin's satellites. Joining an Eastern Locarno pact without German participation and in which France assumed no direct obligations to the Baltic states would have left them at the mercy of the Kremlin. The only option left was that of a Baltic entente.

When Lithuanian foreign minister Lozoraitis returned from Moscow, he once more pressed Latvia and Estonia to summon a conference on the matter of a Baltic entente. Litvinov, perhaps anticipating that the Eastern pact project would fail, had used "potent arguments" on Lozoraitis in favor of Lithuania's joining a Baltic entente. Estonia and Latvia, who had also received encouragement from the Soviets, agreed to meet with Lithuania.[74]

With Moscow's blessings representatives from the three states gathered in Riga on August 29, 1934, and on the evening of that same day initialed a "Treaty of Entente and Collaboration." The agreement called for lending "mutual political and diplomatic assistance" in international relations, although "specific problems" (i.e., Vilna and Memel) were excepted. The new treaty had no military clause and could not be considered to have extended, abrogated, or replaced the Latvian-Estonian defensive alliance. Questions of defense were not discussed. The treaty merely provided for political, diplomatic, and consular cooperation by means of periodic conferences of the foreign ministers of the three states. It was formally signed on September 12, 1934, at Geneva.[75]

After more than a decade of opposition, Moscow encouraged the formation of the Baltic entente in 1934 because of her distrust of German intentions. *Izvestiiâ*, which in the past had condemned efforts at Baltic rapprochement, now wrote that the agreement would help consolidate the independence and security of the Baltic states. Naturally, the signatories of the treaty must, in

Izvestiia's words, "guard against the influence of certain imperial-
istic circles which desire to use the Baltic states for purposes
which have nothing to do with their own security and independence."[76]

Coming after years of pious lip service to the cause of Baltic
solidarity, the entente treaty of 1934 was anticlimactic. It was not
even as strong as the treaty drafted at Bulduri fourteen years earlier. The passage of time had weakened rather than strengthened
the elements for Baltic union. Out of the diplomatic maelstrom of
1933-34 Latvia had snatched—nothing. The Baltic entente of
1934 had no significance as a security measure. Latvia's quest for
security had reached a dead end in 1934. The three Baltic states
then entered upon that condition of pathetic *immobilité* in
which World War II overwhelmed them.

9

Conclusion:

The Limitations

of Small Power Diplomacy

Latvia's quest for security was an exercise in frustration which ended in futility. The frenzied signing of protocols, conventions, treaties, and pacts was a "symptom of insecurity rather than an effective guarantee of safety."[1] In simple terms a small state's security is determined by three elements: the threatening power or powers; the supporting power or powers; and, the small state's own resources and efforts.[2] For Latvia and the other Baltic states the three elements all told against them. They were threatened, finally, by two great powers; there were no supporting powers; and their own resources were thin. Latvia's situation was, of course, rendered more dangerous by her geographical isolation from potential great power allies and her strategic exposure to potential and actual great power enemies. The immutable factors of geography aside, could this political situation have been avoided or if not avoided could it have been alleviated?

The dangerous situation might have been obviated had the Latvian nation found a home in a truly democratic Russian federation. But even the Russian Provisional Government of 1917 was uninterested in autonomy for a unified Latvian state, while, after the triumph of the Bolsheviks, the Latvians had to choose between Lenin's dictatorship and the reactionary chauvinism of the Russian Whites. The Latvians, therefore, had no option but to seek salvation in independence. A Latvian republic

founded upon land reform and the principles of bourgeois democracy could not have existed in either Lenin's Soviet federation or in a Russia reconstituted by the reactionary Whites.
Latvia's situation was compelled by necessity.

Could the dangerous political situation have been alleviated?
As this study has demonstrated, the Latvians tried every humanly
conceivable alternative. The pooling of military strength in a
Baltic league involving Poland and Finland would have significantly enhanced the region's security. Meierovics helped formu-
late this aim during the first few years of independence. But the
cumulative effects of a thousand years of bitter history militated
against an effective Baltic league.[3]

Narrow egoistic nationalism, petty ambition, and personal
jealousies inhibited fruitful collaboration. Meierovics himself
was rather ambigious in his pursuit of the Baltic alliance. However, it was Poland's dream of restoring the boundaries of 1772 and
of playing a great power role in Eastern Europe which ruined
the early and best chances for political and military union of the
Baltic and border states. The Bulduri Conference of 1920, organized by Meierovics, and providing the chief opportunity for a
regional military pact, was destroyed by Poland's seizure of Vilna.
The Vilna question, as these pages have shown, thereafter poison-
ed Baltic relations at every turn.

Even if a Baltic pact had been consummated at Bulduri or, later,
at Warsaw, or Helsinki, it was "quite clear that the whole Baltic
combination would have a solid foundation only if it were at
least morally supported by a Great Power of the first rank."[4]
The ethnic, political, and economic weaknesses of the Baltic region made outside assistance crucial in case of a military conflict with one of the neighboring great powers.

No one understood these facts better than Meierovics. But as
we have seen, the western powers were indifferent to the fate of
the Baltic states. Britain and France had no real interests at stake
there. It is startling to recall that as early as the spring of 1926
Britain decided she should not object to the eventual absorption
of the Baltic states by Soviet Russia. The position of the western
powers altered not one whit from that time forward. Neither
would Weimar Germany challenge Soviet interests in the Baltic.

Disillusioned by the western powers, Meierovics, shortly before
his death, launched his despairing gamble: he would abandon

Poland and the Baltic league concept for collaboration with Germany and Russia. After an interruption, during which Ulmanis tried to restore the orientation to Poland and the western powers, Felikss Cielēns resumed the gamble. He also elaborated the "Eastern Locarno" idea. It was all to no avail.

Berlin and Moscow easily absorbed these efforts of the Baltic diplomats into their own policy of keeping Poland isolated. Indeed, the history of Latvian diplomacy provides instructive insights into the decade-long operation of Soviet-German friendship. If they could be so successful in the days of their weakness, what could Berlin and Moscow not accomplish in the fullness of their power? The middle years of the 1920s provide a dim preview of 1939 and beyond.

By the end of 1927, then, all the security expedients and options had been considered, investigated, and fruitlessly pursued; none could be achieved: no Baltic league; no commitment from a western power; no Eastern Locarno; no real chance of collaboration with Germany. Latvia's ultimate end and that of her sister states was settled long before Ribbentrop and Molotov signed their fatal agreement. Yet Weimar Germany and Soviet Russia could not in 1928 consummate their opportunities; both had first to regain power.

Germany's recovery of power was accompanied by the rise of National Socialism which ideology interrupted the old Berlin-Moscow link. Latvia seemed at last in 1933 to have a real option in foreign policy. Vilhelms Munters tried to achieve an understanding with the new Germany. In his efforts he was seconded by the German minister in Riga and by minor National Socialist figures. He did not succeed, however; Germany chose Warsaw as her temporary partner to the east.

There followed then a shadowy reenactment of Meierovics's diplomacy of the early 1920s. There was Salnais's desperate and unsuccessful attempt to bring Sweden and Finland into a common alliance with Estonia and Latvia. But Sweden would not—indeed, could not—play the "Baltic Britain" to the little "Belgiums" across the sea. Another ghost of the 1920s, Cielēns's Eastern Locarno, reappeared in slightly altered form. But France would give Latvia no direct guarantees under the proposed Eastern security pact of 1934. Without such pledges and without German participation, the Pact would have delivered the Baltic states up to the Kremlin.

Everyone knew what the "protection" of Moscow meant. Therefore, only the three-state entente and despairing declarations of absolute neutrality were the final options for security. But the ability to shoot back and the certainty of doing so is the last defense even of neutrality. A small state must maximize its military potential in order to make an attack by a big power as costly as possible.[5] Switzerland with her marvelous geographical advantages has pursued this policy for centuries. But Baltic geography, a modest population, and an agrarian economy frustrated this tactic for Latvia and her sister republics.

The Latvian political arena was dominated by agrarian-bourgeois combinations that established Latvia's economy and politics on an agricultural base. For social and political reasons, the agrarians resisted attempts by Social Democrats to revive Latvia's prewar industrial complex. These considerations were at the root of the bitter clashes between Ulmanis and Cielēns in 1926-1927 over foreign and domestic policy. Postwar circumstances made it difficult in any case, but the failure to rebuild the prewar industries, especially the metal-working industries, precluded a modern military force. Latvia was dependent upon outside assistance for military equipment and supplies. No such outside assistance existed. Baltic neutrality remained unarmed, naked to its enemies.

In the late 1930s a Baltic newspaper carried a cartoon showing a double headed Latvia with one smiling face turned toward Berlin and Warsaw while the other face, with an equally kind smile, looked toward Moscow. From East, South, and West, the smiles were met with the muzzles of cannon. Underneath the drawing were the words: "Let others conduct war; thou, happy Latvia, smilest!"[6] Smiles, alas, are no substitutes for troops and armaments and bullets.

In moving to the Baltic entente Latvia and her partners were following to fatal conclusion the logic of their situation and, apparently, also the conventional advice of political science. That advice holds that a small state's security is best achieved in a multilateral alliance system containing big and little powers. If such a mixed alliance system is not possible, then the weak state "probably should choose a Small Power alliance in preference to an unequal bilateral alliance. . . . An alliance with a single

Great Power ought to be chosen only if all other alternatives are proscribed. . . ."[7] The Baltic Entente of 1934 seemed to fit this prescription.

But the entente had no significance whatever as a security measure. Coming after fifteen years of strident declarations in support of the principle of Baltic unity, the entente between Latvia, Estonia, and Lithuania was a monument to the failure of an ideal. Military matters were explicitly excluded from the treaty. The agreement was not really due to Baltic initiative; Latvia and Estonia had hesitated throughout the spring of 1934 about including Lithuania in their defensive alliance and, indeed, never did.

The treaty of Baltic entente was fostered by Soviet Russia in order to provide a kind of buffer zone between herself and National Socialist Germany. As such, the Baltic entente of 1934 was not a step toward Baltic unity or toward a solution of the Baltic security problem. This final achievement in Baltic diplomacy marked simply an interim stage in the struggle between neighboring great powers for control of the *Baltikum.*

There are, after all, exceedingly narrow limits to the effectiveness of goodwill and guile as diplomatic strategies for a small power menaced by large powers. Such ploys are no substitutes for maximum development of military resources and foreign backing. In 1928, shortly after the realities of the Baltic situation had begun to reveal their stark outlines, one observer wrote of the Baltic states: "Their future is tied to that of the European peace, the treaties, and the Geneva spirit. Here, more than elsewhere, the wisdom of the large states is for the security of the small the only decisive guarantee."[8] Political wisdom is, unfortunately, in notoriously short supply among all powers, big and small. The Baltic states only partially fulfilled a Biblical injunction: while being as harmless as doves they were not as wise as serpents. On the other hand, "wise" action aggrandizing Germany and Soviet Russia could hardly contribute to the security of their small neighbors. The fate of the Baltic states is a lasting testimonial to that brutal fact.

Notes

Notes to Chapter 1

1. The term "Baltic states" as used in this study refers to Estonia, Latvia, and Lithuania. In contemporary journalism the phrase often meant Finland, Estonia, and Latvia. A convenient introduction to the literature on this area is provided by Zelma Alexandra Ozols, *Latvia: A Selected Bibliography* (Washington: Karl Karusa, 1963), and by Georg von Rauch, *Geschichte der baltischen Staaten* (Stuttgart, Berlin, Cologne: W. Kohlhammer Verlag, 1970). An excellent introduction to the early history of the region is provided by Reinhard Wittram, *Baltische Geschichte: Die Ostseelande Livland, Estland, Kurland 1180-1918* (Munich: Verlag R. Oldenbourg, 1954).

2. In 1914, the population was 2,552,000; in 1920, it was 1,596,181; and in 1935, 1,950,502. For full statistical analysis, see *Latvia: Country and People*, ed. J. Rutkis (Stockholm: Latvian National Foundation, 1967), chapter IV; Roderick von Ungern-Sternberg, "Bevölkerungsprobleme Lettlands," *Osteuropa*, XII (December, 1936), 155-173; *The Baltic States: A Survey of the Political and Economic Structure and the Foreign Relations of Estonia, Latvia, and Lithuania*, prepared by the Public Information Department of the Royal Institute of International Affairs (London: Oxford University Press, 1938), p. 33. This last item is cited hereafter as *Baltic States: Survey*.

3. Latgale's total population in 1935 was 567,164. Of this figure, Latvians accounted for 61.32 percent; Great Russians for 27.15 percent; Jews for 4.93 percent; Poles for 3.45 percent; White Russians for 2.45 percent; all others for 0.7 percent. See *Latvju Enciklopēdija* (Stockholm: Apgāds Trīs zvaigznes, 1950-1955), p. 1226. On conflicts between German and Latvian Lutheran authorities, see Wilhelm von Rüdiger, *Aus dem Letzten Kapitel deutsch-baltischer Geschichte in Lettland: Erster Teil, 1919-1945* (Gern bei Eggenfelden/Bayern: Published by the author, 1954), pp. 24-25.

4. Estimates of the amount of industrial material moved into the Russian interior range from 20,000 to 60,000 boxcar loads. Edgar Anderson, "The U.S.S.R. Trades with Latvia: The Treaty of 1927," *Slavic Review*, XXI, No. 2 (June, 1962), 296-297; Hans Westenberger, "Die handelspolitischen und wirtschaftlichen Beziehungen Deutschlands und Lettlands bis zum Abschluss des deutsch-lettländischen Vertrages vom 28. Juni 1926," *Osteuropa*, I, No. 11/12 (1925-26), 662; R. von Freymann, "Der lettländisch-russische Friedensvertrag und seine Verwirklichung," *Rigasche Zeitschrift für Rechtswissenschaft*, I, No. 4 ("Sonderbeilage," 1926/1927), 1-34; "Latvia," *The Economic Review*, XIV, No. 7 (August 13, 1926), 148; Edward William Polson Newman, *Britain and the Baltic* (London: Methuen and Co., 1930), p. 89.

5. Arnolds Spekke, *History of Latvia: An Outline* (Stockholm: M. Goppers, 1951), p. 365; Daniel Pernak, *Les Relations économiques de la France et de la Lettonie* (Toulouse: Imprimerie Regionale, 1930), p. 92. The war ravaged 1,729,828 hectares of tilled soil (28.3 percent of the total), a fact reflected in the drop of the grain harvest from 15.3 million quintals in 1914 to 7.5 million quintals in 1920.

6. Kārlis Kalnins, "Economic Structure and Resources," in *Crossroad Country: Latvia*, edited by Edgars Andersons (Waverly, Iowa: Latvju Grāmata, 1953), pp. 96-98; F. W. von Bülow, "Social Aspects of the Agrarian Reform in Latvia," *International Labour Review*, XX, No. 1 (July, 1929), 35-66.

7. Pernak, *Les Relations économiques de la France et de la Lettonie*, pp. 93-94.

8. *Latvia: Country and People*, pp. 432-434; *Baltic States: Survey*, pp. 123; 145-447.

9. In 1930, when there had been a quite modest industrial recovery, the German legation in Riga reported: "Since Latvia's own factories are not set up for the manufacture of military equipment the country is dependent upon foreign support in the event of war." Tippelskirch (Riga) to Foreign Ministry (Berlin), February 25, 1930, in *Auswärtiges Amt* (Records of the German Foreign Ministry on Microfilm, United States National Archieves, Microcopy T-120), Reel 5770, Serial K2333, Frame K664436. This source hereafter will be cited as *Auswärtiges Amt* with reel, serial, and frame numbers separated by diagonal lines.

10. *Latvia: Country and People*, pp. 237-238; *Latvju Enciklopēdija*, p. 354; *Riga Times*, October 10, 1925.

11. Arnold John Zucher, *The Experiment with Democracy in Central Europe* (New York: Oxford University Press, 1933), pp. 79-80, 86, 141, 143, 178-181, 191. The text of the Latvian constitution may be found in *Latvian-Russian Relations: Documents* (Washington: Latvian Legation, 1944), pp. 238-244; see also *Latvia: Country and People*, pp. 239-242.

12. André Tibal, *La Constitution lettone* ("Problèmes politiques contemporains de l'Europe orientale"; Paris: Centre européen de la Dotation Carnegie, 1930), pp. 20-25. The 17 parties of the 150-seat

Constituent Assembly fell into four categories: ethnic minorities with 17 seats; Social Democrats and Radical Democrats with 63 seats; bourgeois center with 15 seats; agrarian parties with 54 seats. See R. T. Clark, "Baltic Politics: Elections in Latvia and Lithuania," *The New Europe*, XVI, No. 197 (July 22, 1920), pp. 28-30.

13. Arthur Brown Ruhl, *New Masters of the Baltic* (New York: E. P. Dutton, 1921), pp. 156-157.

14. Albats was deported by Soviet authorities following the occupation of Latvia in 1941. *Latvju Enciklopēdija*, p. 38.

15. *Le Corps diplomatique en Lettonie, 1918-1938* (Riga: Ministère des affaires étrangères de Lettonie, 1938); *Latvia: Country and People*, p. 226.

16. Even routine international contacts were hindered by an officious bureaucracy. Latvia was now independent of Russia—but not of Russian practices. Foreign visitors found themselves drowned in red-tape. Entrance permits, exit permits, money permits, and special permits for personal effects such as typewriters and cameras baffled and enraged foreign businessmen. T. R. Ybarra, "The Self-Extermination of Self-Determination," *New York Times Book Review and Magazine*, October 23, 1921, p. 7.

17. Ruhl, *New Masters of the Baltic*, pp. 151-152; John A. Gade (U.S. Commissioner to the Baltic, Riga) to Secretary of State, April 27, 1920, in Department of State Decimal Files, 1910-1929, Record Group 59, National Archives of the United States, Document No. 860n.00/2; Evan E. Young (Riga) to Secretary of State, July 1, 1920, *ibid.*, Doc. No. 860n00/9 (this source will hereafter be cited as National Archives followed by the document number); London *Times*, July 6, 1920. A similar dispute between Latvia and Lithuania over the coastal town of Polangen was also mediated by the British. Wever (German chargé, Riga) to Foreign Ministry, January 25, 1921, *Auswärtiges Amt*, 5770/ K2331/K663715-K663716.

18. *Vossische Zeitung*, November 9, 1922.

19. *Riga Times*, March 28, 1925. This tendency Latvians shared with other East European diplomats. See Josef Hanč, *Tornado across Eastern Europe* (New York: Greystone Press, 1942), p. 73.

20. On economic and cultural achievements during independence, see chapters five and six of *Latvia: Country and People*, and the pamphlet *Latvia* (Washington: The Latvian Legation, 1966).

21. On this point see the discussion by Edward Beneš, "The Problem of the Small Nations after the War," *Slavonic Review*, IV, No. 11 (December, 1925), 257-277.

22. *Frankfurter Zeitung*, May 18, 1924.

23. Xenia Joukoff Eudin, "Soviet National Minority Policies, 1918-1921," *Slavonic and East European Review*, XXI, No. 57 (November, 1943), 38-40; *Soviet Documents on Foreign Policy*, ed. Jane Degras (3 vols.; London: Oxford University Press, 1951-1953), Vol. I, p. 129.

24. For this whole period on the formation of Latvia, see Edgars Andersons, *Latvijas vēsture 1914-1920* (Stockholm: Daugava, 1967); Albert N. Tarulis, *Soviet Policy toward the Baltic States, 1918-1940.* (Notre Dame, Indiana: Notre Dame University Press, 1959); Stanley W. Page, *The Formation of the Baltic States* (Cambridge: Harvard University Press, 1959); Jürgen von Hehn, "Die Entstehung der Staaten Lettland und Estland, der Bolschewismus und die Grossmächte," *Forschungen zur osteuropäischen Geschichte*, IV (1956), 103-218; Hehn, "Lettland zwischen den Mächten 1918-1920," *Jahrbücher für Geschichte Osteuropas*, XI, No. 1 (March, 1963), 37-45. On the treaty of peace with Russia, see *Latvian-Russian Relations: Documents*, p. 70.

25. Speaking on the occasion of the Estonian peace treaty, Lenin remarked: "This concession has not been made for eternity. Estonia passes now through a Kerensky period. . . . *The workers will over-turn this authority and create a Soviet Estonia which will conclude a new peace treaty with us.*" E. Sobolevitch, *Les États Baltes et la Russie sovietique*, p. 53, quoted in Hugo Vītols, *La Mer Baltique et les états baltes* (Paris: F. Loviton and Co., 1935), p. 289 (italics in the original).

26. Hauschild, "Memorandum on the Baltic States," June 30, 1925, *Auswärtiges Amt* 3876/K243/K072248-K072250. I have taken the liberty of translating into English the titles of memoranda and other lengthy documents referring to the Baltic states.

27. Vitols, *La Mer Baltique et les états baltes*, p. 290.

28. Fritz Fischer, *Germany's Aims in the First World War* (New York: W. W. Norton, 1967), pp. 456-472, 598-608; Douglas Adolph Unfug, "German Policy in the Baltic States, 1918-1919," (Unpublished Ph. D. Dissertation, Yale University, 1960), *passim*; Werner Basler, *Deutschlands Annexionspolitik in Polen und im Baltikum 1914-1918* ("Veröffentlichungen des Instituts für Geschichte der Völker der UdSSR an der Martin Luther Universität Halle-Wittenberg," Series B, Volume III; Berlin: Rütten and Loening, 1962); Herbert A. Grant-Watson, *The Latvian Republic: The Struggle for Freedom* (London: George Allen and Unwin, 1965); Gerd Linde, "Um die Angliederung Kurlands und Litauens: Die deutschen Konzeptionen für die Zukunft der ehemals russicher Randgebiete vom Sommer 1918," *Jahrbücher für Geschichte Osteuropas*, X, No. 4 (December, 1962), 563-580; Hans-Erich Volkmann, "Probleme des deutsch-lettischen Verhältnisses zwischen Compiègne und Versailles," *Zeitschrift für Ostforschung*, XIV, No. 4 (December, 1965), 713-126; see also the articles by Hehn cited in note 25 above.

29. The literature on the German military involvement in the Baltic in 1918-1919 is extensive. In addition to the works cited in the preceding note, see the following: Rüdiger von der Goltz, *Meine Sendung in Finnland und im Baltikum* (Leipzig: Koehler, 1920); Goltz, *Als politischer General im Osten* (Leipzig: Koehler, 1936); J. G. P. M. Benoist-Mèchin, *Histoire de l'armée allemende 1918-1945*, (Vol. II; Paris: Éditions Albin Michel, 1945), pp. 15-60; Robert G. L. Waite, *Vanguard*

of Nazism: The Free Corps Movement in Germany 1918-1923 (Cambridge: Harvard University Press, 1952), Chapter V: "The Baltic Adventure"; Warren E. Williams, "Die Politik der Allierten gegenüber den Freikorps im Baltikum 1918-1919," *Vierteljahrsheft für Zeitgeschichte*, XII, No. 2 (April, 1964), 147-169; Vilnis Sīpols, *Die ausländische Intervention in Lettland 1918-1920* (Berlin: Ruetten and Loening, 1961), pp. 159-170.

30. J. Y. Simpson, "Great Britain and the Baltic States," *Nineteenth Century and After*, XCIV (October, 1923), 619.

31. W. F. Hallgarten, "General Hans von Seeckt and Russia, 1920-1922", *Journal of Modern History*, XXI, No. 1 (March, 1949), 29; Friedrich von Rabenau, *Seeckt: Aus seinem Leben 1918-1936* (Leipzig: Hase und Koehler Verlag, 1940), p. 252; Francis L. Carsten, *Reichswehr und Politik 1918-1933* (Cologne and Berlin: Kiepenheuer and Witsch, 1964), pp. 78-79.

32. *Verhandlungen des Reichstags: Stenographische Berichte*, 53rd Session, 21 January 1921 (Berlin: Norddeutsche Buchdruckerei, 1921), Vol. CCCXLVI, p. 1989; *Vossiche Zeitung*, January 22, 1921.

33. *Jaunākās Zinas*, January 29, 1921, enclosure to report of Wever (German chargé, Riga) to Foreign Ministry, February 1, 1921, *Auswärtiges Amt*, 5770/K2331/K663750-K663751; *Latvijas Kāreivis*, February 3, 4, 1921, enclosures to report of Wever to Foreign Ministry, February 8, 1921, *ibid.*, K663766-K663767. *Jaunākās Zinas* (Latest News) was an organ of the democratic center while *Latvijas Kāreivis* (Latvian Warrior) was issued by the Latvian Army. These press enclosures (and others subsequently cited from the *Auswärtiges Amt*) are German translations of articles from the cited Latvian newspapers.

34. The appointment of Baron Adolf Georg Oskar von Maltzan as head of the Eastern Division (1921) and later (1923) as State Secretary signaled the beginning of a new era. Maltzan was well-known for his opposition to the wartime annexationists and his appointment was hailed by the Latvian press. Hajo Holborn, "Diplomats and Diplomacy in the Early Weimar Republic," in *The Diplomats 1919-1939*; edited by Gordon A. Craig and Felix Gilbert (2 vols.; New York: Atheneum Press, 1965), Vol. I, *The Twenties*, pp. 148-154; Herbert von Dirksen, *Moscow, Tokyo, London: Twenty Years of German Foreign Policy* (Norman: University of Oklahoma Press, 1952), pp. 26, 56; press summary as enclosure to report of the German Legation in Riga to the Foreign Ministry, November 8, 1921, *Auswärtiges Amt*, 5770/K2331/K663849-K663850; Wallroth (Riga) to Foreign Ministry, January 3, 1923, *ibid.*, K664041-K664043.

35. "Report of the State Commissioner for Public Order to the Foreign Ministry," March 15, 1921, *Auswärtiges Amt*, 5770/K2331/K663786; "Memorandum on the Relationship of Germany to the Border States," June 11, 1921, *ibid.*, 5159/K1752/K429126-K429129. See also the excellent study by J. W. Hiden, "The Baltic Germans and German Policy toward Latvia after 1918," *Historical Journal*, XIII, No. 2 (1970), 295-317.

36. He succeeded Maltzan as head of the Eastern Division, a position which he retained until 1928 when he was appointed ambassador to Sweden. *Wer ist's?* (9th ed.; Berlin: Verlag Degener, 1928), p. 1641; Wilhelm von Rüdiger, *Aus dem letzten Kapitel deutsch-baltischer Geschichte in Lettland: Zweiter Teil, 1919-1939* (Hannover-Wulfel: By the author, 1955), p. 32; Wipert von Blücher, *Deutschlands Weg nach Rapallo: Erinnerungen eines Mannes aus dem zweiten Gliede* (Wiesbaden: Lines Verlag, 1951), p. 113.

37. Wallroth to Foreign Ministry, November 21, 1921, *Auswärtiges Amt*, 5770/K2331/K663865; Wallroth to Foreign Ministry, January 15, 1922, *ibid.*, K663875-K663876.

38. Hermann Felix Crohn-Wolfgang, *Lettlands Bedeutung für die östliche Frage* (Berlin: Walther de Gruyter, 1923), pp. 6-7, 10, 11, 56.

39. Oskar Grosberg, "Lettlands Wirtschaft in zehn Jahren," *Osteuropa*, IV (September, 1929), 837-844; Hans Westenberger, "Die handelspolitischen und wirtschaftlichen Beziehungen Deutschlands und Lettlands bis zum Abschluss des deutsch-lettländischen Vertrages vom 28. Juni 1926," *Osteuropa*, I (1925/1926), 656-667; H. E. Ronimois, *Russia's Foreign Trade and the Baltic Sea* (London: Boreas Publishing Co., 1946), pp. 34-40, especially Table 9, p. 35.

40. "Memorandum for State Secretary von Maltzan," December 7, 1923, *Auswärtiges Amt*, 3875/K243/K071356; Adolf Koester (Riga) to Foreign Ministry, December 8, 1923, *ibid.*, K071376. In October, 1923, General Hans von Seeckt sought to impress Stresemann that the "interests of Germany and Russia run parallel in borderstate policy." See Carsten, *Reichswehr und Politik*, p. 155.

41. Harry Gabrielsky, "Polens aussenpolitische Ideologie," *Osteuropa*, VII, No. 8 (May, 1932), 44-45; M. K. Dziewanowski, "Pilsudski's Federal Policy," *Journal of Central European Affairs*, X, No. 2 (July, 1950), 118-119; Taras Hunczak, "'Operation Winter' and the Struggle for the Baltic," *East European Quarterly*, IV, No. 1 (March, 1970), 40-57.

42. In a press statement of April 14, 1920, the Polish chargé said: "In the Latgallian question it was for Latvia to turn rather to Poland than to Russia. Dünaburg and the railroad would have to remain open for the Polish army even in case of peace being concluded between Latvia and Soviet Russia." John A. Gade (U.S. Commissioner, Riga) to Secretary of State, April 27, 1920, National Archives, Doc. No. 860n00/4. See also Vilnis Sipols, *Die ausländische Intervention in Lettland 1918-1920*, pp. 212, 216-219, especially p. 218 n.102.

43. Harald Laeuen, *Polnische Tragödie* (2nd ed.; Stuttgart: Steingrüben Verlag, 1956), pp. 17 n.74, 290; Josef Hanč, *Eastern Europe* (London: Museum Press, 1943), p. 51; Casimir Smogorzewski, *La Pologne Restaurée* (Paris, 1927), quoted in S. Konovalov, *Russo-Polish Relations* (Princeton: Princeton University Press, 1945), p. 78.

44. Erich Wallroth (Riga) to Foreign Ministry, September 29, 1922, *Auswärtiges Amt*, 5380/K1967/K510537.

45. Edgar Anderson, "An Undeclared Naval War: The British-Soviet Struggle in the Baltic 1918-1920," *Journal of Central European Affairs*,

XXII, No. 1 (April, 1962), 43-78; Anderson, "The British Policy toward the Baltic States, 1918-1920," *ibid.*, XIX, No. 3 (October, 1959), 276-289; Albert N. Tarulis, *American-Baltic Relations 1918-1922: The Struggle over Recognition* (Washington: Catholic University of America Press, 1965); U.S. Congress, Senate, *The Baltic Provinces: Report of the Mission to Finland, Estonia, Latvia, and Lithuania on the Situation in the Baltic Provinces*, 66th Congress, 1st Session, Senate Document No. 105 (Washington: Government Printing Office, 1919); Jürgen von Hehn, "Die Entstehung der Staaten Lettland und Estland, der Bolschewismus und die Grossmächte," *Forschungen zur osteuropäischen Geschichte*, IV (1956), 103-218: Hehn, "Lettland zwischen den Mächten 1918-1920," *Jahrbücher für Geschichte Osteuropas*, XI (March, 1963), 37-45.

46. Felikss Cielēns, **Laikmetu mainā: atminas un atzinas** [At the Turning of Epochs: Reflections and Reminiscences] (3 vols.; Lidingo, Sweden: Memento, 1961-1964), vol. II, pp. 62-63, 64-65; *Memorandum on Latvia Addressed to the Peace Conference by the Lettish Delegation* (Paris, 1919), in National Archives, Doc. No. 860n.01/35; Tarulis, *American-Baltic Relations*, pp. 51, 169, 195.

47. Sīpols, *Die ausländische Intervention in Lettland*, pp. 163-165, 189, 208-209, 212, 216-220; Bohdan Halaychuk, "The Peace of Riga: The End of the Anti-Bolshevik Front," *The Ukranian Quarterly*, XII, No. 3. (September, 1956), 244-250.

48. Quoted in *New York Times*, December 17, 1920. The story of the Baltic states' search for diplomatic recognition is fully detailed in Tarulis, *American-Baltic Relations*, which supercedes the older work of Malbone W. Graham, *The Diplomatic Recognition of the Border States. Part III: Latvia* ("Publications of the University of California at Los Angeles in Social Sciences," Vol. III, No. 4) (Berkeley: University of California Press, 1941).

49. "Z. Meierovics un Musu de jure" [Meierovics and *de jure* Recognition], in Edvarts Virza, editor, *Z. A. Meierovics: Latvijas primā ārlietu ministra darbības atcerei veltīts rakstu krājums* [Z. A. Meierovics: A Collection of Essays in Memory of Latvia's First Foreign Minister] (Riga: Z. A. Meierovica pieminas fonda izdevums, 1935), pp. 171-172 (this work will hereafter be cited as Virza, ed., *Meierovics*); Count Carlo Sforza, *Diplomatic Europe since the Treaty of Versailles*, (New Haven: Yale University Press, 1928), pp. 74-76; *Latvian-Russian Relations: Documents*, p. 81; chargé (Riga) to Foreign Ministry (Berlin), January 11, 1921, *Auswärtiges Amt*, 5769/K2329/K663102; Tarulis, *American Baltic Relations*, pp. 313, 327 note 50.

50. *Papers Relating to the Foreign Relations of the United States, 1922* (2 vols.; Washington: Government Printing Office, 1938), II, 870-873.

51. This problem is treated at some length in Louis Tissot, *La Baltique: Situation des pays riverains de la Baltique: Importance économique et stratégique de la "Méditerranée du Nord"* (Paris: Payot, 1940); see also F. de Jessen, "Problèmes actuels et futurs des voies d'accès à la

baltique," in *La Pologne et la baltique: Conférences données à la Bibliothèque polonaise de Paris* ("Problèmes politiques de la Pologne contemporaine," Vol I) (Paris: Gebethener et Wolff, 1931), pp. 145-161; Arthur Taska, "Dominum maris baltici und die Sowjetunion," in *Pro Baltica: Mélanges dédiés à Kaarel R. Pusta*, edited by Jüri G. Poska (Stockholm: Publication du Comité des Amis de K. R. Pusta, 1965), pp. 203-212; Waldemar Westergaard, *Political and Military Factors: The Baltic* (Berkeley: University of California, 1941).

52. J. Y. Simpson, "Great Britain and the Baltic States," *Nineteenth Century and After*, XCIV (October, 1923), p. 621; see also E. W. Polson Newman, "Great Britain and the Baltic," *ibid.*, CIV (November, 1928), 607-617. Throughout 1920 the British warned Latvia against any close connection with Poland, while France and Poland sought to preserve a united anti-Bolshevik front. The English feared that France, through Warsaw, would extend her influence to the Baltic and replace British dominance there. See Sīpols, *Die ausländische Intervention in Lettland*, p. 211. For general treatment of this problem see Arnold Wolfers, *Britain and France between Two Wars: Conflicting Strategies of Peace from Versailles to World War II* (New York: W. W. Norton Co., 1966).

53. Benjamin Siew, *Lettlands Volks- und Staatswirtschaft* (Riga: Müller'sche Buchdruckerei, 1925), p. 213.

54. Koester (Riga) to Foreign Ministry, September 10, 1923, *Auswärtiges Amt*, 5777/K2361K668765-K668767. A Franco-Latvian commercial agreement was not signed until October, 1924, and France was never a serious threat to the primacy of Germany and Britain in Baltic commerce. See Pernak, *Les Rélations économiques de la France et de la Lettonie*, for details.

Notes to Chapter 2

1. Edgar Anderson, "Toward the Baltic Entente: The Initial Phase," in *Pro Baltica: Mélanges dédiés à Kaarel R. Pusta*, ed. Jüri G. Poska (Stockholm: Publication du Comité des Amis de K. R. Pusta, 1965), pp. 41-61; Taras Hunczak, "'Operation Winter' and the Struggle for the Baltic," *East European Quarterly*, IV, No. 1 (March, 1970), 40-57; N. Kaasik, "L'Evolution de l'union baltique," *Revue générale de droit internationale publique*, XLI (September/October, 1934), 631-647.

2. Kaarel Robert Pusta, "Le Statut juridique de la mer baltique à partir du XIXe siècle," *Recueil des cours 1935: Académie de droit internationale* (Paris: Librairie du Recueil Sirey, 1935), LII, pp. 165-166; Pusta, "La Question baltique dans le problème européen," *Revue politique et parlementaire*, LVII (March, 1955), 268-276; Ants Piip, "The Baltic States as a Regional Unity," *Annals of the American Academy of Political and Social Science*, CLXVIII (July, 1933), 171-177.

3. London *Times*, January 12, 21, 24, 1920; see also, Virza, ed.,

Meierovics, pp. 40-41, 70; Sīpols, *Die ausländische Intervention in Lettland*, pp. 193-94, 200-210.

4. *Vossiche Zeitung* (Berlin), November 9, 1922; *Riga Times*, August 29, 1925; Hehn, "Die Entstehung der Staaten Lettland und Estland," *Forschungen zur Osteuropäischen Geschichte*, IV, 115; Virza, ed., *Meierovics*, pp. 179-194, 209.

5. Virza, ed., *Meierovics*, pp. 23-28.

6. *Ibid.*, pp. 209-214; Uldis Germanis, "Latvijas neatkarības idejas attīstība [Development of the Latvian Independence Idea], *Jaunā Gaita*, XII, No. 61 (1967), 38-47; *ibid.*, No. 62 (1967), 26-37.

7. *Vossische Zeitung*, November 9, 1922; Virza, ed., *Meierovics*, p. 122.

8. *Riga Times*, August 29, 1925; Vitols, *La Mer baltique et les états baltes*, p. 273. Between 1921 and 1924, Meierovics held the prime ministership as well as the portfolio for foreign affairs. He was never a tribune of the people nor a popular favorite nor a dramatic orator. He played his role like the head of a liberal English government. A sense of compromise, a feeling for correctness, an absence of haughtiness, a kind and dignified bearing characterized his parliamentary leadership. See Cielēns, *Laikmetu mainā*, II, p. 172.

9. Vitols, *La Mer baltique*, p. 295; Bronius Kazlauskas, *L'Entente baltique*, (Paris: Imprimerie des Presses Modernes, 1939), p. 83; Raymond Leslie Buell, *Europe: A History of Ten Years* (New York: Macmillan, 1928), p. 237.

10. Vitols, *La Mer baltique*, p. 295; André Tibal, "La Politique d'après-guerre des états riverains de la baltique" in *La Pologne et la baltique*, I, p. 113.

11. See the works cited in notes 9 and 10 above.

12. Background on the Bulduri Conference may be found in London *Times*, January 26, 1920; Evan E. Young (Riga) to Secretary of State, June 29, 1920, National Archives, Doc. No. 860n.01/9. The *Brīvā Zeme* article is quoted in *Bulletin publié par le ministère des affaires étrangères de Latvia*, August 5, 1920, enclosure to report of Young to Secretary of State, August 9, 1920, National Archives, Doc. No. 860.01/14; the statement by Meierovics is found in the above-named *Bulletin*, August 17, 1920, quoted in "Baltic Entente," *Contemporary Review*, CXVIII (October, 1920), 580.

13. Evan Young (Riga) to Secretary of State, August 18, 1920, National Archives, Doc. No. 860n.01/17. The prime minister, Karlis Ulmanis, later emphasized to the press that the term "Baltic Union" was misleading. The new states did not propose to surrender their sovereignty but merely to harmonize economic regulations and arrange the coordination of defense if their independence was threatened. See *New York Times*, October 18, 1920.

14. *Minutes of the Baltic Conference Held at Bulduri in Latvia in 1920* (Washington: The Latvian Legation, 1960), pp. 22, 42-43.

15. Wasilewski had attempted in 1920 to exact territorial and other concessions from Latvia as the price for Polish aid in clearing

Latgale of Soviet Russian troops. Sīpols, *Die ausländische Intervention in Lettland*, pp. 212, 216-220. In his study of Polish-Latvian relations in the winter of 1919-1920, Hunczak ignores the Polish demands on Latvia. See his "'Operation Winter' and the Struggle for the Baltic," *East European Quarterly*, IV, No. 1 (March, 1970), pp. 56-57.

16. *Minutes of the Baltic Conference Held at Bulduri, passim.* This aspect of the conference's work is summarized in "Baltic Problems," *European Economic and Political Survey*, III, No. 7 (December 15, 1927), 215-216; and in Kazlauskas, *L'Entente baltique*, pp. 102-105.

17. The text of the treaty may be read as an enclosure to a report by Evan E. Young to Secretary of State, December 13, 1920, National Archives, Doc. No. 860n.01/22.

18. *Minutes of the Baltic Conference Held at Bulduri*, pp. 49-50, 52-53, 55-56; Young (Riga) to Secretary of State, September 7, 9, 1920, National Archives, Doc. Nos. 860n.01/19, 860n.01/20.

19. According to figures submitted by the states at the Moscow disarmament conference in 1922, Poland would maintain a standing army of 280,000; Latvia of 19,000; Estonia of 16,000, and Finland of 28,000, for a total of 343,000. Assuming 20,000 for Lithuania, we arrive at a total for the the five states of over 360,000 men. See London *Times*, December 14, 1922; Louis Fischer, *The Soviets in World Affairs*, 2nd ed., 2 vols. (Princeton: Princeton University Press, 1951, I, pp. 377-381; "Moscow Conference," *European Economic and Political Survey*, I, No. 16 (April 30, 1926), 12-13.

20. This is the contention of Karlis R. Dzelzītis, "The Problem of the United Baltic States," in *First Conference on Baltic Studies: Summary of Proceedings*, Ivar Ivask, editor (Tacoma, Washington: Pacific Lutheran University Press, 1969), pp. 22-23.

21. Alfred Erich Senn, *The Great Powers, Lithuania and the Vilna Question, 1920-1928* ("Studies in East European History," Vol. XI; Leiden: E. J. Brill, 1966), pp. 36-52.

22. The Polish chaplain who accompanied Zeligowski's forces later revealed to the American minister in Kaunas that the real intention of the move was to "establish a Catholic State which would also include Latgalia" as a connecting body between Poland and Lithuania. See Owen J. C. Norem, *Timeless Lithuania* (Chicago: Amerlith Press, 1943), pp. 106, 196.

23. Cielēns, *Laikmetu mainā*, II, pp. 158-159.

24. Cielēns boasted later that his party had prevented the alliance with Poland in 1929. Adolf Koester (German minister, Riga) to Foreign Ministry, February 11, 1924, *Auswärtiges Amt*, 5769/K2329/K663272-K663273.

25. Wever (German chargé, Riga) to Foreign Ministry, January 22, 1921, *Auswärtiges Amt*, 5769/K2329/K663108.

26. Young (Riga) to Secretary of State, December 6, 1920, National Archives, Doc. No. 860n.01/23.

27. *New York Times*, December 26, 1920.

28. Wever to Foreign Ministry, December 25, 1920, *Auswärtiges Amt*,

5380/K1969/K510752.

29. Young to Secretary of State, March 2, May 23, 1927, National Archives, Doc. Nos. 860n.01/28, 760m.60P/1; Sīpols, *Slepenā Diplomātija: Buržuāziskās Latvijas ārpolitika 1919.-1932. gadā* [Secret Diplomacy: Bourgeois Latvian Foreign Policy 1919-1932] (Riga: Izdevnieciba Liesma, 1965), pp. 86-87.

30. Sīpols, *Slepenā diplomātija*, pp. 88-89; Anderson, "Toward the Baltic Union, 1920-1927," *Lituanus*, XII, No. 2 (Summer, 1966), 35, 36-37.

31. Sīpols, *Slepenā diplomātija*, p. 91; F. H. Lyon, "Baltic Alliances: Finland at the Cross-Roads," *Fortnightly Review*, CXXI (February, 1924), 310-311.

32. *New York Times*, July 28, 1921.

33. "Failure of the Baltic League," *Current History*, XIV, No. 6 (September, 1921), 1062-1063; London *Times*, July 29, 1921; Virza, ed., *Meierovics*, pp. 82-83.

34. *Soviet Documents on Foreign Policy*, J. Degras, ed., I, pp. 285-286; Widenfeld (Moscow) to Foreign Ministry, February 9, 1922, *Auswärtiges Amt*, 5380/K1967/K510437; League of Nations, *Official Journal* (Special Supplement No. 13): *Records of the Fourth Assembly, Text of the Debates* (Geneva, 1923), pp. 74-75. On the Karelian question in general, see Clarence Jay Smith, *Finland and the Russian Revolution, 1917-1922* (Athens, Georgia: University of Georgia Press, 1958), pp. 190-205. In this matter, the Lithuanians supported the Soviets, desiring to retain Soviet backing for their claim to Vilna. See Senn, *The Great Powers, Lithuania and the Vilna Question*, p. 108.

35. Ago von Maltzan (Berlin) to German missions in Eastern Europe, February 21, 1922, *Auswärtiges Amt*, 5770/K2331/K663884-K663887.

36. "Memorandum of a Conversation with Latvian Foreign Minister Meierovics," March 7, 1922, as enclosure to a report of Evan E. Young to Secretary of State, March 8, 1922, National Archives, Doc. No. 860n.-01/47.

37. Meierovics' interview in the *Gazeta Poranna*, March 17, 1922, quoted in a despatch from the German Legation in Warsaw to the Foreign Ministry, March 22, 1922, *Auswärtiges Amt*, 5770/K2331/-K663888.

38. Meirovics' interview in the *Gazeta Warszawska*, March 17, 1922, quoted in *ibid.*, K663890-K663891.

39. Widenfeld (Moscow) to Foreign Ministry, March 15, 1922, *Auswärtiges Amt*, 3883/K253/K076953.

40. Adolf Koester (Riga) to Foreign Ministry, December 8, 1923, *Auswärtiges Amt*, 3875/K243/K071366-K071368; London *Times*, March 16, 1922.

41. Erich Wallroth (Riga) to Foreign Ministry, March 22, 1922, *Auswärtiges Amt*, 2558/5173/E306643; Kazlauskas, *L'Entente baltique*, pp. 108-109.

42. *Frankfurter Zeitung*, March 16, 1922. The previous year many patriotic Latvians had been angered by the appearance of a geography

work in Polish which showed the boundaries of a "United Poland" including Lithuania, Courland (Kurzeme), White Russia and Ukraine. Sīpols, *Slepenā diplomātija*, p. 86.
43. Cielēns, *Laikmetu mainā*, II, pp. 163-165.
44. Wallroth (Riga) to Foreign Ministry, September 9, 1922, *Auswärtiges Amt*, 5770/K2331/K663987.
45. Robert Machray, "The Baltic League," *Fortnightly Review*, CXVII(May, 1922), 738-740, 742-743; Lyon, "Baltic Alliances: Finland at the Cross-Roads," *ibid.*, CXXI (February, 1924), 305-306; see also, John H. Wuorinen, *A History of Finland* (New York: Columbia University Press, 1965), pp. 300-301.

Notes to Chapter 3

1. Benndorf (Warsaw) to Foreign Ministry, March 19, 1922, *Auswärtiges Amt*, 5380/K1967/K510447.
2. W. P. Potjomkin (V. P. Potëmkin), *Geschichte der Diplomatie*, Vol. III, p. 202, quoted in Hans von Rimscha, "Die Baltikumpolitik der Grossmächte," *Historische Zeitschrift*, CLXXVII, No. 2 (April, 1954), 284.
3. "Protocole de clôture de la réunion des délégués gouvernments d'Esthonie, de Lettonie, de Pologne, et de la R. S. F. des S. de Russie, tenue à Riga les 29 et 30 mars 1922," in *Auswärtiges Amt*, 2558/5173/E306638-E306641; Evan E. Young (Riga) to Secretary of State, April 17, 1922, National Archives, Doc. No. 860i.00/29; Sīpols, *Slepenā diplomātija*, p. 113.
4. *New York Times*, April 3, 1922.
5. Wallroth (Riga) to Foreign Ministry, May 23, 1922, *Auswärtiges Amt*, 5770/K2331/K663910.
6. *Ibid.*, K663911.
7. Maltzan (Genoa) to Foreign Ministry, April 28, 1922, *ibid.*, 5159/K1752/K429142.
8 Maltzan to Foreign Ministry, April 27, 1922, *ibid.*, K429148.
9. Wallroth (Riga) to Foreign Ministry, September 6, 1922, *ibid.*, 5770/K2331/K663980-K663981.
10. Z. Meierovics, "La Lettonie et l'accord avec les Soviets," *L'Europe Nouvelle*, V, No. 19 (May 13, 1922), 588-589.
11. *Brīvā Zeme*, August 31, 1922, enclosure to report of Wallroth to the Foreign Ministry, September 6, 1922, *Auswärtiges Amt*, 5770/K2331/K663981; A. Birznieks, "Amtinas par Z. Meierovica austrumu politiku," in Virza, ed., *Meierovics*, pp. 86-87.
12. Quoted in report of F. W. B. Coleman (Riga) to Secretary of State December 22, 1922, National Archives, Doc. No. 860n.00/24; Coleman to Secretary of State, January, 1923, *ibid.*, Doc. No. 860n.00/25.
13. *Izvestiia*, June 14, 1922, as enclosure to a report of Widenfeld (Moscow) to Foreign ministry, June 16, 1922,*Auswärtiges Amt*, 5380/

K1967/K510490-K510492.

14. Adolf Koester (Riga) to Foreign Ministry, December 8, 1923, *ibid.*, 3875/K243/K071369-K071370; Benndorff (Warsaw) to Foreign Ministry, September 22, 1922, *ibid.*, 5380/K1967/K510517-K510519; Wallroth (Riga) to Foreign Mcnistry, September 29, 1922, *ibid.*, 5770/K2331/K663992-K663995.

15. Rauscher (Warsaw) to Foreign Ministry, October 7, 1922, *ibid.*, 5380/K1967/K510550-K510551; Olshausen (Kaunas) to Foreign Ministry, October 21, 1922, *ibid.*, K510564.

16. Hentig (Tallinn) to Foreign Ministry, October 11, 1922, *ibid.*, K510560-K510561; Sīpols, *Slepenā diplomātija*, pp. 117-118.

17. "Polish *aide mémoire* to the German Government on the Moscow Conference," December 22, 1922, in *Auswärtiges Amt*, 5380/K1967/K510621-K510623. The text of the projected nonaggression and arbitration convention was published by the Latvian Telegraph Agency and appears in the London *Times*, December 21, 1922. For additional press accounts, see London *Times*, December 14, 1922; *New York Times*, December 15, 1922; and *Frankfurter Zeitung*, December 14, 1922. A general summary is to be found in a report of Consul Edwards (Kaunas), as enclosure no. 1 to report of Frederick W. B. Coleman (Riga) to Secretary of State, January 11, 1923, National Archives, Doc., No. 860m.00/45. See also Fischer, *The Soviets in World Affairs*, I, pp. 377-379.

18. Koester to Foreign Ministry, December 8, 1923, *Auswärtiges Amt*, 3878/K243/K071370-K071371. This summary report was written a year after the conference.

19. "Ārpolitika," *Latvju Enciklopēdija*, pp. 110-111; see also Koester (Riga) to Foreign Ministry, June 29, 1923, *Auswärtiges Amt*, 5769/K2329/K663240.

20. It took several months to negotiate a "preliminary" treaty for a Latvian-Estonian customs union (November, 1922). The treaty provided for a mixed commission to work out the details of common tariff legislation but the commission did not meet until October, 1924. See Benjamin Siew, *Lettlands Volks- und Staatswirtschaft* (Riga: Mueller'sche Buchdruckerie, 1925), pp. 205-206, 210-212. On talks among the three Baltic states, see *Rigasche Nachrichten*, February 24, 1923, enclosure No. 1 to report of Coleman to Secretary of State, March 2, 1923, National Archives, Doc. No. 860i.00/42; *Jaunākās Zinas*, June 29, 1923, enclosure No. 1, to report of Coleman to Secretary of State, July 6, 1923, *ibid.*, Doc. No. 860p.00/41.

21. Coleman to Secretary of State, August 3, 1923, *ibid.*, Doc. No. 860p.00/42; report of Consul Harold B. Quarton (Tallinn) for July, 1923, enclosure to report of Coleman to Secretary of State, August 25, 1923, *ibid.*, Doc. No. 860i.00/53.

22. The Saeima was a single-chamber body of 100 seats. In 1922 leftist parties held 38 seats; bourgeois center, 13; agrarians, 25; rightest parties, 9; ethnic parties, 15 seats. *Baltic States: Survey*, p. 52.

23. *Latvju Enciklopēdija*, p. 396.

24. This summary of Cielēns's views is based on a lengthy article writ-

ten by him in 1924. *Sociāldemokrats*, February 10, 1924, enclosure No. 1 to report of Koester to Foreign Ministry, February 11, 1924, *Auswärtiges Amt*, 5769/K2329/K663272-K6633274. The Germans looked with favor on Cielēns because of his non-chauvinist position respecting the German minority in Latvia and because of his general anti-French and anti-Polish attitudes. See report of Koester to Foreign Ministry, March 12, 1923, *ibid.*, 5770/K2331/K664063-K664065.

25. Wever (German secretary of legation, Riga) to Foreign Ministry, January 31, 1923, *ibid.*, 5769/K2329/K663210-K663212; Koester to Foreign Ministry, February 9, 1923, *ibid.*, K663215-K663216.

26. *New York Times*, November 5, 1923.

27. Koester to Foreign Ministry, October 29, 1923,*Auswärtiges Amt*, 5380/K1967/K510649; *Brīvā Zeme*, Nos. 187, 188, quoted in "Baltic Security Pact Negotiations," *European Economic and Political Survey*, II, No. 2 (September 30, 1926), 51.

28. Kopp's demands were later formalized into four points of a draft protocol: (1) a pledge of complete neutrality and nonparticipation in any form of blockade in case Germany's form of government altered; (2) a Latvian pledge guaranteeing the Soviets free transit to third counries "regardless of their domestic political form"; (3) a benevolent neutrality to be preserved in case a third power attacked one of the protocol signatories; (4) a Soviet guarantee of the "complete invulnerability" of Latvia's frontiers. See "Draft Latvian-Soviet Protocol," enclosure to a report of Koester to Foreign Ministry, January 28, 1924, *Auswärtiges Amt*, 3883/K253/K077062; also, *Dokumenty vneshneĭ politiki SSSR*, Vol. VI (Moscow: Gosudarstvenoe izdatel'stvo politicheskoĭ literatury, 1962), p. 593, n. 4; Sīpols, *Slepenā diplomātija*, pp. 122-123; Rantzau (Moscow) to Foreign Ministry, October 30, 1923, *Auswärtiges Amt*, 1466/3015/D596321.

29. According to one Latvian diplomat, Kopp asked "unofficially" about the possibility of sending Russian troops across Latvia. See Karlis V. Ozols, *Memuary poslannika* (Paris: Dom knigi, 1938), p. 163. Kopp's counterpart in Tallinn, L. Stark, was reported to have endeavored "in a threatening way...to see that Estonia would assist Soviet Russia in the transport of arms and ammunitions as well as in other ways." See report of Consul Harold B. Quarton (Tallinn) for November, 1923, as enclosure No. 1 to report of Coleman (Riga) to Secretary of State, January 14, 1924, National Archives, Doc. No. 860i.00/58. On the other hand, Fischer quotes an unnamed official in the Foreign Commissariat as saying, regarding movement of troops through the border states, that "such thoughts in that absolute form, we actually did not have." See *The Soviets in World Affairs*, Vol. I, p. 458. See also "Āpolitika," *Latvju Enciklopēdija*, pp. 112-113; Sīpols, *Slepenā diplomātija*, p. 123.

30. *Latvian-Russian Relations: Documents*, pp. 246-247; Report of Consul Harold B. Quarton (Tallin) for October, 1923, enclosure No. 1 to report of Coleman to Secretary of State, November 22, 1923, National Archives, Doc. No. 860i.00/56; Vitols, *La Mer baltique et les états baltes*, p. 304.

31. Anderson, "Toward the Baltic Union," *Lituanus*, XII, No. 2, (Summer, 1966), 44. In 1935 Latvian military elements included 2,000 officers and 4,000 permanent cadre with 9,000 to 13,500 obligated draftees. There were 1,000 officers and 17,000 cadre (noncommissioned officers) in the reserves. The air corps consisted of 550 men; the naval force of 450 men. See *Latvju Enciklopēdija*, p. 354.

32. Maltzan (London) to Foreign Ministry, November 24, 1923, *Auswärtiges Amt*, 1466/3015/K596323; Theodor Rothstein, "Die auswärtige Politik der U. S. S. R.," *Osteuropa*, III (1927/1928), 133.

33. "Ārpolitika," *Latvju Enciklopēdija*, p. 113; Sīpols, *Slepenā diplomātija*, p. 123. John D. Gregory, who was in charge of the Northern European section of the British Foreign Office, wrote in 1928, that the Baltic states "will always look for a moral support to us, though not, I trust, for military protection in a grave emergency." John D. Gregory, *On the Edge of Diplomacy: Rambles and Reflections 1902-1928* (London: Hutchinson and Co., 1929), p. 188.

34. Jane Degras, ed., *Soviet Documents on Foreign Policy*, Vol. I, p. 421.

35. Koester to Foreign Ministry, February 11, 16, 25, 1924. *Auswärtiges Amt*, 3883/K253/K077074, K077077-K077078, K077079, K077081-K077082; Koester to Foreign Ministry, March 15, 1924, *ibid.*, K077091-K077093; Reisser (Riga) to Foreign Ministry, March 22, 26, 1924, *ibid.*, K077093, K077099; Sīpols, *Slepenā diplomātija*, p. 125.

36. "Memorandum for State Secretary von Maltzan," December 7, 1923, *Auswärtiges Amt*, 3875/K243/K071356; "Memorandum concerning France, Poland, Russia and the Border States," *ibid.*, K071341. This last memorandum bears the date February 6, 1924, on 3607/9768/E686536, but was prepared at the beginning of December, 1923.

37. Koester to Foreign Ministry, December 8, 1923, *ibid.*, 3875/K243/K071376. General Hans von Seeckt had written Stresemann in almost identical terms about six weeks earlier: "The interests of Germany and Russia thus run parallel in border state policy." Quoted in Carsten, *Reichswehr und Politik 1918-1933*, p. 155.

38. *Baltic States: Survey,*, pp. 94-95; Senn, *The Great Powers, Lithuania, and the Vilna Question*, pp. 107-108, 109, 114-115, 118, 121, 125-126, 127-13.

39. The Lithuanians put forward an ambitious program which recalled in its completeness the work of the Bulduri Conference. The Lithuanians even visualized the standardization of military equipment and the establishment of a single manufacturing plant for arms and ammunition. But the Lithuanians emphasized they would never make concessions on Memel nor surrender claims to Vilna. F. W. B. Coleman (Riga) to Secretary of State, October 13, 1923, National Archives, Doc. No. 860p.00/45; *Jaunākās Zinas*, October 15, 1923, enclosure No. 1 to report of Coleman to Secretary of State, October 29, 1923, *ibid.*, Doc. No. 860n.00/45; Coleman to Secretary of State, November 7, 1923, *ibid.*, Doc. No. 760m.60p/2;

Report of Consul Clement S. Edwards (Kaunas), November, 1923, enclosure No. 1 to report of Coleman to Secretary of State, December 10, 1923, *ibid.*, Doc. No. 860m.00/61; Reisser (Riga) to Foreign Ministry, December 17, 1923, *Auswartiges Amt*, 3875/K243/K071400-K071401; Koester to Foreign Ministry, November 26, 1923, *ibid.*, 1466/3015/ D596324.

40. *Jaunākās Zinas*, March 17, 1923, enclosure No. 1 to report of Coleman (Riga) to Secretary of State, March 31, 1923, National Archives, Doc. No. 860n.00/30.

41. Koester to Foreign Ministry, December 8, 1923, *Auswärtiges Amt*, 3875/K243/K071372-K071373.

42. Koester to Foreign Ministry, November 30, 1923, *ibid.*, Frame K071337; memorandum for State Secretary von Maltzan, December 7, 1923, *ibid.*, Frame K071352; *Jaunākās Zinas*, November 13, 1923, Enclosure No. 1 to report of Coleman to Secretary of State, National Archives, Doc. No. 860n.00/47; *Latvijas Kāreivis* (Latvian Warrior), December 18, 1923, enclosure No. 1 to report of Coleman to Secretary of State, December 22, 1923, *ibid.*, Doc. No. 860n.00/49.

43. Koester to Foreign Ministry, November 26, 1923, *Auswärtiges Amt*, 1466/3015/D596324. In this stand, Meierovics enjoyed the full support of the Social Democrats. Koester to Foreign Ministry, December 11, 1923, *ibid.*, 3875/K243/K071396-K071397.

44. Soviet Russia made the same proposal to Warsaw, Tallinn, and Kaunas. Koester to Foreign Ministry, November 26, 1923, *ibid.*, 1466/ 3015/K596325.

45. Koester to Foreign Ministry, January 5, 1924, *ibid.*, 3607/9768/ E686528-E686529.

46. Koester to Foreign Ministry, January 16, 1924, *ibid.*, 1466/3015/ D596329-D596330; Koester to Foreign Ministry, January 19, 1924, *ibid.*, 3875/K243/K071451-K071458.

47. The Polish military attaché in Riga arrogantly told a member of the German legation that Poland "would simply sell Latvia to Russia" if the Baltic state tried again to follow an "anti-Polish policy." Koester to Foreign Ministry, January 19, 1924, *ibid.*, 3875/K243/K071458.

48. Sēja, formerly minister to Kaunas, was characterized by a German observer as a "politically weak bureaucrat who has no really important foreign policy convictions." Koester to Foreign Ministry, February 2, 1924, *ibid.*, K071496. Sēja, born in 1885, had gone into exile after the 1905 revolution and completed his education in France. Besides his year as foreign minister, he served as envoy to Washington from 1925-1927, and as chargé d'affaires in London from 1927-1931. In the latter year he returned to his first post, Kaunas. He was arrested by the Gestapo in 1944, but released in 1945 in Poland. He was then deported to Soviet Russia in 1946. *Latvju Enciklopēdija*, p. 2260.

49. London *Times*, February 19, 1924; Robert Machray, "The Baltic Situation," *Fortnightly Review*, CXXII (July, 1924), 47; *Frankfurter*

Zeitung, March 6, 1924; Rauscher (Warsaw) to Foreign Ministry, February 21, 1924, *Auswärtiges Amt*, 3875/K243/K071524-K071526; German legation in Helsinki to Foreign Ministry, July 28, 1924, *ibid.*, K071771-K071773.

50. Koester to Foreign Ministry, February 11, 1924, *ibid.*, 3606/9768/E686544.

51. Koester to Foreign Ministry, November 17, 1924, *ibid.*, 3883/K253/K077128.

52. Riesser (Riga) to Foreign Ministry, July 28, 1924, *ibid.*, 5777/K2361/K668770-K668773

53. Koester to Foreign Ministry, February 2, 1925, *ibid.*, 1466/3015/D596348.

54. Coleman to Secretary of State, November 8, 1923, *Papers Relating to the Foreign Relations of the United States: 1923* (Washington: Government Printing Office, 1938), Vol. II, p. 772; *Kölnische Zeitung*, December 3, 1924.

55. Georg von Rauch, *Geschichte der baltischen Staaten* (Stuttgart: W. Kohlhammer Verlag, 1970), pp. 99-104; "Ārpolitika," *Latvju Enciklopēdija*, p. 113; Walter Assmus, "Entwicklungstendenzen im baltischen Raum," *Zeitschrift für Geopolitik*, V, No. 7 (July, 1928), 564-565.

56. Sīpols, *Slepenā diplomātija*, pp. 136-137.

57. Völkers (Helsinki) to Foreign Ministry, January 20, 1925, *Auswärtiges Amt*, 5769/K2329/K663239. Völkers reported that a Lithuanian diplomat had noted with satisfaction that Meierovics had "astonishingly revised his former polonophile position."

58. Semen Ivanovich Aralov (Soviet Plenipotentiary in Riga) to Victor L. Kopp (Collegium of the People's Commissariat of Foreign Affairs, Moscow) January 7, 1925, *Dokumenty vneshneĭ politiki SSSR*, Vol. VIII, pp. 21-22; Sīpols, *Slepenā diplomātija*, p. 138.

59. Extracts from Chicherin's report to the Central Executive Committee, October 18, 1924, in J. Degras, ed., *Soviet Documents on Foreign Policy*, Vol. I, p. 407.

60. Koester to Foreign Ministry, January 7, 1925, *Auswärtiges Amt*, 1466/3015/D596347.

61. Aralov (Riga) to Kopp (Moscow), January 7, 1925, *Dokumenty vneshneĭ politiki SSSR*, Vol. VIII, p. 22.

62. *Ibid.*, pp. 22-23; Report of Consul Harold B. Quarton (Tallinn) for January, 1925, enclosure No. 1 to report of Coleman (Riga) to Secretary of State, March 11, 1925, National Archives, Doc. No. 860i.00/112.

63. *Frankfurter Zeitung*, January 16, 17, 1925.

64. "Procès verbal de clôture," January 17, 1925, in *Auswärtiges Amt*, 3876/K243/K071799-K071805; "Convention de conciliation et d'arbitrage," January 17, 1925, *ibid.*, Frames K071806-K071816. To call this arbitration agreement "a juridical act of the first magnitude" for Baltic unity is a gross exaggeration (Kazlauskas, *L'Entente baltique*, p. 127). Almost equally exaggerated is Buell's remark that the convention was "regarded as a victory for Poland over Russia in the Baltic area." See

Raymond Leslie Buell, *Europe: A History of Ten Years* (New York: Macmillan Co., 1928), p. 238. For more sober appraisal, see the summaries of the conference by German diplomats: Völkers (Helsinki) to Foreign Ministry, January 20, 1925, *Auswärtiges Amt*, 5769/K2329/K663288-K663291; Rauscher (Warsaw) to Foreign Ministry, January 30, 1925, *ibid.*, 3876/K243/K071780.

Notes to Chapter 4

1. Frederick W. B. Coleman (U. S. Minister, Riga) to Secretary of State, July 6, 1925, National Archives, Doc. No. 869n.00/65.

2. The article in the *Manchester Guardian* was quoted and commented upon at length in *Rigas Zinas*. The latter was translated and appears in *Riga Times*, March 28, 1925.

3. *Gustav Stresemann; Vermächtnis: Der Nachlass in drei Bänden*, Henry Bernhard, editor. (Berlin: Verlag Ullstein, 1932), Vol. II, pp. 91-93, as quoted in Henry L. Bretton, *Stresemann and the Revision of Versailles: A Fight for Reason* (Stanford: Stanford University Press, 1953), p. 118.

4. *Deutsche Allgemeine Zeitung*, June 18, 1926, in *Auswärtiges Amt*, 3876/K243/K072216. Some of the documents for the years 1925-1933 which I have cited in this study from *Auswärtiges Amt* (Records of the German Foreign Ministry on Microfilm, United States National Archives, Microcopy T-120), are now appearing in print in Series B of *Akten zur Deutschen Auswärtigen Politik, 1918-1945, aus dem Archiv des Auswärtigen Amts* (Göttingen, 1966, et seq.).

5. Koester to State Secretary von Schubert, March 28, 1925, *Auswärtiges Amt*, 1466/3015/D596357-D596358.

6. Koester, memorandum of April 24, 1925, *ibid.*, 2310/4561/E153689-E153690.

7. Koester to Wallroth (Berlin), June 29, 1925, *ibid.*, E153742. A somewhat chagrined Koester insisted to Berlin that the idea was his not Meierovics's.

8. Dirkson, memorandum of June 8, 1925, *ibid.*, 2777/5462/E373578.

9. Schubert, "Notes on the Possible Conclusion of a Guarantee Pact between Germany, Russia and the Border States," April 24, 1925, *ibid.*, 2310/4561/E153694-E153696.

10. Stresemann to Koester, May 2, 1925, *ibid.*, 1466/3015/D596385-D596387. Preliminary drafts of this letter may be read in the Dirksen *Handakten*, *ibid.*, 2777/5462/E373584-E373586; E373588-E373590; E373595-E373597.

11. Scubert, "Memorandum of a Conversation with Latvian Minister Oskars Voits," June 23, 1925, *Auswärtiges Amt*, 2574/5265/E319780-E319781.

12. Koester to Foreign Ministry, May 20, 1925, *ibid.*, 3876/K243/ K072133-K072134; Koester to Foreign Ministry, June 4, 1925, *ibid.*, K072165; Koester to Foreign Ministry, May 25, 1925, *ibid.*, K072149-K072150. A visit by the Lithuanian envoy in Riga to Tallinn failed to move Pusta. See Koester to Foreign Ministry, May 29, 1925, *ibid.*, K072153. On Estonian obstinacy, see Koester to Foreign Ministry, June 18, 1925, *ibid.*, K072221; report of Consul Groeninger (Tallinn) for June, 1925, enclosure to report of Coleman to Secretary of State, July 16, 1925, National Archives, Doc. No. 860i.00/124.

13. Coleman to Secretary of State, July 6, 1925, National Archives, Doc. No. 860p.00/70; "Communiqué of the Lithuanian Foreign Ministry," July 2, 1925, *Auswärtiges Amt*, 3876/K243/K072265-K072266; *Deutsche Allgemeine Zeitung*, June 18, 1925, *ibid.*, K072216.

14. Frank (Tallinn) to State Secretary von Schubert, July 17, 1925, *ibid.*, 2310/4561/E153770.

15. *Riga Times*, July 4, 1925; Coleman to Secretary of State, July 6, 1925, National Archives, Doc. No. 860p.00/70. Koester to Foreign Ministry, June 27, 1925, *Auswärtiges Amt*, 1466/3015/D596388; *ibid.*, 5770/K2331/K664191; Koester to Foreign Minister, July 2, 1925, *ibid.*, 5769/K2329/K663320. A group of Baltic Germans were in the process of presenting a petition to the League of Nations alleging that the Latvian land reform constituted political discrimination against the German minority. The petition was dismissed in 1926. See André Tibal, *La réforme agraire lettone* ("Problèmes politiques contemporains de l'Europe orientale"; Paris Centre européen de la Dotation Carnegie 1930), pp. 14-20; *Frankfurter Zeitung*, June 21, 1926; Koester to Foreign Ministry, August 18, 1925, *Auswärtiges Amt*, 5769/K2329/ K663337.

16. Schubert, "Memorandum on the Visit of Latvian Foreign Minister Meierovics," July 3, 1925, *Auswärtiges Amt*, 2310/4561/E153752.

17. Koester to Foreign Ministry, June 29, 1925, *ibid.*, 2310/4561/ E153742; Koester to Foreign Ministry, August 18, 1925, *ibid.*, 5769/ K2329/K663333-K663334; *Riga Times*, July 11, 1925.

18. *Frankfurter Zeitung*, July 6, 1925; Frank (Tallinn) to State Secretary von Schubert, July 17, 1925, *Auswärtiges Amt*, 2310/4561/E153773.

19. London *Times*, January 31, 1925.

20. *Riga Times*, July 25, 1925; Koester to Foreign Ministry, August 18, 1925, *Auswärtiges Amt*, 5769/K2329/K663334; State Secretary von Schubert, memorandum of February 15, 1926, *ibid.*, 2311/4561/E153192-E153193. While in London, Meierovics signed a debt settlement agreement with the British. See "Latvia," *Economic Review*, XII, No. 12 (September 18, 1925), 250. V. Sīpols asserts that London urged Meierovics to move toward an alliance with Poland but available evidence indicates the contrary. See his *Slepenā diplomātija*, p. 142.

21. Riesser (Riga) to Foreign Ministry, August 5, 1925, *Auswärtiges Amt*, 5769/K2329/K663328; Koester to Foreign Ministry, August 18, 1925, *ibid.*, K663335.

22. *Riga Times*, August 1, 1925; Koester to Foreign Ministry, August 24, 1925, *Auswärtiges Amt*, 3876/K243/K072362-K072363. Meierovics gave Koester a quite detailed report on his visit to the European capitals. The Latvian foreign minister displayed a marked distrust of Poland in this conversation.

23. *Ibid.*, K072361.

24. London *Times*, July 15, 1925, Frank (Tallinn) to Foreign Ministry, August 1, 1925, *Auswärtiges Amt*, 3883/K253/K077132.

25. Brockdorff-Rantzau to Foreign Ministry, July 15, 1925, *ibid.*, 2310/4561/E153765; Frank to Foreign Ministry, July 16, 1925, *ibid.*, E153768.

26. *New York Times*, August 2, 1925. The Soviet naval demonstration at the Belts was part of a persistent Soviet effort to close the Baltic Sea to the warships of all non-littoral states. As one contemporary observer put it, closing the Baltic Sea would give the Soviets the opportunity to do to the Baltic peoples "what she had already done to the peoples of Ukrainia, Georgia, and the Caucasus." Litvinov had "regretfully" declined to discuss naval disarmament at the Moscow Disarmament Conference of 1922 and would not participate in a Baltic naval conference held in Riga in July, 1923. The western powers first obtained some impression of Soviet ambitions in 1924 at the Rome Conference of Naval Experts. At that time the Soviet delegate demanded that Russia have a maximum limit of 490,000 tonnage in capital ships rather than the 110,000 suggested by the experts. The Soviets offered to compromise on 280,000 tons if the Powers would agree to close the Baltic and Black Seas to the warships of non-littoral states. On this problem see the following: Chief of the Naval Office (Reichswehrministerium) to the Foreign Ministry, May 7, 1924, *Auswärtiges Amt*, 5108/L798/L235028-L235034; F. de Jessen, "Problèmes actuels et futurs des voies d'accès à la baltique," in *La Pologne et la baltique*, pp. 145-161; A. Taska, "Dominum maris baltici und die Sowjetunion," in *Pro Baltica*, pp. 203-212.

27. Koester to Foreign Ministry, August 17, 1925, *Auswärtiges Amt*, 3883/K253/K077133.

28. Koester to Foreign Ministry, August 24, 1925, *ibid.*, K077135-K077136.

29. Riesser (Riga) to Foreign Ministry, July 31, 1925, *ibid.*, 5769/K2329/K663323.

30. Koester to Foreign Ministry, August 18, 1925, *ibid.*, 3876/K243/K072341-K072342.

31. Ewald Ammende, "Der Zusammenbruch des baltischen Blocks," *Frankfurter Zeitung*, September 26, 1925. Ammende had been Meierovics's press representative at Genoa in 1922.

32. Koester to Wallroth, June 29, 1925, *Auswärtiges Amt*, 2310/4561/E153742; Schroetter (Kaunas) to Foreign Ministry, September 13, 1925, *ibid.*, 3876/K243/K072421-K072422; Hauschild (Helsinki) to Foreign Ministry, August 25, 1925, *ibid.*, 2310/4561/E153788-E153789; Coleman to Secretary of State, July 6, 1925, National Archives, Doc. No. 860p.00/

70; Sforza, *Diplomatic Europe*, p. 78; Sīpols, *Slepenā diplomātija*, p. 143.
33. Koester to Foreign Ministry, August 21, 1925, *Auswärtiges Amt*, 1466/3015/D596394-D596395; Koester to Foreign Ministry, August 24, 1925, *ibid.*, 3876/K243/K072363; Koester to Foreign Ministry, August 22, 1925, *ibid.*, 277/5462/E373553; Koester to Foreign Ministry, August 22, 1925, *ibid.*, 1466/3015/D596396; Sīpols, *Slepenā diplomātija*, p. 144; *Frankfurter Zeitung*, September 26, 1925; Assmus, "Entwicklungstendenzen im baltischen Raum," *Zeitschrift für Geopolitik*, V (July, 1928), 565; Kazlauskas, *L'Entente Baltique*, pp. 127-129, 141-142.
34. Viktor Zinghaus, *Führende Köpfe der baltischen Staaten* (Kaunas, Leipzig, Vienna: Ostverlag der Buchhandlung Pribačis, 1938), pp. 122-123; *Riga Times*, August 29, 1925; *Economic Review*, XII, No. 2 (September 18, 1925), 250.
35. Koester to Foreign Ministry, August 24, 1925, *Auswärtiges Amt*, 3883/K253/K077136; Dirksen to Koester, August 29, 1925, *ibid.*, 2777/5462/E373547.

Notes to Chapter 5

1. *Riga Times*, December 19, 1925, February 13, 1926; "Memorandum on an Eastern Locarno," February 15, 1926, *Auswärtiges Amt*, 3877/K244/K072738-K072745; Sīpols, *Slepenā Diplomātija*, p. 148.
2. Hauschild (Helsinki) to Foreign Ministry, November 17, 1925, *Auswärtiges Amt*, 3877/K244/K072509; Rafael Erich, "Quelques observations concernant la possibilité d'assurer l'integrité territoriale et l'indépendence des états secondaires que se trouvent dans une situation singulièrement exposée," *Revue de droit internationale*, 3rd series, VI (1925), pp. 349-363.
3. Rosenberg (Stockholm) to Foreign Ministry, November 21, 1925, *Auswärtiges Amt*, 3877/K244/K072492-K072498; Rhomberg (Oslo) to Foreign Ministry, November 24, 1925, *ibid.*, K072507; Legation in Copenhagen to Foreign Ministry, November 25, 1925, ibid., K072504-K072505; Hauschild (Helsinki) to Foreign Ministry, January 16, 1926, *ibid.*, 2311/4561/E153862-E153863.
4. Hey (Moscow) to Foreign Ministry, December 12, 1925, *ibid.*, 2310/4561/E153849; London *Times*, November 25, 1925; "Foreign Policy of the U.S.S.R.," *European Economic and Political Survey*, I, No. 7 (December 21, 1925), p. 10.
5. *Die Welt am Montag*, April 12, 1926, in *Auswärtiges Amt*, 2777/5462/E373877-E373878: Christian Höltje, *Die Weimarer Republik und das Ostlocarno-Problem, 1919-1934: Revision oder Garantie der deutschen Ostgrenze von 1919* (Würzburg: Holzner Verlag, 1958), pp. 3, 5-6, 254-256.
6. "Memorandum concerning the Economic and Political Situation of Lithuania," December 9, 1925, *Auswärtiges Amt*, 2310/4561/E153685.

7. Quoted in Koester to Foreign Ministry, November 10, 1925, *ibid.*, 5769/K2329/K663343-K663344.

8. Rosenberg (Stockholm) to Foreign Ministry, March 4, 1926, *ibid.*, 3877/K244/K072831; Coleman (Riga) to Secretary of State, February 27, 1926, National Archives, Doc. No. 860n.00/65.

9. Koester to Foreign Ministry, January 14, 1926, *Auswärtiges Amt*, 3877/K244/K072641; Koester to Foreign Ministry, February 1, 1926, *ibid.*, 5769/K2329/K663345; Brockdroff-Rantzau (Moscow) to Foreign Ministry, February 21, 1926, 2777/5462/E373943. Albats may have been encouraged by some remarks made by Chicherin as he paused in Riga on his way home from Germany: "Particularly good are the relations between Latvia and the Soviet Union, the attitudes being based upon friendship and confidence. We desire to intensify these friendly relations." *Riga Times*, January 2, 1926.

10. Koester to State Secretary von Schubert, January 25, 1926, *Auswärtiges Amt*, 2777/5462/E373961; Koester to Schubert, January 30, 1926, *ibid.*, E373960.

11. Brockdorff-Rantzau to Foreign Ministry, February 21, 1926, *ibid.*, E373960.

12. Koester to Foreign Ministry, February 22, 1926, *ibid.*, E153962; Wallroth (Berlin) to Rauscher (Warsaw), February 12, 1926, *ibid.*, 3877/K244/K072753-K072754; Koester to Foreign Ministry, March 6, 1926, *ibid.*, K072838-K072839.

13. John D. Gregory, "Memorandum on the Foreign Policy of His Majesty's Government with a list of British Commitments in their Relative Order of Importance," April 10, 1926, *Documents on British Foreign Policy*, Series IA *(1925-1929)*, Vol. I, *The Aftermath of Locarno, 1925-1926* (London: H. M. Stationery Office, 1966), p. 866. The British position regarding the Baltic states underwent no change in subsequent revisions of this important policy statement. *See ibid.*, Vol. II, p. 800.

14. Frank (Tallinn) to Foreign Ministry, February 5, 1926, *Auswärtiges Amt*, 2777/5462/E373957; Brockdorff-Rantzau (Moscow) to Foreign Ministry, March 4, 1926, *ibid.*, E373905-E373907; Sīpols, *Slepenā diplomātija*, pp. 153-154.

15. Koester to Foreign Ministry, March 6, 1926, *Auswärtiges Amt*, 2311/4561/E153946; Hauschild (Helsinki) to Foreign Ministry, March 17, 1926, *ibid.*, 3877/K244/K072989.

16. Draft of a letter from Stresemann to Brockdorff-Rantzau, February, 1926, *ibid.*, 2777/5462/E373915-E373916; Stresemann to Brockdorff-Rantzau, February 24, 1926, *ibid.*, 2311/4561/E153921-E153923.

17. Brockdorff-Rantzau to Foreign Ministry, March 4, 6, 7, 1926, *ibid.*, 2777/5462/E373904-E373909.

18. The Soviets signed such treaties with several states as follows: Turkey, December 17, 1925; Germany, April 24, 1926; Afghanistan, August 31, 1926; Lithuania, September 28, 1926; Persia, October 1, 1927. See Malbone W. Graham, "The Soviet Security Treaties," *American Journal of International Law*, XXIII, No. 2 (April, 1929), 336-350; also, Koester to

Foreign Ministry, March 19, 1926, *Auswärtiges Amt*, 3877/K244/ K072908.

19. "Extracts from a Conversation between State Secretary von Schubert and Litvinov on August 5, 1926," *Auswärtiges Amt*, 2311/4561/ E154167. Later in the year a Soviet spokesman said: "The Soviet Government cannot, however, agree to conclude a collective treaty in which the U.S.S.R. was one of the contracting parties and the other Poland together with the Baltic States, *because that would mean ourselves creating an anti-Soviet coalition.*" Degras, ed., *Soviet Documents on Foreign Policy*, II, p. 139 (italics in the original). See also Harvey L. Dyck, *Weimar Germany and Soviet Russia, 1926-1933: A Study in Diplomatic Instability* (New York: Columbia University Press, 1966), pp. 38-41.

20. Koester to Foreign Ministry, March 19, 1926, *Auswärtiges Amt*, 3877/K244/K072908.

21. Gregory Rutenberg, "The Baltic States and the Soviet Union," *American Journal of International Law*, XXIX, No. 4 (October, 1935), 598-615, especially, pp. 605-606.

22. Koester to Foreign Ministry, March 23, 1926, *Auswärtiges Amt*, 2311/4561/E153963-E153966.

23. Frank (Tallinn) to Foreign Ministry, April 27, 1926, *ibid.*, E154008-E154009; Koester to Foreign Ministry, May 5, 1926, *ibid.*, E154025; see also, 1466/3015/D596418-D596419; London *Times*, April 29, 30, 1926; *New York Times*, April 30, 1926. More detail on the Lithuanian issue may be had in Schroetter (Kaunas) to Foreign Ministry, March 27, 1926, *Auswärtiges Amt*, 3877/K244/K072934-K072935. Litvinov told Rantzau that Lithuania put special value on the separate treaty and that therefore a collective treaty with the Baltic states would not be signed. Brockdorff-Rantzau to Foreign Ministry, April 23, 1926, *ibid.*, 2777/5462/E373955. Out of consideration for their German partner, the Soviets rejected a Lithuanian proposal to include the Memel territory in the treaty. Schubert to Brockdorff-Rantzau, April, 1926, *ibid.*, E373851 (this document has been damaged). See further, Senn, *The Great Powers, Lithuania and the Vilna Question*, pp. 164-165.

24. "Die Antwortnote an Russland," *Rigasche Rundschau*, May 8, 1926, enclosure to report of Koester to Foreign Ministry, May 8, 1926, *Auswärtiges Amt*, 3878/K244/K073222; *Sevodnia* (Riga), May 8, 1926, in "Political Alignments in the Baltic," *European Economic and Political Survey*, I, No. 18 (May 31, 1926), 15. For Estonian and Finnish replies, see "*Promemoria*" of the Estonian Government to the Soviet Government, enclosure to report of Frank to Foreign Ministry, May 8, 1926, *Auswärtiges Amt*, 3878/K244/K073201-K073202; "Les 'Conclusions' du gouvernment finlandais," May 5, 1926, *ibid.*, K073209-K073212.

25. Koester to Foreign Ministry, May 9, 1926, *ibid.*, 1466/3015/ D496429; Koester to Foreign Ministry, May 27, 1926, *ibid.*, D596437-D596438.

26. The latest study of Pilsudski's seizure of power concludes that the foreign situation was only a "marginal factor" in the coup. Joseph

Rothschild, *Pilsudski's Coup d'état* ("East Central European Studies of Columbia University"; New York: Columbia University Press, 1966), p. 296.

27. Hauschild (Helsinki) to Foreign Ministry, May 14, 1926, *Auswärtiges Amt*, 1466/3015/D596431: Hauschild to Foreign Ministry, May 26, 1926, *ibid.*, 2311/4561/E154071; J. C. White (chargé, Riga) to Secretary of State, June 7, 1926, National Archives Doc. No. 860p.00/95; Sīpols, *Slepenā diplomātija*, p. 155.

28. Koester to Foreign Ministry, May 27, 1926, *Auswärtiges Amt*, 1466/3015/D596435-D596436; Senn, *The Great Powers, Lithuania and the Vilna Question*, p. 170.

29. The treaty was signed on June 28, 1926. See Koester to Wallroth, June 29, 1926, *Auswärtiges Amt*, 2574/5265/E319760-E319761; Westengerger, "Die handelspolitischen und wirtschaftlichen Beziehungen Deutschlands und Lettlands," *Osteuropa*, I, (1925/1926), 659-660; "Latvia," *Economic Review*, XIV. No. 7 (August 13, 1926), 149; *Frankfurter Zeitung*, June 29, 1926.

30. Brockdorff-Rantzau (Moscow) to Foreign Ministry, May 26, 1926, *Auswärtiges Amt*, 3878/K244/K073274; Brockdorff-Rantzau to Foreign Ministry, May 27, 1926, *ibid.*, 2311/4561/E154074-E154075; Brockdorff-Rantzau to Foreign Ministry, June 12, 1926, *ibid.*, 2777/5462/E373779-E373781.

31. *Riga Times*, May 22, June 19, July 13, 1926; *Rigasche Rundschau*, May 18, 1926, quoted in "Political Alignments in the Baltic," *European Economic and Political Survey*, I, No. 18 (May 31, 1926), 16; *Frankfurter Zeitung*, June 1, 1926.

32. *Latvis*, June 13, 1926, as enclosure to report of Koester to Foreign Ministry, June 19, 1926, *Auswärtiges Amt*, 3883/K253/K077155-K077157.

33. *Latvia: Country and People*, pp. 220, 239-241; René Puaux, "Karlis Ulmanis, Latvia's Dictator," *Living Age*, CCCL (June, 1936), 323-325.

34. Koester to Foreign Ministry, May 7, 1926, *Auswärtiges Amt*, 1466/3015/D596421; also 3878/K244/K073329.

35. Riesser (Riga) to Foreign Ministry, July 22, 1926, *ibid.*, 3878/K244/K073433-K073434.

36. Report of Consul Groeninger (Tallinn) for July, 1926, enclosure No. 1 to report of Coleman (Riga) to Secretary of State, August 20, 1926, National Archives, Doc. No. 860i.00/141; Frank (Tallinn) to Foreign Ministry, July 20, 1926, *Auswärtiges Amt*, 2311/4561/E154117; Reisser (Riga) to Foreign Ministry, July 21, 1926, *ibid.*, E154118. See also *Izvestiîa*, August 3, 1926, quoted in "Baltic Security Pact Negotiations," *European Economic and Political Survey*, II, No. 2 (September 30, 1926), 54; London *Times*, July 1ɔ, 26, 1926.

37. Schroetter (Kaunas) to Foreign Ministry, July 28, 1926, *Auswärtiges Amt*, 2311/4561/E154139; Riesser (Riga) to Foreign Ministry, July 28, 1926, *ibid.*, 2777/5462/E374091. The Poles had indeed made overtures to Kaunas. See Wallroth's memorandum, June 23, 1926, *ibid.*, E373763-E373765.

38. Coleman (Riga) to Secretary of State, August 2, 1926, National Archives, Doc. No. 860p.00/98.

39. Brockdorff-Rantzau to Foreign Ministry, July 21, 1926, *Auswärtiges Amt*, 2777/5462/E373772.

40. *Riga Times*, October 2, 1926; Senn, *The Great Powers, Lithuania and the Vilna Question*, pp. 174-175.

41. Koester to Foreign Ministry, October 4, 1926, *Auswärtiges Amt*, 2311/4561/E154180.

42. Koester to Foreign Ministry, October 5, 1926, *ibid.*, E154181-E154182; Sīpols, *Slepenā diplomātija*, pp. 160-161.

43. *Riga Times*, October 23, 1926; Koester to Foreign Ministry, October 14, 1926, *Auswärtiges Amt*, 2311/4561/E154184; Koester to Foreign Ministry, October 26, 1926, *ibid.*, E154188-E154189.

44. Koester to Foreign Ministry, November 26, 1926, *ibid.*, E154203-E154204.

Notes to Chapter 6

1. *Riga Times*, April 1, 1927.

2. The key materials for an understanding of Cielēns's views are his memoirs and the reports of the German minister in Riga to Berlin. Cielēns's interviews and speeches were also faithfully reproduced in the English-language *Riga Times* (especially the issues of March 19, April 1, July 15, and August 19, and October 1, 1927). See his *Laikmetu mainā*, Vol. II, pp. 162-163. 294-295, 326ff. Among the German dispatches from Riga to Berlin see the following: March 31, 1926, *Auswärtiges Amt*, 5769/K2329/K663357; January 12, 1927, *ibid.*, 1466/3015/D596464; February 11, 1927, *ibid.*, 5769/K2329/K663349. Also consult the report of Louis Sussdorf, Jr., (U. S. chargé, Riga) to Secretary of State, April 17, 1930, National Archives, Doc. No. 760p.00/19.

3. Koester to Foreign Ministry, December 29, 1926, *Auswärtiges Amt*, 2311/4561/E154207.

4. Koester to Foreign Ministry, January 6, 1927, *ibid.*, E154211-E154212; January 10, 1927, E154226. Koester noticed a strong pro-Polish element in the Latvian army, and expected, despite Cielēns's assurances, that in case of a Polish-Soviet conflict, the Latvian military would attempt, "legally or illegally," to side with Poland. State Secretary von Schubert relayed this information to the German embassy in Moscow on January 20, 1927, *ibid.*, E154238.

5. State Secretary von Schubert to German Embassy, Moscow, January 31, 1927, *ibid.*, E154243-E154244.

6. Schubert to Koester, January 20, 1927, *ibid.*, E154240.

7. Koester to Foreign Ministry, January 14, 1927, *ibid.*, E154235.

8. Brockdorff-Rantzau to Foreign Ministry, January 21, 1927, *ibid.*, 2777/5462/E373722.

9. Senn, *The Great Powers, Lithuania and the Vilna Question*, pp. 179-184.

10. Cielēns, *Laikmetu mainā*, Vol. II, 294-295.

11. Koester to Foreign Ministry, February 2, 1927, *Auswärtiges Amt*, 2311/4561/E154252.

12. Koester to Foreign Ministry, January 19, 1927, *ibid.*, E154236.

13. Koester to Foreign Ministry, February 15, 1927, *ibid.*, 5769/K2329/K663352-K663353.

14. Koester to Foreign Ministry, February 2, 1927, *ibid.*, 2311/4561/E154253.

15. Koester to Foreign Ministry, February 17, 1927, *ibid.*, E154273.

16. Koester to Foreign Ministry, February 23, 1927, *ibid.*, 1466/3015/D596471.

17. Louis Sussdorf, Jr. (chargé, Riga) to Secretary of State, April 17, 1930, National Archives, Doc. No. 760p.00/19. See also F. W. B. Coleman to Secretary of State, December 20, 1927, *ibid.*, Doc. No. 860n.00/68.

18. Koester to Foreign Ministry, February 15, 1927, *Auswärtiges Amt*, 5769/K2329/K663353; *Riga Times*, February 12, 1927; "Estonia and Latvia," *European Economic and Political Survey*, II, No. 13 (March 15, 1927), 377-378; J. Hahn, "Die Wirtschaftspolitik der baltischen Staaten," *Rigaer Wirtschaftszeitung*, No. 22 (November, 1928), as abstracted in *Osteuropa*, IV (December, 1928), 214-215. The Latvian-Estonian treaty initially attracted wide and favorable attention. See Otto Erwin von Scala. "Der lettländisch-estländische Zollunionvertrag--Ein Vorbild für ein deutsch-österreichesches Zoll- und Wirtschaftsbündnis," *Nationalwirtschaft: Blätter für organischen Wirtschaftsaufbau*, I, (1927), 62-68.

19. Frank (Tallinn) to Foreign Ministry, February 27, 1927, *Auswärtiges Amt*, 2311/4561/E154288-E154289. The Estonian-Polish treaty contained the "Baltic" but not the "Russian" clause. The Russian and Baltic clauses were invariably placed in the commercial treaties signed by the Baltic states; it allowed them the privilege of granting economic and tariff concessions to each other and to Russia above and beyond the usual most-favored nation stipulation. See Pernak, *Les Rélations économiques de la France et de la Lettonie*, pp. 103-104.

20. Koester to Foreign Ministry, February 22, 1927, *Auswärtiges Amt*, 2311/4561/E154274.

21. M.W. Graham, "Soviet Security Treaties," *American Journal of International Law*, XXIII, No. 2 (April, 1929), 344. See also Cielēns, *Laikmetu mainā*, Vol. II, pp. 325-326.

22. State Secretary von Schubert to Brockdorff-Rantzau, February 11, 1927, *Auswärtiges Amt*, 1466/3015/D596462-D596463.

23. Koester to Foreign Ministry, February 25, 1927, *ibid.*, 2311/4561/E154282-E154283; Koester to Foreign Ministry, March 5, 1927, *ibid.*, E154311-E154313; Koester to Wallroth, March 5, 1927, *ibid.*, 2573/5265/E319713-E319714; London *Times*, March 5, 1927.

24. Koester to Foreign Ministry, March 11, 1927, *Auswärtiges Amt*, 2311/4561/E154319-E154320; London *Times*, March 11, 1927; *Riga Times*, March 19, 1927.

25. "Cielēns's Speech on Negotiations with the Soviet Russians, March 10, 1927," in *Auswärtiges Amt*, 2573/5265/E319704-E319707; Cielēns, *Laikmetu mainā*, Vol. II, pp. 326-327.

26. Koester to Foreign Ministry, March 8, 1927, *Auswärtiges Amt*, 1466/3015/D596482-D596483; Otto Hoetzsch, "Innere Lage und Mächtebeziehungen der Randstaaten," *Osteuropa*, II, (1926/27), 351; London *Times*, March 14, 1927.

27. Koester to Foreign Ministry, March 8, 1927, *Auswärtiges Amt*, 2311/4561/E154356.

28. Brockdorff-Rantzau to Foreign Ministry, March 24, 1927, *ibid.*, 1466/3015/D596356.

29. Reinhardt (Riga) to Foreign Ministry, May 4, 1927, *ibid.*, 2311/4561/E154377. Cielēns was complimented by Reinhardt on Latvia's progress as a "zone of order" (*Ordnungszelle*) in the Baltic region. Cielēns, who saw Ulmanis pass by outside, remarked to Reinhardt: "If only the Fat One does not disturb our orderliness, throw my foreign policy overboard, and put us in Poland's wake!" He obviously still feared a coup attempt by his agrarian rival.

30. *New York Times*, March 12, 1927.

31. Report of Consul Harry E. Carlson (Tallinn) for April, 1927, enclosure No. 1 to report of Coleman to Secretary of State, May 16, 1927, National Archives, Doc. No. 860i.00/152.

32. Pannwitz (Warsaw) to Foreign Ministry, March 12, 1927, *Auswärtiges Amt*, 3878/K244/K073888.

33. Report of Consul Harry E. Carlson (Tallinn) for April, 1927, enclosure No. 1 to report of Coleman to Secretary of State, National Archives, Doc. No. 860i.00/152; Frank (Tallinn) to Foreign Ministry, March 18, 1927, *Auswärtiges Amt*, 3879/K244/K073969; London *Times*, March 14, 19, 1927. On Čakste's death see *ibid.*, March 15, 1927.

34. The formal break came on May 26, 1927, following the "Arcos affair." See *Survey of International Affairs 1927* (London: Oxford University Press, 1929), pp. 266-271; *Documents on British Foreign Policy*, Series IA, Vol. III, *European and Naval Questions, 1927* (London: His Majesty's Stationery Office, 1970), Doc. Nos. 191, 193, 194, 204.

35. London *Times*, March 14, 1927.

36. Koester to Foreign Ministry, March 11, 1927, *Auswärtiges Amt*, 3878/K244/K073872-K073873; London *Times*, March 18, 1927.

37. Wallroth to Reinhardt (Riga), May 18, 1927, *Auswärtiges Amt*, 5770/K2331/K664274-K664277; Dirksen, "Memorandum for Stresemann," September 12, 1927, *ibid.*, 1466/3015/D596502-K596506.

38. Augur, "The Foreign Policy of Germany, Soviet Russia, and Felikss Cielēns," *Latvis*, July 13, 1927, enclosure to report of Koester to Foreign Ministry, July 22, 1927, *ibid.*, 5380/K1969/K510783; Koester to Foreign Ministry, July 14, 1927, *ibid.*, 2778/5462/E374297. Koester described the owner of *Latvis*, Arvēds Bergs, as "an intimate of the British Legation."

39. Count Bassewitz (in the Eastern Division), memorandum of March 31, 1927, *ibid.*, E374286.

40. The British would have been more disturbed had they known that Brockdorff-Rantzau had suggested to Berlin a rather thoroughgoing Reich involvement in Latvian affairs *via* the Baltic-German political party. Brockdorff-Rantzau's suggestion was correctly rejected by the Foreign Ministry for several political reasons, but basically because, as Wallroth put it, "Riga is not Memel." See Wallroth, "Notes on Brockdorff-Rantzau's Telegram," December 19, 1927, *Auswärtiges Amt*, 2311/4561/E154401-E154402.

41. Edgar Anderson, "The U.S.S.R. Trades with Latvia: The Treaty of 1927," *Slavic Review*, XXI, No. 2 (June, 1962), 296-321; Fischer, *Soviets in World Affairs*, Vol. II, p. 519; Mousset, "Les Marches septentrionales de l'Europe: une enquête aux pays baltes," *L'Europe Nouvelle*, XI, No. 558 (October 20, 1928), 1415.

42. S. I. Aralov had stated that signing the nonaggression pact would facilitate economic discussions. See also Rykov's speech of April 18, 1927, to the Fourth All-Union Congress of Soviets, *Izvestiîa*, April 20, 1927, quoted in "Russian Foreign Relations," *European Economic and Political Survey*, II, No. 19 (June 15, 1927), 636.

43. *Latvian-Russian Relations: Documents*, pp. 148-159. The Soviet insistence on credits rendered the promised purchase of industrial goods in the amount of 40 million lats of little value. See Coleman to Secretary of State, October 10, 1927, National Archives, Doc. No. 660 p. 6131/25; *Riga Times*, May 6, June 3, June 17, 1927.

44. Koester to Wallroth, November 11, 1927, *Auswärtiges Amt*, 2573/5263/E319677.

45. *Revaler Bote*, September 3, 1927, enclosure to report of Weyrauch to Foreign Ministry, September 7, 1927, *ibid.*, 3879/K244/K074398-K074399. Part of this newspaper article is quoted in Assmus, "Entwicklungstendenzen im baltischen Raum," *Zeitschrift für Geopolitik*, V, No. 7 (July, 1928), 569. The German-language papers in Reval and Riga each supported the governments of their respective republics.

46. *Frankfurter Zeitung*, October 1, 7, 1927; "Baltic Problem," *European Economic and Political Survey*, III, No. 7 (December 15, 1927), 215, 217; Oswald Zienau, "Die sowjetrussisch-lettischen und estnischen Handelsbeziehungen," *Osteuropa*, V, No. 4 (January, 1930), 258-259; Anderson, "U.S.S.R. Trades with Latvia," *Slavic Review*, XXI, No. 2 (June, 1962), 309; Report of Consul Harry E. Carlson (Tallinn) for September, 1927, enclosure No. 1 to report of Coleman to Secretary of State, October 10, 1927, National Archives, Doc. No. 860i.00/157. On Estonian irritation with Latvia, see further Coleman to Secretary of State, October, 24, 1927, *ibid.*, Doc. No. 860p.00/115; Coleman to Secretary of State, August 13, 1927, *ibid.*, Doc. No. 860p.00/114; Coleman to Secretary of State, November 2, 1927, *ibid.*, Doc. No. 660p.6131/31; London *Times*, September 2, 1927; Koester to Foreign Ministry, August 30, 1927 *Auswärtiges Amt*, 2777/5462/E373623; *Sociāldemokrats*, August 27, 1927 , *ibid.*, 3879/K244/K074378.

47. Quoted in Weyrauch (Tallinn) to Foreign Ministry, August 24, 1927, *ibid.*, K074344-K074345.

48. *Sociāldemokrats*, August 27, 1927, enclosure to report of Koester to Foreign Ministry, August 27, 1927, *ibid.*, K074378.

49. Stuart R. Schram, "L'Union sovietique et les états baltes," in *Les Frontières européennes de l'U.R.S.S. 1917-1941* ("Cahiers de la fondation nationale des sciences politiques," No. 85; Paris: Armand Colin, 1957), p. 84.

50. "Latvia between Two Worlds," *The Economist*, CVI (May 19, 1928), 1024.

51. Paul Schiemann, "Die baltischen Staaten und Russland," *Frankfurter Zeitung*, October 30, 1927.

52. London *Times*, June 2, 1927; *Frankfurter Zeitung*, June 3, 1927.

53. *Brīvā Zeme*, June 2, 1927, quoted in Schram, "L'Union sovietique et les etats balts," *Les Frontières européennes de l'U.R.S.S.*, pp. 83-84; *Latvis*, May 10, 1927, quoted in *ibid.*, p. 83.

54. *Riga Times*, June 3, 1927. In 1919 and 1920 Cielēns had strongly urged Meierovics not to fight the western powers' anit-Bolshevik war for them when these powers would not grant aid and *de jure* recognition to Latvia. In the face of English criticism, Meierovics had undertaken armistice and peace negotiations with the Soviet Russians. See Cielēns, *Laikmetu mainā*, II, pp. 62-65, 88-100.

55. Russia, according to Voldemaras, would welcome the stabilization of her 1,500 kilometer Baltic frontier. The Poles would have to disgorge some territory, and transfer Vilna and Grodno to Lithuania, but would then be able to reduce their military expenditure. Since Poland was not included in Voldemaras' suggested guarantee scheme, it was almost an open invitation to Germany and Russia to revise their respective Polish frontiers. See E. J. Harrison, ed., *Lithuania 1928* (London: Hazell, Watson and Viney, Ltd., 1928), pp. 56-58. A Lithuanian journal, *Lietuva*, noted on March 26, 1927: "The fate of Eastern Europe lies in the hands of Germany and Russia. Yet their time has not quite come for disposing of that fate." Quoted in a report of Hans Moraht (Kaunas) to Foreign Ministry, March 28, 1927, *Auswärtiges Amt*, 2778/5462/E374153.

56. Cielēns, *Laikmetu mainā*, Vol. II, pp. 338-339, 340-342; report of Consul R. W. Heingartner (Kaunas) for March, 1927, enclosure No. 1 to report of Louis Sussdorff, Jr. (chargé, Riga) to Secretary of State, April 25, 1927, National Archives, Doc. No. 860m.00/128; Hans Moraht (Kaunas) to Foreign Ministry, March 26, 1927, *Auswärtiges Amt*, 2777/5462/E373680; *Frankfurter Zeitung*, June 2, 1927. When Voldemaras came to Riga in mid-March, 1927, for the funeral of President Čakste, the two foreign ministers signed a number of administrative agreements on transit and trade. The Latvian leftist press put great significance on such collaboration and Cielēns told the foreign affairs commission of the Saeima that as long as Estonia remained under English-Polish influence, Latvia had to seek closer relations with Lithuania. Koester to Foreign Ministry, March 22, 1927, *Auswärtiges Amt*, 1466/3015/D596487-D596488.

57. Koester to Foreign Ministry, March 11, 1927, *ibid.*, 2311/4561/E154321-E154322.

58. "Copy of a Speech by Cielēns, March 10, 1927," *ibid.*, 2778/5462/ E374196; Koester to Foreign Minisrty, March 31, 1927, *ibid.*, 5769/ K2329/K663356; London *Times*, March 11, 1927; *Riga Times*, March 19, 1927.

59. Schiemann, "Die baltischen Staaten und Russland," *Frankfurter Zeitung*, October 30, 1927.

60. Hōltje, *Die Weimarer Republik und das Ostlocarno-Problem 1919-1934*, treats this question at length. Speaking in Frankfurt early in March 1927, Count Cuno von Westarp claimed that all the Reichstag parties agreed that an Eastern Locarno was "unthinkable." London *Times*, March 5, 1927.

61. Stresemann to German Envoys in Paris, London, Moscow, Rome, Washington, Warsaw, Riga, Tallinn, Kaunas, Helsinki, Bucharest, March 21, 1927, *Auswärtiges Amt*, 2311/4561/E154332-E154335. See also Josef Korbel, *Poland between East and West: Soviet and German Diplomacy toward Poland, 1919-1933* (Princeton: Princeton University Press, 1963), pp. 231-233.

62. *Riga Times*, October 1, 1927. See also, K. R. Pusta, "Le Statut de la mer baltique à partir du XIXe siècle," *Academie de droit internationale, Recueil des Cours 1935*, Vol. LII, pp. 149-150; Newman, *Britain and the Baltic*, p. 21.

63. *Riga Times*, October 1, 1927. Poland drew up another version of an Eastern Locarno and presented it at Geneva to a caucas of delegates from the Little Entente and Baltic and Scandinavian powers. *New York Times*, July 22, 1927; *Frankfurter Zeitung*, September 5, 6, 7, 1927; Ludwig Zimmermann, *Deutsche Aussenpolitik in der Āra der Weimarer Republik* (Göttingen, Berlin, Frankfurt: Musterschimdt-Verlag, 1958), pp. 341-343; Harald von Reikhoff, *German-Polish Relations, 1918-1933* (Baltimore and London: The Johns Hopkins Press, 1971), pp. 235-248.

64. Hugh F. Spender, "Security and Disarmament, Cross Currents at Geneva," *Fortnightly Review*, CXXVIII (November, 1927), 601, 605-607.

65. League of Nations, *Official Journal* (Special Supplement No. 54): *Records of the Eighth Ordinary Session of the Assembly, Plenary Meetings, Text of the Debates* (Geneva, 1927), pp. 44-45, 46; see also the press account in *Riga Times*, September 16, 1927.

66. Cielēns, *Laikmetu mainā*, Vol. II, pp. 362-363. Interestingly enough, later in the year, Briand spoke of the need for a collective security system which would include Finland, Latvia, Estonia, Poland, and Roumania. Briand's idea consisted of a nonaggression pact among these states to be guaranteed by France, England, and Russia. See Ludwig Zimmermann, *Deutsche Aussenpolitik in der Āra der Weimarer Republik*, pp. 343-344.

67. Cielēns, *Laikmetu maina*, Vol. II, pp. 364-365; Stresemann, "Memorandum concerning a Conversation with Latvian Foreign Minister Cielēns," September 12, 1927, *Auswärtiges Amt*, 2311/4561/E154390-E154391; Dirksen, memorandum of September 12, 1927, *ibid.*, 1466/3015/ D596504; *Gustav Stresemann: His Diaries, Letters and Papers*, ed. Eric

Sutton (London: Macmillan, 1940), Vol. III, pp. 258, 368.

68. Dirkson to von Hassell (Copenhagen), August 1928, *Auswärtiges Amt*, 3880/K244/K0714714. (This file damaged by fire.) A Latvian diplomat also recalls Stresemann's negative attitude. See Edgars Kreewinsch, *Vinās dienās*, [In Days Gone By] (Melbourne: Austrālijas Latvietis, 1966), p. 183.

69. Cielēns, *Laikmetu mainā*, Vol. II, pp. 366-367; *Gustav Stresemann: Diaries, Letters, Papers*, Vol. III, p. 263; James Corbett, "Sir Austen Chamberlain and the League," *Fortnightly Review*, CXXVIII (November, 1927), 681-682.

70. *Gustav Stresemann: Diaries, Letters, Papers*, Vol. III, p. 263.

71. "Record of an Interview on September 13, 1927, between Latvian Foreign Minister Cielēns and Under-Secretary General of the League of Nations, McKinnon Wood" [marked "GANZ GEHEIM!"], *Auswärtiges Amt*, 2778/5462/E374125-E374127.

72. F. W. B. Coleman to Secretary of State, August 13, 1927, National Archives, Doc. No. 860p.00/114; London *Times*, September 14, 1927; Zienau, "Die sowjetrussisch-lettischen und estnischen Handelsbeziehungen," *Osteuropa*, V (January, 1930), 255-56.

73. *Latvis*, May 10, 1927, quoted in Schram, "L'Union sovietique et les états balts," *Les Frontières européennes de l'U.R.S.S.*, p. 83.

74. Cielēns, *Laikmetu mainā*, Vol. II, p. 337; Anderson, "U.S.S.R. Trades with Latvia," *Slavic Review*, XXI, No. 2 (June, 1962), 315.

75. Reinhardt (Riga) to Foreign Ministry, January 3, 1928, *Auswärtiges Amt*, 5769/K2329/K663363.

76. London *Times*, October 27, 1927.

77. *Frankfurter Zeitung*, October 27, 1927; Robert Machray, "Poland and the Baltic," *Fortnightly Review*, CXXIX (January, 1928), 96.

78. *Frankfurter Zeitung*, October 1, 30, 1927; Reinhardt to Foreign Ministry, January 3, 1928, *Auswärtiges Amt*, 5769/K2329/K663363; *Survey of International Affairs 1927*, p. 221.

79. Koester to Wallroth, November 11, 1927, *Auswärtiges Amt*, 2573/5265/E319677; Koester to Foreign Ministry, December 17, *ibid.*, 1466/3015/D596515-D596516.

Notes to Chapter 7

1. F. W. B. Coleman to Secretary of State, November 21, 1929, National Archives, Doc. No. 860p.00/131.

2. *Latvju Enciklopēdija*, p. 182. Balodis subsequently served as minister to Helsinki 1931-1933; after Soviet occupation of Latvia, he was deported to the Soviet interior in 1941.

3. *Riga Times*, February 16, 1928.

4. Koester to Foreign Ministry, February 14, 1928, *Auswärtiges Amt,* 2778/5462/E374223-E374224; Otto Hoetzsch, "Die osteuropäischen Randstaaten," *Osteuropa,* III (July, 1928), 687.

5. Schroetter (Tallinn) to Foreign Ministry, December 28, 1929, *Auswärtiges Amt,* 3880/K244/K074933-K074935.

6. Harry E. Carlson (chargé, Tallinn) to Secretary of State, September 17, 1931, National Archives, Doc. No. 760i.60P/31.

7. Coleman to Secretary of State, September 1, 1931, *ibid.,* Doc. No. 860i.31.

8. Felix Cole (chargé, Riga) to Secretary of State, December 5, 1931, *ibid.,* Doc. No. 760n.00/20.

9. Cielēns, *Laikmetu mainā,* Vol. II, p. 341.

10. League of Nations, *Official Journal* (Special Supplement No. 64): *Records of the Ninth Ordinary Session of the Assembly, Plenary Meetings, Text of the Debates* (Geneva, 1928), pp. 88-89.

11. Koester to Foreign Ministry, May 6, 1924, *Auswärtiges Amt,* 3873/K243/K071635; Henri de Monfort, "L'Aspect européen de l'expérience baltique," *La Pologne et la baltique,* p. 132; Robert Machray, "The Peace of the Baltic," *Fortnightly Review,* CXXX (November, 1928), 649-650. In view of the Soviet manipulation of trade for political ends, the opening of the railroad would hardly have altered Liepāja's situation. See also report of Consul Clement S. Edwards (Kaunas), enclosure No. 1 to report of Coleman to Secretary of State, February 18, 1924, National Archives, Doc. No. 860m.00/65.

12. Consul Hugh S. Fullerton (Kaunas) to Secretary of State, October 24, 1928, National Archives, Doc. No. 760n.60P/15.

13. Louis Sussdorf, Jr. (Riga) to Secretary of State, November 28, 1930, *ibid.,* Doc. No. 760m.60P/29; Hugh S. Fullerton (chargé, Kaunas) to Secretary of State, January 26, 1932, *ibid.,* Doc. No. 760m.00/37.

14. See the enclosure to report of Stieve to Foreign Ministry, July [?], 1928 *Auswärtiges Amt,* 3880/K244/K074727-K074729 (burned file).

15. Reinhardt (chargé, Riga) to Foreign Ministry, April 30, 1928, *ibid.,* 2778/5462/E374254.

16. Stieve to Foreign Ministry, August 24, 1928, *ibid.,* 3880/K244/ K074741-K074743. See also, Joseph Beck, *Dernier rapport: Politique polonaise 1926-1939* (Neuchâtel: Éditions de la Baconnière, 1951), pp. 77-78.

17. Stieve to Foreign Ministry, December 21, 1929, *Auswärtiges Amt,* 3880/K244/K074929-K074930. See further *Latvis,* November 24, 1930, enclosure of Stieve to Foreign Ministry, December 6, 1930, *ibid.,* 5769/ K2329/K663405; Coleman to Secretary of State, June 19, 1931, National Archives, Doc. No. 760p.61/63.

18. Stieve to Foreign Ministry, August 1, 1928, *Auswärtiges Amt,* 3880/K244/K074734; Stieve to Foreign Ministry, November 30, 1928, *ibid.,* 5375/K1951/K507261-K507264.

19. *Baltic States: Survey,* p. 33.

20. Stieve to Foreign Ministry, October 29, 1931, *Auswärtiges Amt*, 5375/K1951/K507274-K057275, K507278.

21. See press enclosures to report of Stieve to Foreign Ministry, October 29, 1931, *ibid.*, K507274-K507278; Šīpols, *Slepenā diplomātija*, pp. 222-223, 224. Lithuanian foreign minister, Dovas Zaunius, spoke to the Germans about the possibility of bringing Latvia into a German-Soviet-Lithuanian orientation. This could be done if Latvia obtained from the Soviets guarantees for her territorial status. Berlin instructed Herbert von Dirksen in Moscow to drop the necessary hints. Litvinov, however, had reservations and Dirksen concluded it was highly unlikely the Soviets would give Riga the kind of firm guarantees desired. Instead, Litvinov merely told the Latvian envoy in Moscow that Latvia need have no fear of the Soviet Union. See Ministerialdirektor Meyer to Stieve, November 9, 1931, *Auswärtiges Amt*, 5375/K1951/K507280-K507282; Meyer to Dirksen, November 9, 1931, *ibid.*, K507283; Dirksen to Foreign Ministry, November 16, 1931, *ibid.*, K507285-K507286; Dirksen to Foreign Ministry, December 5, 1931, *ibid.*, K507295-K507296; Weyrauch (Riga) to Foreign Ministry, November 21, 1931, *ibid.*, K507291-K507293.

22. Felix Cole (Riga) to Secretary of State, December 5, 1931, National Archives, Doc. No. 760n.00/20.

23. Levetzow (Copenhagen) to Foreign Ministry, May 6, 1930, *Auswärtiges Amt*, 3880/K244/K075040. The occasion of the remark was an address to the Conservative Club of Copenhagen. By "Central Europe," Bergs meant, of course, Germany.

24. London *Times*, March 3, 1928. For Groener's lengthy speech defending his naval construction program, see *Verhandlungen des Reichstags, Stenographische Berichte* (399th Session, 14 March 1928) (Berlin: Reichsdruckerei, 1928), Vol. CCCXCV, pp. 13376-13379.

25. London *Times*, March 19, 20, 1928; *ibid.*, May 18, 1931.

26. Quoted in André Tibal, "La Politique d'après-guerre des états riverains de la baltique," in *La Pologne et la baltique*, pp. 108-109.

27. *Ibid.*, p. 109.

28. London *Times*, August 12, 13, 15, 1930.

29. Tippleskirch (chargé, Riga) to Foreign Ministry, August 16, 1930, *Auswärtiges Amt*, 5770/K2331/K664374.

30. Stieve to Foreign Ministry, October 11, 1930, *ibid.*, K664377.

31. "Interpellation Dr. Frick, Kasche und Genossen über Sicherstellung der Rechte der Baltikumkämpfer," *Verhandlungen des Reichstags: Anlagen Nr. 1 bis 400 zu den Stenographischen Berichten* (Berlin: Julius Sittenfeld, 1931), Vol. CDXLVIII, Appendix No. 312.

32. On this controversial point see Douglas A. Unfug, "German Policy in the Baltic States, 1918-1919" (Unpublished dissertation, Yale University, 1960), pp. 277-285, who puts the argument to rest in favor of the Latvian interpretation. See also Hans-Erich Volkmann, "Probleme des deutsch-lettischen Verhältnisses," *Zeitschrift für Ostforschung*, XIV (December, 1965), p. 719; Waite, *Vanguard of Nazism*, p. 104. Among those who maintain that Ulmanis promised grants of land to German

volunteers is Benoist-Méchin, *Histoire de l'armée allemande 1918-1945*, Vol. II (Paris: Éditions Albin Michel, 1954), p. 17.

33. Stieve to Foreign Ministry, December 3, 1930, *Auswärtiges Amt*, 1466/3015/D596556; Ministeraldirektor Oskar Trautmann, notes [on the German-Latvian Agreement of December, 1918], December 10, 1930, *ibid.*, D596558-D596561.

34. Adolf Hitler, *Mein Kampf* (New York: Reynal and Hitchcock, 1941), pp. 950-951.

35. London *Times*, June 9, 1931.

36. Robert Machray, "The Baltic States, Some Personal Impressions," *The Central European Observer*, X, No. 39 (September 23, 1932), 551; "British Policy in the Baltic," *Fortnightly Review*, CXL (October, 1933), 405.

37. *Jaunākās Zinas*, November 13, 1930, enclosure to report of Stieve to Foreign Ministry, November 15, 1930, *Auswärtiges Amt*, 5769/K2329/K663390.

38. *Brīvā Zeme*, December 12, 1930, enclosure to report of Stieve to Foreign Ministry, December 18, 1930, *ibid.*, 5770/K2331/K664389-K664393.

39. Esmond Ovey to Sir John Simon, January 19, 1932, *Documents on British Foreign Policy*, 2nd Series (1930-1934), Vol. VII, No. 149, p. 230; Machray, "Baltic States," *Central European Observer*, X, No. 39 (September 23, 1932), 550.

40. William E. Scott, *Alliance against Hitler: Origins of the Franco-Soviet Pact* (Durham, N. C.: Duke University Press, 1962), pp. 15, 31.

41. Renner (Helsinki) to Foreign Ministry, September 9, 1931, *Auswärtiges Amt*, 3605/9756/E685682. See also Dyck, *Weimar Germany and Soviet Russia*, pp. 236-237, 242.

42. Litvinov's offer to Warsaw was made on October 14, and November 22, 1931. Stieve to Foreign Ministry, December 14, 1931, *Auswärtiges Amt*, 3605/9756/E685688; Scott, *Alliance against Hitler*, pp. 31, 33, 38.

43. *Latvian-Russian Relations: Documents*, pp. 170-171.

44. Finland signed on January 21, 1932; Poland initialed a draft on January 25 and signed on July 25, 1932; Latvia, as stated, on February 5, 1932; Estonia on May 4, 1932; Lithuania, of course, had signed such a pact in September, 1926. *Survey of International Affairs, 1934* (London: Oxford University Press, 1935), p. 409; Tarulis, *Soviet Policy toward the Baltic States*, pp. 80-81.

45. Cielēns, "Concerning the Russo-Polish and Franco-Russian Non-aggression Pacts," *Sociāldemokrats*, December 2, 1932, enclosure No. 1 to report of Weyrauch (Riga) to Foreign Ministry, December 7, 1932, *Auswärtiges Amt*, 5769/K2329/K663431-K663433.

46. Cielēns, *Laikmetu mainā*, Vol. II, pp. 461-462; *Sociāldemokrats*, No. 190, [September, 1932.], enclosure to report of Stieve to Foreign Ministry, September 10, 1932, *Auswärtiges Amt*, 5769/K2329/K663424-K663425.

47. Cielēns, *Laikmetu mainā*, Vol. II, pp. 449-457; *Sociāldemokrats*, No. 196 [September, 1932], enclosure to report of Stieve to Foreign Ministry, September 10, 1932, *Auswärtiges Amt*, 5769/K2329/K663426-K663427.

48. The lat was a gold standard currency exactly equal to the Swiss franc. The impact of the depression on Latvia may best be seen in the excellent statistical tables in *Baltic States: Survey*, pp. 160-163, 165-166. Adding to Latvia's difficulties was the fact that between 1920 and 1932, Latvia never had a favorable balance of trade. See charts in *ibid.*, pp. 122, 156, 166.

49. *Latvju Enciklopēdija*, p. 257.

50. *Latvia: Country and People*, pp. 239-240.

51. Martius to Foreign Ministry, January 21, 1933, *Auswärtiges Amt*, 3506/9020/E632012-E632014; Martius to Foreign Ministry, February 4, 1933, *ibid.*, E632018-E632020.

52. Blodnieks enjoyed the support of Karlis Ulmanis' Farmers' Union. See Blodnieks, *The Undefeated Nation* (New York: Robert Speller, 1960) pp. 219-220. Atis Kenins, the chauvinist minister of education in the preceding cabinet, retained his portfolio. See London *Times*, March 23, 1933.

53. *Latvju Enciklopēdija*, p. 2247; "Memorandum for the Visit of Latvian Foreign Minister Salnais," October 11, 1933, *Auswärtiges Amt*, 1466/3015/D596596.

54. Robert P. Skinner (Riga) to Secretary of State, March 29, 1933, National Archives, Doc. No. 760p.00/22.

55. Martius to Foreign Ministry, March 18, 1933, *Auswärtiges Amt*, 3506/9018/E631816. The Latvian-German controversy over the Latvian socialist press may be followed in diplomatic correspondence appearing in *ibid.*, E631848-E631871.

56. *New York Times*, June 15, 1933.

57. *Ibid.*, June 17, 1933; Ministerialdirektor Meyer, "Memorandum of a Conversation with Latvian Minister Kreewinsch," June 14, 1933, *Auswärtiges Amt*, 3506/9018/E631886-E631890; Martius to Foreign Ministry, July 14, 1933, *ibid.*, E631891-E631892; "Copy of a Radio Speech by Latvian Foreign Minister Salnais," January 9, 1934, enclosure to report of Martius to Foreign Ministry, January 11, 1934, *ibid.*, 3081/6604/E495849; Otto Hoetzsch, "Russland und Osteuropa: Übersicht," *Osteuropa*, IX (February, 1934), 306.

58. Felix Cole (chargé, Riga) to Secretary of State, June 30, 1933, National Archives Doc. No. 860p.021/11; Martius to Foreign Ministry, June 2, 1933, *Auswärtiges Amt*, 3506/9018/E631883.

59. Jürgen von Hehn, "Vilhelms Munters: Von Aussenminister des freien Lettland zum Verteidiger der Sowjetpolitik," *Osteuropa*, XIII (May, 1963), 326-327; Zinghaus, *Führende Köpfe der baltischen Staaten*, pp. 120-125; Kreewinsch, *Vinās dienās*, pp. 224-231, 245. Kreewinsch probably gives the fairest estimate of Munters' chequered career.

60. "Memorandum for the Visit of Latvian Foreign Minister Sal-

nais," October 11, 1933, *Auswärtiges Amt*, 1466/3015/D596596-D596597.

61. Martius to Foreign Ministry, March 23, 1933, *ibid.*, 3506/9018/E631825-E631826; Martius to Foreign Ministry, August 26, 1933, *ibid.*, E631898-E631899; Martius to Foreign Ministry, September 5, 1933, *ibid.*, E631902-E631906.

62. Martius to Foreign Ministry, December 1, 1933, *Documents on German Foreign Policy 1918-1945*, Series C (1933-1937), Vol. II (October 14, 1933-June 13, 1934) (Washington: Government Printing Office, 1959) No. 155, p. 289.

63. The episode may be followed in an exchange of memoranda and letters from April 4, 1934, to June 14, 1934, between Captain Ernst Munzinger, the Foreign Ministry, and the Reichsbank, in 3506/9019/E631932-E631938, E631942-E631944, E631950. An even earlier suggestion of Reich help to the Latvian Farmers' Union had been made by Friedrich Stieve in a letter to Ministerialdirektor Oskar Trautmann, February 6, 1929, in 2604/5551/E390178-E390179.

64. *Documents on German Foreign Policy*, Series C, Vol. II, p. 289.

65. *Diplomat in Berlin 1933-1939: Papers and Memoirs of Jozef Lipski, Ambassador of Poland* (New York and London: Columbia University Press, 1969), p. 133.

66. *New York Times*, April 27, 1933. Alfred Rosenberg was a Baltic-German from Tallinn (Reval). He had left Russia to escape the revolution and had become one of Hitler's earliest recruits. See Alan Bullock, *Hitler: A Study in Tyranny* (revised ed.; New York: Bantam Books, 1961) pp. 54, 272-273.

67. Martius to Foreign Ministry, July 14, 1933, *Auswärtiges Amt*, 3506/9018/E631892-E631893; Sir John Simon to Sperling (Helsinki), January 19, 1934, *Documents on British Foreign Policy*, 2nd Series Vol. VII, No. 565. pp. 641-642.

68. *Latvian-Russian Relations: Documents*, pp. 175-178; London *Times*, July 4, 1933; Martius to Foreign Ministry, July 14, 1933, *Auswärtiges Amt*, 3605/9756/E685725-E685726; *Survey of International Affairs, 1934* (London; Oxford University Press, 1935), p. 379.

69. Cielēns, *Laikmetu mainā*, Vol. II, p. 461.

70. League of Nations, *Official Journal* (Special Supplement No. 115): *Records of the Fourteenth Ordinary Session of the Assembly, Plenary Meetings, Text of the Debates* (Geneva, 1933), pp. 53, 54, 55.

Notes to Chapter 8

1. Felix Cole to Secretary of State, October 3, 1933, National Archives, Doc. No. 760p.00/24.

2. Sir Hughe M. Knatchbull-Hugessen, *Diplomat in Peace and War* (London: John Murray, 1949), p. 64.

3. Luther (Washington) to Foreign Ministry, January 6, 1934, *Auswärtiges Amt*, 3081/6604/E495777; *New York Times*, January 6, 1934. A territorial deal was actually considered in early 1935. See Gerhard L. Weinberg, *The Foreign Policy of Hitler's Germany: Diplomatic Revolution in Europe 1933-1936* (Chicago and London: University of Chicago Press, 1970), p. 193 n. 65.

4. For details see *Diplomat in Berlin: Lipski*, pp. 94-130; and Weinberg, *Foreign Policy of Hitler's Germany*, pp. 57-74, which cites the relevant German documentation.

5. "Memorandum of a Conversation on January 30, 1934, with General Aleksanders Kalejs," enclosure No. 1 to report of Cole to Secretary of State, February 16, 1934, National Archives, Doc. No. 760p.00/25. See further Martius to Foreign Ministry, February 9, 1934, *Auswärtiges Amt*. 3025/6603/E495299-E495300; see also Tripier (Riga) to Flandin (Paris), March 25, 1936, *Documents diplomatiques français 1932-1939*. 2nd Series (1936-1939), Vol. I (January 1-March 31, 1936) (Paris: Imprimerie Nationale, 1963), No. 501, p. 654.

6. "Soviet Note of December 21, 1933," enclosure to report of Martius to Foreign Ministry, January 11, 1934, *Auswärtiges Amt*, 3081/6604/E495836; *Diplomat in Berlin: Lipski*, pp. 131-134.

7. Martius to Foreign Ministry, January 4, 1934, *Auswärtiges Amt*, 3081/6604/E495750-E495751; "Memorandum of a Conversation with Hans Laretei, Assistant Estonian Minister for Foreign Affairs," enclosure No. 3, Carlson (Tallinn) to Secretary of State, January 8, 1934, National Archives, Doc. No. 760n.00/41; Knatchbull-Hugessen to Sir John Simon, January 5, 1934, *Documents on British Foreign Policy*, 2nd Series, Vol. VII, No. 552, pp. 630-631.

8. Edward Albright (Helsinki) to Secretary of State, January 12, 1934, National Archives, Doc. No. 760n.00/43; "Memorandum on Developments in Baltic Pact Matters," April 4, 1934, *Auswärtiges Amt*, 3025/6603/E495391; Knatchbull-Hugessen to Sir John Simon, January 14, 1934, *Documents on British Foreign Policy*, 2nd Series, Vol. VII, No. 561, p. 637; London *Times*, January 5, 1934.

9. Felix Cole to Secretary of State, January 25, 1934, National Archives, Doc. No. 760n.00/47; John Cudahay (Warsaw) to Secretary of State, January 10, 1934, *ibid.*, Doc. No. 760n.00/49; Erskine (Warsaw) to Sir John Simon, January 7, 1934, *Documents on British Foreign Policy*, 2nd Series, Vol. VII, No. 556, pp. 632-633; Viscount Chilston (Moscow) to Sir John Simon, January 7, 1934, *ibid.*, No. 557, p. 634; Nadolny to Foreign Ministry, January 16, 1934, *Documents on German Foreign Policy*, Series C, Vol. II, No. 187, p. 369.

10. "Polish Note [to Latvian Government] of December 28, 1933," enclosure to report of Martius to Foreign Ministry, January 11, 1934, *Auswärtiges Amt*, 3081/6604/E495837. The Polish note had an additional paragraph stating that the declaration would not be made without the consent of the Baltic states. See also, Joseph Beck, *Dernier rapport: Politique polonaise 1926-1939* (Neuchâtel: Édition de la Bacconnière, 1951), p. 36.

11. "Internal Memorandum of the Latvian Foreign Ministry on the Situation of the Baltic States," enclosure No. 1 to report of Martius to Foreign Ministry, February 9, 1934, *Auswärtiges Amt,* 3025/6603/ E495302-E495305. Nadolny, Germany's ambassador in Moscow, shared Riga's opinion of Polish motives. Nadolny to Foreign Ministry, January 10, 1934, *ibid.,* 3081/6604/E495818-E495819.

12. "Notes of an Oral Report of Foreign Minister Salnais to President Kviesis," enclosure No. 2 to report of Martius to Foreign Ministry, January 26, 1934, *ibid.,* 3025/6603/E495276. Martius obtained these notes from an informant in the Latvian foreign ministry. It is interesting that the prospect described by Salnais was partially fulfilled six years later in June, 1940, although at that time the Soviets acted with a German rather than a Polish partner.

13. Nadolny to Foreign Ministry, January 16, 1934, *Documents on German Foreign Policy,* Series C, Vol. II, No. 187, pp. 367-369; "Conclusions of the Latvian, Finnish, and Estonian Foreign Ministries on the Soviet-Polish Declaration Offer, January 6, 1934," enclosure to report of Martius to Foreign Ministry, January 11, 1934, *Auswärtiges Amt,* 3081/6604/E495838; "Press Summary," enclosure No. 2 to report of Felix Cole to Secretary of State, January 25, 1934, National Archives, Doc. No. 760n.00/47; *New York Times,* January 6, 21, 1934; London *Times,* January 8, 9, 1934.

14. Martius to Foreign Ministry, January 5, 1934, *Auswärtiges Amt,* 3081/6604/E495749. In a different context, the Soviets expressed almost identical concern with Finnish domestic politics in 1958 and, more strikingly, in 1961 and in 1970. See David Vital, *The Survival of Small States: Studies in Small Power-Great Power Conflicts* (London, New York, Toronto: Oxford University Press, 1971), pp. 107-109, 115.

15. *Izvestiia,* July 26, 1930, quoted in *Documents on British Foreign Policy,* 2nd Series, Vol, VII, No. 92, pp. 145-146; Karl Radek, "German Imperialism and the Fascization of the Baltic States," *Izvestiia,* December 17, 1933, enclosure No. 1 to report of Felix Cole to Secretary of State, January 25, 1934, National Archives, Doc. No. 760n.00/47.

16. Extracts from a speech by Litvinov on foreign affairs, December 29, 1933, in Degras, ed., *Soviet Documents on Foreign Policy,* Vol. III, pp. 53-54.

17. Knatchbull-Hugessen to Sir John Simon, January 24, 1934, *Documents on British Foreign Policy,* 2nd Series, Vol. VII, No. 567, pp. 643-644.

18. Internal Memorandum of the Latvian Foreign Ministry," enclosure to report of Martius to Foreign Ministry, February 9, 1934, *Auswärtiges Amt,* 3025/6603/E495303. There is some evidence that Poland declined a Soviet attempt to "guarantee the *domestic* security of the Baltic states." See Moltke (Warsaw) to Foreign Ministry, January 7, 1934, *ibid.,* 3081/6604/E495778-E495779.

19. *Paevaleht,* January 4, 1934, enclosure No. 1 to report of Carlson (Tallinn) to Secretary of State, January 8, 1934, National Archives, Doc. No. 760n.00/41. In 1935 a Soviet representative told the Finnish prime

minister that in case of war between Russia and Germany, the Soviets would occupy Finland. Latvia, Estonia, and Lithuania did ultimately suffer this fate. Vital, *Survival of Small States*, p. 104.

20. The best introduction to the fascinating topic of fascist and semi-fascist organizations in Latvia is provided by Jürgen von Hehn, *Lettland zwischen Demokratie und Diktatur; Zur Geschichte des lettländischen Staatsstreichs von 15. Mai 1934 (Jahrbücher zur Geschichte Osteuropas*, Beiheft 3; Munich: Isar Verlag, 1957), especially pp. 22-26. See also dispatches from Riga to the German foreign ministry, during the months of April, May, June, and July, 1934: *Auswartiges Amt*, 3506/9020/E632023-E632039; 3506/9019/E631932-E631950.

21. *Sociāldemokrats*, January 14, 1934, enclosure to report of Martius to Foreign Ministry, January 16, 1934, *ibid.*, 3081/6604/E495874.

22. *Latvijas Kāreivis*, January 12, 13, 1934, enclosure to report of Martius to Foreign Ministry, January 13, 1934, *ibid.*, E495870-E495871.

23. German Legation (Helsinki) to Foreign Ministry, March 17, 1933, 3605/9756/E685697; M. L. Strafford (chargé, Kaunas) to Secretary of State, May 19, 1933, National Archives, Doc. No. 760n.00/38; *New York Times*, April 25, 1933.

24. Karlis Ozols, *Memuary poslannika*, pp. 255-257; Martius to Foreign Ministry, March 23, 1933, *Auswärtiges Amt*, 3506/9018/E631826-E631827; Felix Cole (Riga) to Secretary of State, May 5, 1933, National Archives, Doc. No. 760n.00/35.

25. In the spring of 1933, Cielēns predicted a German-Polish war by 1935. "The Hitlerites have piled up more psychological high explosives than Germany had ready in 1914," he wrote. See *Jaunākās Zinas*, March 27, 1933, enclosure to report of Robert P. Skinner to Secretary of State, March 31, 1933, National Archives, Doc. No. 760n.00/31.

26. M. L. Strafford (chargé, Kaunas) to Secretary of State, May 10, 1933, National Archives, Doc. No. 760n.00/37; German Legation (Kaunas) to Foreign Ministry, May 4, 1933, *Auswärtiges Amt*, 3605/9756/E685718.

27. Stafford to Secretary of State, May 19, 1933, National Archives, Doc. No. 760n.00/38; Martius to Foreign Ministry, May 24, 1933, *Auswartiges Amt*, 3605/9756/E685722.

28. "Latvian-Finnish Protocol of Agreement, December 8, 1933," enclosure to report of Martius to Foreign Ministry, December 23, 1933, *ibid.*, E685738-E685739. See also Edgar Anderson, "Toward the Baltic Union, 1927-1934," *Lituanus*, XIII, No. 1 (Spring, 1967), 5-28.

29. Knatchbull-Hugessen to Sir John Simon, January 24, 1934, *Documents on British Foreign Policy*, 2nd Series, Vol. VII, No. 567, p. 645; Felix Cole to Secretary of State, January 29, 1934, National Archives, Doc. No. 760i.060P/37.

30. "Notes of an Oral Report of Foreign Minister Salnais to President Kviesis," enclosure No. 2 to report of Martius to Foreign Ministry, January 26, 1934, *Auswärtiges Amt*, 3025/6603/E495274.

31. Knatchbull-Hugessen to Sir John Simon, January 24, 1934, *Docu-*

ments on British Foreign Policy, 2nd Series, Vol. VII, No. 567, pp. 645-646.

32. Martius to Foreign Ministry, February 23, 1934, *Auswärtiges Amt*, 3025/6603/E495340; Buesing (Helsinki) to Foreign Ministry, January 20, 1934, *ibid.*, E495215.

33. "Memorandum of a Conversation with General Kalejs," enclosure No. 3 to report of Cole to Secretary of State, February 16, 1934, National Archives, Doc. No. 760p.00/25.

34. Martius to Foreign Ministry, February 9, 1934, *Auswärtiges Amt*, 3025/6603/E495299-E495300.

35. M. L. Strafford (Kaunas) to Secretary of State, March 1, 1934, National Archives, Doc. No. 760n.00/53; Knatchbull-Hugessen to Sir John Simon, February 1, 1934, *Documents on British Foreign Policy*, 2nd Series, Vol. VII, No. 571, p. 654.

36. Dirksen to Foreign Ministry, March 21, 1933, *Auswärtiges Amt*, 3605/9756/E685704-E685705; Martius to Foreign Ministry, March 15, 1933, *ibid.*, E685699-E685701.

37. Frederick P. Latimer (chargé, Tallinn) to Secretary of State, October 3, 1933, National Archives, Doc No. 760n.61/40.

38. Nadolny to Foreign Ministry, January 10, 1934, *Auswärtiges Amt*, 3081/6604/E485817-E495818.

39. Martius to Foreign Ministry, February 16, 1934, *ibid.*, 3025/6603/E495323-E495324.

40. Felix Cole to Secretary of State, April 17, 1934, National Archives, Doc. No. 760i.6011/1; Kazlaukas, *L'Entente baltique*, pp. 142-143.

41. Blodnieks, *Undefeated Nation*, pp. 215-226. For details of the Ulmanis reform scheme, see Hehn, *Lettland zwischen Demokratie und Diktatur*, pp. 29-39.

42. Otto Hoetzsch, "Russland und Osteuropa: Übersicht," *Osteuropa*, IX, (April, 1934), 427; *Vossische Zeitung*, March 18, 1934.

43. Nadolny to Foreign Ministry, March 28, 1934, *Documents on German Foreign Policy*, Series C, Vol. II, No. 362, p. 684; Rudolf Nadolny, *Mein Beitrag* (Wiesbaden: Limes Verlag, 1955), p. 166. Russian and German texts of Litvinov's draft protocol appear as enclosures to report of Nadolny to Foreign Ministry, March 29, 1934, *Auswärtiges Amt*, 3025/6603/E495389-E495390. Litvinov's words, "previously a part of the former Russian Empire," were not merely descriptive, but designed to exclude Memel from the declaration. Krestinsky and Voroshilov stressed this point to Nadolny at dinner on March 28. Nadolny to Foreign Ministry, March 29, 1934, *Documents on German Foreign Policy*, Series C, Vol. II, No. 364, p. 686.

44. Nadolny to Foreign Ministry, April 3, 1934, *Documents on German Foreign Policy*, Series C, Vol. II, No. 375, pp. 701-702. Nadolny failed to convince Neurath and Hitler of the necessity of good relations with Moscow and was forced to resign his position. See his *Mein Beitrag*, pp. 166-169. Additional information on Nadolny and the Baltic guarantee proposal may be had in Gustav Hilger and Alfred G. Meyer, *The Incom-*

patible Allies: A Memoir-History of German-Soviet Relations, 1918-1941 (New York: Macmillan Co., 1953), pp. 261-267; and in Weinberg, *Foreign Policy of Hitler's Germany*, pp. 180-183.

45. Neurath to Nadolny, April 9, 1934, *Documents on German Foreign Policy*, Series C, Vol. II, No. 390, pp. 731-734.

46. Statement by Litvinov to the German Ambassador, April 21, 1934, in Degras, ed., *Soviet Documents on Foreign Policy*, Vol. III, pp. 79-83.

47. Neurath to Ambassadors and Ministers in London, Rome, Paris, Warsaw, Kaunas, Riga, Tallinn, Helsinki, April 21, 1934, *Auswärtiges Amt*, 3072/6610/E497856; Martius to Foreign Ministry, April 23, 1934, *Documents on German Foreign Policy*, Series C, Vol. II, No. 415, pp. 764-766; Neurath to Martius, April 25, 1934, *ibid.*, No. 425, p. 777.

48. Nadolny to Neurath, April 26, 1934, *ibid.*, No. 427, p. 780; State Secretary von Bülow to Martius, April 25, 1934, *Auswärtiges Amt*, 3072/6610/E497861-E497862; Sir John Simon to Torr (Riga), May 11, 1934, *Documents on British Foreign Policy*, 2nd Series, Vol. VII, No. 596, p. 689; London *Times*, April 26, 27, 1934.

49. Press summaries as enclosures to report of Weyrauch to Foreign Ministry, April 28, 1934, *Auswärtiges Amt*, 3072/6610/E497952-E497953, E497974.

50. *Ibid.*, E497954-E497957; Martius to Foreign Ministry, April 25, 1934, *ibid.*, E497877.

51. Carlson (Tallinn) to Secretary of State, April 27, 1934, National Archives, Doc. No. 760n.00/55; Strafford (Kaunas) to Secretary of State, May 7, 1934, *ibid.*, Doc. No. 760n.00/64; *Jaunākās Zinas*, April 26, 1934, enclosure to report of Weyrauch (Riga) to Foreign Ministry, April 26, 1934, *Auswärtiges Amt*, 3072/6610/E497865; Torr (Riga) to Sir John Simon, April 28, 1934, *Document on British Foreign Policy*, 2nd Series, Vol. VII, No. 593, pp. 681-684.

52. Kazlauskas, *L'Entente baltique*, pp. 144-146; Otto Hoetzsch, "Das politische Kräftespiel im Osteuropa," *Osteuropa*, IX (June, 1934) 514-515; Weyrauch to Foreign Ministry, April 28, 1934, *Auswärtiges Amt*, 3072/6610/E497975-E497976; Martius to Foreign Ministry, May 4, 1934, *ibid.*, E497592; memorandum of July 18, 1934, *ibid.*, 3073/6611/E498183.

53. Reinebeck (Tallinn) to Foreign Ministry, May 12, 1934, *Auswärtiges Amt*, 3073/6611/E498105.

54. *New York Times*, May 25, 1934; *Survey of International Affairs, 1934*, p. 413.

55. Martius to Foreign Ministry, May 25, 1934, *Auswärtiges Amt*, 3073/6611/E498135; Preston (Kaunas) to Torr (Riga), May 26, 1934, *Documents on British Foreign Policy*, 2nd Series, Vol. VII, No. 600, pp. 691-692.

56. This position was taken so that Munters could attend for Latvia. Ulmanis, who was foreign minister as well as prime minister, had pulled off his *coup d'état* on May 15, 1934, and was too busy consolidating the new regime to leave the country. After establishing his dictatorship, he made no particular changes in Latvian foreign policy. See Hehn,

Lettland zwischen Demokratie und Diktatur, pp. 48-52; Wipert von Blücher, *Gesandter zwischen Diktatur und Demokratie: Erinnerungen aus den Jahren 1935-1944* (Wiesbaden: Limes Verlag, 1951), p. 104; Martius to Foreign Ministry, May 19, 1934, *Auswärtiges Amt*, 3506/9020/E632057-E632071; Carlson (Tallinn) to Secretary of State, May 25, 1934, National Archives, Doc. No. 860p.00/184.

57. W. J. Gallman (chargé, Riga) to Secretary of State, July 12, 1934, National Archives, Doc. No. 760i.60Pll/2; William M. Gwynn (chargé, Riga) to Secretary of State, September 6, 1934, *ibid.*, Doc. No. 760n.00/87; William C. Bullitt (Moscow) to Secretary of State, July 12, 1934, *ibid.*, Doc. No. 760n.00/79. On Stasys Lozoraitis, see Zinghaus, *Führende Köpfe*, pp. 20-22.

58. Knatchbull-Hugessen to Sir John Simon, July 14, 1934, *Documents on British Foreign Policy*, 2nd Series, Vol. VI, No. 506, p. 842. See also Karlheinz Gehrmann, *Die Baltischen Staaten: Eine Brücke zwischen Ost und West* (Berlin: Verlagsanstalt Otto Stollberg, 1939), pp. 84-85.

59. Martius to Foreign Ministry, July 16, 1834, *Auswärtiges Amt*, 3073/6611/E498191-E498193; *Ost-Express*, July 12, 1934, in *ibid.*, E498182.

60. London *Times*, December 6, 1927; Otto Hoetzsch, "Russlands Aussenpolitik zu Beginn 1928," *Osteuropa*, III, (1927/28), 252; Zimmermann, *Deutsche Aussenpolitik*, pp. 343-344. Poland had tried to resurrect the concept in 1931. See John N. Willys (Warsaw) to Secretary of State, October 22, 1931, *Foreign Relations of the United States, 1931*, Vol. I, p. 602; memorandum by the Secretary of State, July 9, 1931, *ibid.*, pp. 596-597.

61. Cielēns, *Laikmetu mainā*, Vol. II, pp. 473-474, 480-482.

62. Scott, *Alliance against Hitler*, pp. 135-138, 168-169, 171, 177; Elizabeth R. Cameron, "Alexis Saint-Léger Léger," in *The Diplomats*, Vol. II, pp. 385-396; Jules Laroche, *La Pologne de Pilsudski: Souvenirs d'une Ambassade, 1926-1935* (Paris: Flammarion, 1953), p. 164; Sir George Clark (Paris) to Sir John Simon, June 14, 1934, *Documents on British Foreign Policy*, 2nd Series, Vol. VI, No. 455, pp. 754-755; Weinberg, *Foreign Policy of Hitler's Germany*, p. 183 n.16.

63. Sir John Simon to Sir Eric Phipps, June 12, 1934, *Documents on British Foreign Policy*, 2nd Series, Vol. VI, No. 450, pp. 746-747; record of an Anglo-French meeting, London, July 10, 1934, *ibid.*, No. 489, p. 821; "Memorandum by State Secretary von Bulow," June 14, 1934, *Documents on German Foreign Policy*, Series C, Vol. III (June 14, 1934-March 31, 1935), No. 1, pp. 1-3; "Circular of the German Foreign Ministry," July 12, 1934, *ibid.*, No. 92, pp. 180-181.

64. Weyrauch (Riga) to Foreign Ministry, June 5, 1934, *Auswärtiges Amt*, 3073/6611/E498151-E498153; Laroche, *La Pologne de Pilsudski*, p. 172; Dodd (Berlin) to Secretary of State, July 7, 1934, *Foreign Relations of the United States, 1934*, Vol. I, p. 494, State Secretary von Bülow to Foreign Minister Neurath, July 23, 1934, *Documents on German For-*

eign Policy, Series C, Vol. III, No. 109, p. 215; Scott, *Alliance against Hitler*, p. 177.

65. Laroche, *La Pologne de Pilsudski*, pp. 165, 173, 178; Weinberg, *The Foreign Policy of Hitler's Germany*, pp. 184-185.

66. William C. Bullitt to Secretary of State, July 30, 1934, *Foreign Relations of the United States 1934*, Vol. I, pp. 506-507; Bullitt to Secretary of State, August 3, 1934, *ibid*., pp. 507-508; Hans Roos, *Polen und Europa: Studien zur polnischen Aussenpolitik* (Tübingen: J. C. B. Mohr, 1957), pp. 204-206; Robert Machray, "The Baltic Pact, Vilna and Memel," *Nineteenth Century and After*, CXVII (May, 1935), 589-590; Hoetzsch, "Russland und Osteuropa: Übersicht," *Osteuropa*, IX (August, 1934), 686-687.

67. Machray, "Baltic Pact, Vilna and Memel," *Nineteenth Century*, CXVII (May, 1935), 590-591; Hoetzsch, "Russland and Osteuropa," *Osteuropa*, IX, (August, 1934), 687.

68. Roos, *Polen und Europa*, p. 206.

69. *Kölnische Zeitung*, quoted in *New York Times*, July 26, 1934; Knatchbull-Hugessen to Sir John Simon, July 18, 1934, *Documents on British Foreign Policy*, 2nd Series, Vol. VII, No. 507, p. 844; Roos, *Polen und Europa*, p. 207; Michele Model, "Le Traité de entente et de collaboration des états baltes," *L'Europe Nouvelle*, XVII, No. 867 (September 22, 1934), 957.

70. Bullitt to Secretary of State, July 30, 1934, *Foreign Relations of the United States, 1934*, Vol. I, p. 506; "Declaration of Secretary General of the Latvian Foreign Ministry, Munters, of July 27, 1934," *Weltgeschichte der Gegenwart in Dokumenten 1934/35*, ed. Michael Freund (2 vols.; Essen: Essen Verlagsanstalt, 1942), Vol. I, pp. 191-192; Moltke (Warsaw) to Foreign Ministry, August 1, 1934, *Documents on German Foreign Policy*, Series C, Vol. III, No. 139, p. 278.

71. *New York Times*, August 1, 1934. Walter Duranty talked with Estonian foreign minister Seljamaa and an unnamed but "important British representative."

72. Bullitt to Secretary of State, July 30, 1934, *Foreign Relations of the United States, 1934*, Vol. I, pp. 505-506; Bullit to Secretary of State, August 3, 1934, *ibid*., p. 507.

73. Kreewinsch, *Vinās dienās*, pp. 169-170; Bülow to Neurath, July 23, 1934, *Documents on German Foreign Policy*, Series C, Vol. III, No. 109, p. 217; Bülow to Neurath, August 16, 1934, *ibid*., No. 162, p. 328; "Memorandum Replying to the French and Russian Proposal for an Eastern Pact," September 8, 1934, *ibid*., No. 200, pp. 396-402; Höltje, *Die Weimarer Republik und das Ostlocarno-Problem*, pp. 226-230.

74. Preston (Kaunas) to Knatchbull-Hugessen (Riga), Augus 16, 1934, *Documents on British Foreign Policy*, 2nd Series, Vol. VII, No. 615, p. 721; Mohrmann (Kaunas) to Foreign Ministry, August 20, 1934, *Auswärtiges Amt*, 3073/6611/E498205-E498206.

75. *Latvian Russian Relations: Documents*, pp. 250-251; William M. Gwynn (Riga) to Secretary of State, September 6, 1934, National

Archives, Doc. No. 760n.00/87; Knatchbull-Hugessen to Sir John Simon, August 30, 1934, *Documents on British Foreign Policy*, 2nd Series, Vol. VII, No. 623, pp. 730-731; Marschall (Riga) to Foreign Ministry, September 1, 1934, *Auswärtiges Amt*, 3073/6611/E498217-E498219 E498226; Rinebeck (Tallinn) to Foreign Ministry, September 5, 1934, *ibid.*, E498247-E498250; Mohrmann (Kaunas) to Foreign Ministry, September 7, 1934, *ibid.*, E498260-E498263.

76. *Izvestiîâ*, September 15, 1934, quoted by the *Ost-Express*, September 15, 1934, in *Auswärtiges Amt*, 3073/6611/E498285.

Notes to Chapter 9

1. Josef Hanč, *Tornado across Eastern Europe* (New York: Greystone Press, 1942), p. 73.

2. Nils Ørvik, "Scandinavian Security in Transition: The Two-Dimensional Threat," *Orbis*, XVI, No. 3 (Fall, 1972), 720-742. See also the interesting but not always convincing argument of V. V. Šveics, *Small Nation Survival: Political Defense in Unequal Conflicts* (New York: Exposition Press, 1970).

3. For a rather romantic interpretation of this point see Herbert Schroeder, *Russland und die Ostsee: Ein Beitrag zum Randstaatenproblem* (Riga: Verlag der Buchhandlung G. Loeffler, 1927), p. 256.

4. *Frankfurter Zeitung*, March 30, 1926; Newman, *Britain and the Baltic*, p. 95.

5. David Vital, *The Survival of Small States*, p. 129.

6. Zinghaus, *Führende Köpfe der baltischen Staaten*, p. 124.

7. Robert L. Rothstein, *Alliances and Small Powers* (New York, London: Columbia University Press, 1968), p. 177, quoted in Robert O. Keohane, "Lilliputians' Dilemmas: Small States in International Politics," *International Organization*, XXIII, (1969), p. 301.

8. Albert Mousset, "Les marches septentrionales de l'Europe: Une enquête aux pays baltes," *L'Europe Nouvelle*, XI, No. 558 (October 20, 1928), p. 1417.

Bibliography

I. *Primary Materials*

A. Unpublished Sources

Germany. Auswärtiges Amt. Archives of the German Foreign Ministry on microfilm deposited in the National Archives of the United States, Washington. Microcopy T-120.

Film Serial Numbers	*Title of File*
3015	Büro des Reichsministers: Akten betreffend Lettland (1922-1935)
4561	Büro des Staatssekretärs: Akten betreffend politische Beziehungen zu den Randstaaten (1925-1929).
5173	Direktoren, Handakten. Hauschild: Randstaaten, Polen, und Finnland (1921-1923).
5265	Direktoren, Handakten. Wallroth: Lettland (1923-1928).
5462	Direktoren, Handakten. Dirksen: Randstaaten, Ostlocarno (1925-1928).
5551	Direktoren, Handakten. Trautmann: Lettland (1928-1931).
6603	Geheimakten 1920-1936. Randstaaten: Sicherheitspakt (Nord-, Ostlocarno, Ostsee Entente, 1934-1935).
6604	Geheimakten 1920-1936. Randstaaten: Sonderheft russisch-polnischer Baltikum-Garantiepakt (1934).

6610　　　Geheimakten 1920-1936. Russland, Baltenstaaten: Politische Beziehungen Russland-
Deutschland und die Garantierung der Unab-
hängikeit der Baltenstaaten (1934).

6611　　　Geheimakten 1920-1936. Russland: Akten betreffend Zusammenschluss der Baltenstaaten
(1934).

9018　　　Abteilung IV. Randstaaten: Akten betreffend
politische Beziehungen Lettlands zu Deutschland (1931-1934).

9019　　　Abteilung IV. Randstaaten, Estland: Politische
Beziehungen Estland-Lettland (1928-1934).

9020　　　Abteilung IV. Randstaaten, Lettland: Innere
Politik, Parlaments- und Parteiwesen (1931-1934).

9756　　　Abteilung IV. Randstaaten: Sicherheitspakt
(Nord-, Ostlocarno, Ostsee Entente, 1931-1934).

9768　　　Abteilung IV. Randstaaten: Politische Beziehung-
en der Randstaaten zu Russland (1924-1934).

K243　　　Geheimakten 1920-1936. Randstaaten-Problem
(Randstaatenbund einschliessend Finnlands und
Polen, 1923-1925).

K244　　　Geheimakten 1920-1936. Randstaaten: Sicherheitspakt (Nord-, Ostlocarno, Ostsee Entente,
1925-1931).

K253　　　Geheimakten 1920-1936. Lettland: Politische
Beziehungen Lettland-Russland (1921-1936).

K1752　　Abteilung IV. Baltikum (Randstaaten: Politische Beziehungen zu Deutschland 1921-1936).

K1951　　Geheimakten 1920-1936. Randstaaten, Lettland:
Politische Beziehungen Lettland-Polen (1928-
1934).

K1967　　Abteilung IV. Baltikum (Randstaaten: Politische Beziehungen zu Russland 1921-1923).

K1969　　Abteilung IV. Lettland: Politische Beziehungen
zu Russland (1920-1934).

K2329　　Abteilung IV. Lettland: Allgemeine auswärtige Politik (1920-1934).

K2331　　Abteilung IV. Lettland: Politische Beziehungen
zu Deutschland (1921-1933).

K2334	Abteilung IV. Lettland: Politische Beziehungen zu Litauen (1920-1930).
K2361	Abteilung IV. Randstaaten (Baltikum): Politische Beziehungen zu England (1923-1934).
L584	Abteilung IV. Polen: Politische Beziehungen Polen-Randstaaten (1920-1929)
L798	Abteilung IV. Russland: Das Ostseeproblem (1924).

United States. Department of State. Decimal Files, 1910-1929, 1930-1939. Record Group 59, National Archives of the United States, Washington.

File Number	*File Description*
660p.6131	Commerce. Commercial treaties, conventions, commercial and trade agreements between Latvia and the Union of Soviet Socialist Republics.
760i.00	Estonia. Political Relations; bilateral treaties.
760i.60p	Estonia. Political Relations; bilateral treaties between Estonia and Latvia.
760m.00	Lithuania. Political Relations; bilateral treaties.
760m.60p	Lithuania. Political Relations; bilateral treaties between Lithuania and Latvia.
760n.00	Baltic Provinces. Political Relations; bilateral treaties.
760n.61	Baltic Provinces. Political Relations; bilateral treaties between the Baltic Provinces and the Union of Soviet Socialist Republics.
760p.00	Latvia. Political Relations; bilateral treaties.
760p.61	Latvia. Political Relations; bilateral treaties between Latvia and the Union of Soviet Socialist Republics.
860i.00	Internal Affairs of States. Estonia. Political Affairs.
860m.00	Internal Affairs of States. Lithuania. Political Affairs.
860n.00	Internal Affairs of States. Baltic Provinces. Political Affairs.
860n.01	Internal Affairs of States. Baltic Provinces. Government.

860p.00   Internal Affairs of States. Latvia. Political Affairs.
860p.021   Internal Affairs of States. Latvia. Foreign Office.

B. Printed Documents

France. Ministère des Affaires Étrangères. *Documents diplomatiques français 1932-1939.* 1st series (1932-1935), Vol. I. 2nd series (1936-1939), Vol. I. Paris: Imprimerie nationale, 1963-1966.

Germany. Archives of the German Foreign Ministry. *Atken zur Deutschen Auswärtigen Politik, 1918-1945, aus dem Archiv des Auswärtigen Amts.* Series B (1925-1933). Göttingen: Vandenhoeck and Rupprecht, 1966. Vol. I.

———. *Documents on German Foreign Policy 1918-1945.* Series C (1933-1937). Washington: Government Printing Office, 1957-1966. Vols. I, I, III.

———. Reichstag. *Verhandlungen des Reichstags: Stenographische Berichte.* Berlin: Various publishers, 1871-1942. Vols. CCCXLVI, CCCXCV, CDXLVIII.

Great Britain. Foreign Office. *Documents on British Foreign Policy 1919-1939.* Edited by E. L. Woodward, Rohan Butler, *et al.* 1st Series (1919-1921), Vol. III. 2nd Series (1930-1934), Vols. VI, VII. Series IA (1925-1929), Vols. I, II, III. London: H. M. Stationery Office, 1946-1970.

Latvia. Ārlietu ministrija. *Le Corps diplomatique en Lettonie, 1918-1938.* Riga: Ministère des affaires étrangères de Lettonie, 1938.

———. Paris Peace Conference, 1919. Latvian Delegation. *Memorandum on Latvia Addressed to the Peace Conference by the Lettish Delegation.* Paris: n. p., 1919.

———. Sūtniecība [Legation]. United States. *Latvian-Russian Relations: Documents.* Complied by Alfreds Bilmanis. Washington: The Latvian Legation, 1944.

———. *Minutes of the Baltic Conference Held at Bulduri in Latvia in 1920.* Washington: The Latvian Legation, 1960.

League of Nations. *Official Journal.* Special Supplement No. 13. *Records of the Fourth Assembly, Plenary Meetings, Text of the Debates.* Geneva, 1923.

———. *Official Journal.* Special Supplement No. 54. *Records of* the Eighth Ordinary Session of the Assembly, Plenary Meetings, Text of the Debates. Geneva, 1927.

———. *Official Journal.* Special Supplement No. 64. *Records of the Ninth Ordinary Session of the Assembly, Plenary Meetings, Text of the Debates.* Geneva, 1928.

———. *Official Journal.* Special Supplement No. 75. *Records of the Tenth Ordinary Session of the Assembly, Plenary Meetings, Text of the Debates.* Geneva, 1929.

———. *Official Journal.* Special Supplement No. 115. *Records of the Fourteenth Ordinary Session of the Assembly, Plenary Meetings, Texts of the Debates.* Geneva, 1933.

Soviet Documents on Foreign Policy. 3 vols. Edited by Jane Degras. New York: Oxford University Press, 1951-1953.

Union of Soviet Socialist Republics. Komissiia po izdaniiu diplomaticheskikh dokumentov. *Dokumenty vneshnei politiki S S S R.* Moscow: Gosudarstvennoe izdatel'stvo politichkeskoi literatury, 1957-1964. Vols. VI, VIII.

United States Congress, House of Representatives. Select Committee to Investigate Communist Aggression and Forced Incorporation of the Baltic States into the U. S. S. R., *Third Interim Report* (83rd Cong., 2nd Sess.). Washington: Government Printing Office, 1954.

———. Senate. *The Baltic Provinces: Report of the Mission to Finland, Estonia, Latvia, and Lithuania on the Situation in the Baltic Provinces by Robert Hale.* (66th Cong., 1st Sess., Senate Doc. 105). Washington: Government Printing Office, 1919.

United States. Department of State. *Papers Relating to the Foreign Relations of the United States, 1919: Russia.* Washington: Government Printing Office, 1937.

———. *Papers Relating to the Foreign Relations of the United States: The Paris Peace Conference, 1919.* 13 vols. Washington: Government Printing Office, 1942-1947. Vol. IV.

———. *Papers Relating to the Foreign Relations of the United States* [annual volumes, 1920-1934]. Washington: Government Printing Office, 1935-1952.

Weltgeschichte der Gegenwart in Dokumenten, 1934/35. 2 vols. Edited by Michael Freund. Essen: Essen Verlagsanstalt, 1942. Vol. I.

C. Memoirs and Accounts by Contemporaries

Ammende, Ewald. "Der Zusammenbruch des baltischen Blocks," *Frankfurter Zeitung*, September 26, 1925.

Bastjānis, Voldemārs. *Demokratiskā Latvija: Vērojumi un vērtējumi* [Democratic Latvia: Observations and Evaluations]. Stockholm: Izdevis Dr. Emils Ogriņš, 1966.

Beck, Joseph. *Dernier rapport: Politique polonaise 1926-1939.* Neuchâtel: Éditions de la Baconnière, 1951.

Berg, Arved. *Latvia and Russia: One Problem of the World Peace Considered.* London: J. M. Dent and Sons, 1920.

Blodnieks, Adolfs. *The Undefeated Nation.* New York: Robert Speller, 1960.

Blücher, Wipert von. *Deutschlands Weg nach Rapallo: Erinnerungen eines Mannes aus dem zweiten Gliede.* Wiesbaden: Limes Verlag, 1951.

_____. *Gesandter zwischen Diktatur und Demokratie: Erinnerungen aus den Jahren 1935-1944.* Wiesbaden: Limes Verlag, 1951.

Cielēns, Felikss. *Laikmetu maiņā: atmiņas un atziņas* [At the Turning of Epochs: Reflections and Reminiscences]. 3 vols, Lidingo, Sweden: Memento, 1961-1964. Vol. II.

Crohn-Wolfgang, Hermann Felix. *Lettlands Bedeutung für die östliche Frage.* Berlin, Leipzig: Walter de Gruyter, 1923.

Dirksen, Herbert von. *Moscow, Tokyo, London: Twenty Years of German Foreign Policy.* Norman: University of Oklahoma Press, 1952.

Erich, Rafael. "Quelques observations concernant la possibilité d'assurer l'integrité territoriale et l'indépendance des états secondaires que se trouvent dans une situation singulièrement exposée," *Revue de droit internationale,* 3rd ser., VI, No. 3 (1925), 349-353.

Grant-Watson, Herbert A. *The Latvian Republic: The Struggle for Freedom.* London: George Allen and Unwin, 1965.

Goltz, Rüdiger von der. *Meine Sendung in Finnland und im Baltikum.* Leipzig: Koehler, 1920.

_____. *Als politischer General im Osten.* Leipzig: Koehler, 1936.

Gregory, John D. *On the Edge of Diplomacy: Rambles and Reflections, 1902-1928.* London: Hutchinson and Co., 1929.

Gustav Stresemann: His Diaries, Letters and Papers. Edited and
translated by Eric Sutton. 3 vols. New York: Macmillan Company, 1935-1940. Vol. III.

Hilger, Gustav, and Meyer, Alfred G. *The Incompatible Allies:
A Memoir-History of German-Soviet Relations, 1918-1941.*
New York: Macmillan Company, 1953.

Knatchbull-Hugessen, Sir Hughe M. *Diplomat in Peace and War.*
London: John Murray, 1949.

Kreewinsch, Edgars. *Vinās dienās* [In Days Gone By]. Melbourne:
Austrālijas Latvietis, 1966.

Laroche, Jules. *La Pologne de Pilsudski: Souvenirs d'une ambassade, 1926-1935.* Paris: Flammarion, 1953.

Lipski, Jozef. *Diplomat in Berlin 1933-1939: Papers and Memoirs of Jozef Lipski, Ambassador of Poland.* New York, London: Columbia University Press, 1968.

Meierovics, Zigfrids. "La Lettonie et l'accord avec les Soviets,"
L'Europe Nouvelle, V, No. 19 (May 13, 1922), 588-589.

Nadolny, Rudolf. *Mein Beitrag.* Wiesbaden: Limes Verlag, 1955.

Norem, Owen J. C. *Timeless Lithuania.* Chicago: Amerlith Press,
1943.

Ozols, Charles. "Russia, Germany, and the Baltic States," *International Affairs*, XIII, No. 4 (July/August, 1934), 558-560.

Ozols, K[arlis] V. *Memuary poslannika.* Paris: Dom knigi, 1938.

Piip, Antonius [Ants]. "Baltic States as a Regional Unity,"
*Annals of the American Academy of Political and Social Sci-
ence*, CLXVIII (July, 1933), 171-177.

Pusta, Kaarel R. "La Question baltique dans le problème européen," *Revue politique et parlementaire*, LVII (March, 1955),
268-275.

_____. "Le Statut juridique de la mer baltique à partir du XIXe
siècle," *Académie de droit internationale, Recueil des Cours,
1935*, Vol. LII, pp. 107-190. Paris: Librairie du Recueil Sirey,
1935.

Rothstein, Theodor. "Die auswärtige Politik der U S S R,"
Osteuropa, III, (1927/1928), 126-135.

Rüdiger, Wilhelm von. *Aus dem letzten Kapitel deutsch-baltischer
Geschichte in Lettland: Erster Teil, 1919-1945.* Gern bei
Eggenfelden/Bayern: By the author, 1954.

_____. *Aus dem letzten Kapitel deutsch-baltischer Geschichte in Lettland: Zweiter Teil, 1919-1939.* Hannover-Wülfel: By the author, 1955.

Schiemann, Paul. "Die baltischen Staaten und Russland," *Frankfurter Zeitung,* October 30, 1927.

———. "Die baltischen Staaten zwischen Ost und West," *Frankfurter Zeitung,* March 30, 1926.

Spekke, Arnolds. *History of Latvia: An Outline.* Stockholm: M. Goppers, 1951.

Vizra, Edvarts (ed.). *Z. A. Meierovics: Latvijas primā ārlietu ministra darbības atcerei veltīts rakstu krājums* [Z. A. Meierovics: A Collection of Essays in Memory of Latvia's First Foreign Minister]. Riga: Z. A. Meieroivca pieminas fonda izdevums, 1935.

II. *Secondary Material*

A. Books

Andersons, Edgars. *Latvijas vēsture 1914-1920.* Stockholm: Daugava, 1967.

The Baltic States: A Survey of the Political and Economic Structure and the Foreign Relations of Estonia, Latvia, and Lithuania. Prepared by the Information Department of the Royal Institute of International Affairs. London: Oxford University Press, 1938.

Basler, Werner. *Deutschlands Annexionspolitik in Polen und im Baltikum 1914-1918.* ("Veröffentlichungen des Instituts für Geschichte der Völker der UdSSR an der Martin Luther Universität Halle-Wittenberg," Series B, Vol. III). Berlin: Rütten and Loening, 1962.

Benoist-Méchin, Jacques G. P. M. *Historie de l'armée allemande, 1918-1945.* 2 vols. Paris: Éditions Albin Michel, 1954. Vol. II.

Bērziņš, Artūrs. *Kārlis Zariņš dzīvē un darbā* [Karlis Zarins: Life and Work]. London: Rūja, 1959.

Bretton, Henry L. *Stresemann and the Revision of Versailles: A Fight for Reason.* Stanford: Stanford University Press, 1953.

Carsten, Francis L. *Reichswehr und Politik 1918-1933.* Cologne, Berlin: Kiepenheuer and Witsch, 1964.

Dennis, Alfred L. P. *The Foreign Policies of Soviet Russia.* New York: E. P. Dutton and Co., 1924.

Dyck, Harvey Leonard. *Weimar Germany and Soviet Russia, 1926-1933: A Study in Diplomatic Instability* ("Studies of the Russian Institute of Columbia University"). New York: Columbia University Press, 1966.

Fischer, Fritz. *Germany's Aims in the First World War.* New York: W. W. Norton, 1967.

Fischer, Louis. *The Soviets in World Affairs.* 2nd ed. 2 vols. Princeton, New Jersey: Princeton University Press, 1951.

Gehrmann, Karlheinz. *Die Baltischen Staaten: Eine Brücke zwischen Ost und West.* Berlin: Verlagsanstalt Otto Stollberg, 1939.

Graham, Malbone W. *The Diplomatic Recognition of the Border States. Part III: Latvia.* ("Publications of the University of California at Los Angeles in Social Sciences," Vol. III, No. 4). Berkeley: University of California Press, 1941.

Hanč, Josef. *Eastern Europe.* London: Museum Press, 1943.

_____. *Tornado across Eastern Europe.* New York: Greystone Press, 1942.

Harrison, Ernest J. (ed.). *Lithuania, 1928.* London: Hazell, Easton and Viney, 1928.

Hehn, Jürgen von. *Lettland zwischen Demokratie und Diktatur: Zur Geschichte des lettländischen Staatsstreichs von 15. Mai 1934.* ("Jahrbücher zur Geschichte Osteuropas," Beiheft 3). Munich: Isar Verlag, 1957.

Höltje, Christian. *Die Weimarer Republik und das Ostlocarno-Problem, 1919-1934: Revision oder Garantie der deutschen Ostgrenze von 1919.* Würzburg: Holzner Verlag, 1958.

Kazlauskas, Bronius. *L'Entente baltique.* Paris: Imprimerie des Presses Modernes, 1939.

Konovalov, S. *Russo-Polish Relations.* Princeton, New Jersey: Princeton University Press, 1945.

Korbel, Josef. *Poland between East and West: Soviet and German Diplomacy toward Poland, 1919-1933.* Princeton, New Jersey: Princeton University Press, 1963.

Laeuen, Harald. *Polnische Tragödie.* 2nd ed. Stuttgart: Steingrüben Verlag, 1956.

Meissner, Boris. *Die Sowjetunion, die baltischen Staaten und das Völkerrecht.* Cologne: Verlag für Politik und Wirtschaft, 1956.

Newman, Edward William Polson. *Britain and the Baltic.* London: Methuen and Co., Ltd., 1930.

Page, Stanley W. *The Formation of the Baltic States.* Cambridge: Harvard University Press, 1959.

Pernak, Daniel. *Les Rélations économiques de la France et de la Lettonie.* Toulouse: Imprimerie Regionale, 1930.

Rabenau, Friedrich von. *Seeckt: Aus seinem Leben 1918-1936.* Leipzig: Hase and Koehler Verlag, 1940.

Rauch, Georg von. *Geschichte der baltischen Staaten.* Stuttgart, Berlin, Cologne: W. Kohlhammer Verlag, 1970.

Riekhoff, Harald von. *German-Polish Relations, 1918-1933.* Baltimore, London: The Johns Hopkins Press, 1971.

Ronimois, H. E. *Russia's Foreign Trade and the Baltic Sea.* London: Boreas Publishing Co., 1946.

Ross, Hans. *Polen und Europa: Studien zur polnischen Aussenpolitik.* Tubingen: J. C. B. Mohr, 1957.

Rothschild, Joseph. *Pilsudski's Coup d'état.* ("East Central European Studies of Columbia University"). New York: Columbia University Press, 1966.

Ruhl, Arthur. *New Masters of the Baltic.* New York: E. P. Dutton and Co., 1921.

Rutkis, J. (ed.). *Latvia: Country and People.* Stockholm: Latvian National Foundation, 1967.

Schroeder, Herbert. *Russland und die Ostsee: Ein Beitrag zum Randstaatenproblem.* Riga: Verlag der Buchhandlung G. Leoffler, 1927.

Scott, William E. *Alliance against Hitler: Origins of the Franco-Soviet Pact.* Durham, North Carolina: Duke University Press, 1962.

Senn, Alfred Erich. *The Great Powers, Lithuania and the Vilna Question, 1920-1928.* ("Studies in East European History," Vol. XI). Leiden: E. J. Brill, 1966.

Sforza, Count Carlo. *Diplomatic Europe since the Treaty of Versailles.* New Haven: Yale University Press for the Institute of Politics, 1928.

Siew, Benjamin. *Lettlands Volks- und Staatswirtschaft.* Riga: Müller'sche Buchdruckerei, 1925.

Sīpols, Vilnis. *Die ausländische Intervention in Lettland, 1918-1920.* (German translation of *Ārvalstu intervencija Latvijā un tās aizkulises 1918-1920).* Berlin: Ruetten and Loening, 1961.

————. *Slepenā diplomātija: Buržuāziskās Lavijas ārpolitika, 1919.-1932. gada.* [Secret Diplomacy: Bourgeois Latvian Foreign Policy, 1919-1932]. Riga: Izdenvniecība Liesma, 1965.

Šveics, V. V. *Small Nation Survival: Political Defense in Unequal Conflicts.* New York: Exposition Press, 1970.

Smith, Clarence Jay. *Finland and the Russian Revolution, 1917-1922.* Athens, Georgia: University of Georgia Press, 1958.

Tarulis, Albert N. *American-Baltic Relations, 1918-1922: The Struggle over Recognition.* Washington: Catholic University of America Press, 1965.

————. *Soviet Policy toward the Baltic States 1918-1940.* Notre Dame, Indiana; University of Notre Dame Press, 1959.

Tibal, Andre. *La Reforme agraire lettone.* ("Problèmes politiques contemporaines de l'Europe orientale"). Paris: Centre européen de la Dotation Carnegie, 1930.

Tissot, Louis. *La Baltique: Situation des pays riverains de la Baltique: Importance économique et stratégique de la "Méditerranée du Nord".* Paris: Payot, 1940.

Toynbee, Arnold. *Survey of International Affairs, 1920-1934.* 11 vols. Issued under the Auspices of the Royal Institute of International Affairs. London: Oxford University Press, 1925-1935.

Unfug, Douglas Adolph. "German Policy in the Baltic States, 1918-1919." Unpublished Ph.D. dissertation, Yale University, 1960.

Vital, David. *The Survival of Small States: Studies in Small Power-Great Power Conflicts.* London, New York, Toronto: Oxford University Press, 1971.

Vitols, Hugo. *La Mer baltique et les états baltes.* Paris: F. Loviton and Co., 1935.

Waite, Robert G. L. *Vanguard of Nazism: The Free Corps Movement in Germany, 1918-1923.* Cambridge: Harvard University Press, 1952.

Weinberg, Gerhard L. *The Foreign Policy of Hitler's Germany: Diplomatic Revolution in Europe 1933-1936.* Chicago, London:

University of Chicago Press, 1970.

Westergaard, Waldemar. *Political and Military Factors: The Baltic.* Berkeley: University of California, 1941.

Wittram, Reinhard. *Baltische Geschichte: Die Ostseelande Livland, Estland, Kurland, 1180-1918.* Munich: Verlag R. Oldenbourg, 1954.

Wuorinen, John Henry. *A History of Finland.* New York: Columbia University Press, 1965.

Zimmermann, Ludwig. *Deutsche Aussenpolitik in der Ära der Weimarer Republik.* Göttingen, Berlin, Frankfurt: Musterschmidt-Verlag, 1958.

Zinghaus, Viktor. *Führende Köpfe der baltischen Staaten.* Kaunas, Leipzig, Vienna: Ostverlag der Buchhandlung Pribačis, 1938.

Zucher, Arnold John. *The Experiment with Democracy in Central Europe.* New York: Oxford University Press, 1933.

B. Articles and Essays

Anderson, Edgar. "The British Policy toward the Baltic States, 1918-1920," *Journal of Central European Affairs,* XIX, No. 3 (October, 1959), 276-289.

———. "Through the Baltic Gate: Impact of the First World War on the Baltic Area," *The Baltic Review,* No. 33 (January, 1967), 3-21.

———. "Toward the Baltic Entente: The Initial Phase," in *Pro Baltica: Mélanges dédiés à Kaarel R. Pusta.* Edited by Jüri G. Poska. Stockholm: Publication du Comité des Amis de K. R. Pusta, 1965.

———. "Toward the Baltic Union, 1920-1927," *Lituanus,* XII, No. 2 (Summer, 1966), 30-56.

———. "Toward the Baltic Union, 1927-1934," *Lituanus,* XIII, No. 1 (Spring, 1967), 5-28.

———. "An Undeclared Naval War: The British-Soviet Struggle in the Baltic, 1918-1920," *Journal of Central European Affairs,* XXII, No. 1 (April, 1962), 43-78.

_____. "The U. S. S. R. Trades with Latvia: The Treaty of 1927," *Slavic Review*, XXI, No. 2 (June, 1962), 296-321.

"Ārpolitika," *Latvju Enciklopēdija*, pp. 99-129. Edited by Arvēds Svābe. Stockholm: Apgāds Tris Zvaīgznes, 1950-1955.

Assmus, Walter. "Entwicklungstendenzen im baltischen Raum," *Zeitschrift für Geopolitik*, (July, 1928), 560-570.

"Baltic Entente," *Contemporary Review*, CXVIII (October, 1920), 579-581.

"Baltic Problems," *European Economic and Political Survey*, III, No. 7 (December 15, 1927), 215-222.

"Baltic Security Pact Negotiations," *European Economic and Political Survey*, II, No. 2 (September 30, 1926), 51-55.

Beneš, Edward. "The Problem of the Small Nations after the World War," *The Slavonic Review*, IV, No. 11 (December, 1925), 257-277.

Bülow, F. W. von. "Social Aspects of Agrarian Reform in Latvia," *International Labour Review*, XX, No. 1 (July, 1929), 35-66.

Cameron, Elizabeth R. "Alexis Saint-Léger Léger," in *The Diplomats 1919-1939*, Vol. II, *The Thirties*, pp. 378-405. Edited by Gordan A. Craig and Felix Gilbert. New York: Atheneum Press, 1965

Clark, R. T. "Baltic Politics: The Elections in Latvia and Lithuania," *The New Europe*, XVI, No. 197 (July 22, 1920), 28-33.

Dzelzītis, Karlis R. "The Problem of the United Baltic States," in *First Conference on Baltic Studies: Summary of Proceedings*. Edited by Ivar Ivask. Tacoma, Washington: Pacific Lutheran University Press, 1969.

Dziewanowski, M. K. "Pilsudski's Federal Policy, 1919-1921," *Journal of Central European Affairs*, X, No. 2 (July, 1950), 113-128; No. 3 (October, 1950), 271-287.

Eccard, Frédéric. "L'Appel des pays baltiques," *Revue des Deux Mondes*, Series 8, XXIII (September, 1934), 199-222.

"Estonia and Latvia: Customs Union," *European Economic and Political Survey*, II, No. 13 (March 15, 1927), 377-378.

Eudin, Zenia Joukoff. "Soviet National Minority Policies, 1918-1921," *Slavonic and East European Review*, XXI, No. 57 (November, 1943), 31-55.

"Failure of the Baltic League," *Current History*, XIV, No. 6 (September, 1921), 1062-1063.

Freymann, R. von. "Der lettländisch-russische Friedensvertrag und seine Verwirklichung," *Rigasche Zeitschrift für Rechts-wissenschaft*, I, 4 ("Sonderbeilage," 1926/1927), 1-34.

Gabrielsky, Harry. "Polens aussenpolitische Ideologie," *Ost-europa*, VII (May, 1932), 422-456.

Germanis, Uldis. "Latvijas neatkarības idejas attīstibā [Development of the Latvian Independence Idea]," *Jaunā Gaita*, XII, No. 61 (1967), 38-47; No. 62 (1967), 26-37.

Gibbons, Herbert Adams. "The International Whirlpool: The Baltic Sea Republics," *Century Magazine*, CI, No. 3 (January, 1921), 375-382.

Graham, Malbone Watson. "Security in the Baltic States," *Foreign Policy Reports*, VII, No. 25 (February 17, 1932), 437-454.

————. "The Soviet Security Treaties," *American Journal of International Law*, XXIII, No. 2 (April, 1929), 336-350.

Grosberg, Oskar. "Lettlands Wirtschaft in zehn Jahren," *Osteuro-pa*, IV (September, 1929), 837-844.

Hahn, John. "Die Wirtschaftspolitik der baltischen Staaten," *Rigaer Wirtschaftszeitung*, No. 22 (November, 1928), abstracted in *Osteuropa*, IV (December, 1928), 214-215.

Halaychuk, Bohdan. "The Peace of Riga: The End of the Anti-Bolshevik Front," *Ukrainian Quarterly*, XII, No. 3 (September, 1956), 244-250.

Hallgarten, George W. F. "General Hans von Seeckt and Russia, 1920-1922," *Journal of Modern History*, XXI, No. 1 (March, 1949), 28-34.

Hehn, Jürgen von. "Die Entstehung der Staaten Lettland Estland, der Bolschewismus und die Grossmächte," *Forsch-ungen zur osteuropäischen Geschichte*, IV (1956), 103-218.

————. "Lettland zwischen den Mächten 1918-1920," *Jahrbücher für Geschichte Osteuropas*, XI (March, 1963), 37-45.

————. "Vilhelms Munters: Vom Aussenminister des freien Lett-land zum Verteidiger der Sowjetpolitik," *Osteuropa*, XIII (May, 1963), 326-327.

Hiden, J. W. "The Baltic Germans and German Policy toward Latvia after 1918," *Historical Journal*, XIII, No.2 (1970), 295-317.

Hoetzsch, Otto. "Innere Lage und Mächtebeziehungen der Randstaaten," *Osteuropa*, II (1926/27), 347-359.

_____. "Die Lage in Polen und den Randstaaten," *Osteuropa*, IX (November, 1933), 69-90.

_____. "Die osteuropäischen Randstaaten im zehnten Jahre ihres Bestehens," *Osteuropa*, III (July, 1928), 677-689.

_____. "Russland und Osteuropa—Monatsübersicht," *Osteuropa*, VII (March, 1932), 348-365; IX (December, 1933), 166-180; (February, 1934), 286-307; (April, 1934), 417-439; (August, 1934), 668-689.

_____. "Russlands Aussenpolitik zu Beginn 1928," *Osteuropa*, III (1927/1928), 241-255.

_____. "Die Situation der grossen Politik in Osteuropa im Herbst 1934," *Osteuropa*, X (November, 1934), 61-80.

Holborn, Hajo. "Diplomats and Diplomacy in the Early Weimar Republic," in *The Diplomats 1919-1939*, Vol. I, *The Twenties*, pp. 123-171. Edited by Gordon A. Craig and Felix Gilbert. New York: Atheneum Press, 1965.

Hunczak, Taras. " 'Operation Winter' and the Struggle for the Baltic," *East European Quarterly*, IV, No. I (March, 1970), 40-57.

Jessen, F. de. "Problèmes actuels et futurs des voies d'accès à la baltique," in *La Pologne et la baltique: Conférences données à la Bibliothèque polonaise de Paris* ("Problèmes politiques de la Pologne contemporaine," Vol. I). Paris: Gebethener et Wolff, 1931.

Kassik, N. "L'Evolution de l'union baltique," *Revue générale du droit international publique*, XLI, No. 5 (September/October, 1934), 631-647.

Kalnins, Karlis. "Economic Structure and Resources," in *Cross Road Country: Latvia*, pp. 95-117. Edited by Edgars Andersons. Waverly, Iowa: Latvju Gramāta, 1953.

Kaslas, Bronis. "A Lesson from History: Upon the Occasion of the Twenty-Fifth Anniversary of the Baltic Entente," *Baltic Review*, No. 18 (November, 1959), 11-20.

Keohane, Robert O. "'Lilliputians' Dilemmas: Small States in International Politics," *International Organization*, XXIII (1969) 291-310.

Laserson, Max M. "Die Verfassungsentwicklung Lettlands," *Jahrbuch des oeffentlichen Rechts der Gegenwart*, IX (1922), 218-226.

"Latvia," *The Economic Review*, XIV, No. 7 (August 13, 1926), 148-150.

"Latvia," *The Economic Review*, XIV, No. 19 (November 5, 1926), 410-413.

"Latvia between Two Worlds," *The Economist*, CVI (May 19, 1928), 1023-1024.

"Latvia," *The Economic Review*, XII, No. 12 (September 18, 1925), 250-252.

"Latvia: New Trend in Foreign Policy," *The Economic Review*, XV, No. 4 (April 15, 1927), 173-175.

"Latvian Farmers' Union," *The Central European Review* ("Special Latvian Number"), No. 61 (July, 1924), 39.

"Latvia: Settlement of Debt with Great Britain," *The Economic Review*, XII, No. 12 (September 18, 1925), 250.

"Latvia: The Transit Trade," *European Finance* (as Monthly Supplement to *Economic Review*), VIII, No. 13 (September 28, 1928), 58-59.

Linde, Gerd. "Um die Angliederung Kurlands und Lituaens: Die deutschen Konzeptionen für die Zukunft der ehemals russischer Randgebiete vom Sommer, 1918," *Jahrbücher für Geschichte Osteuropas*, X (December, 1962), 563-580.

Lyon, F. H. "Baltic Alliances: Finland at the Cross-Roads," *Fortnightly Review*, CXXI (February, 1924), 301-311.

Machray, Robert. "A Baltic League," *Fortnightly Review*, CX (July, 1921), 54-56.

————. "The Baltic League," *Fortnightly Review*, CXI (May, 1922), 734-743.

————. "The Baltic Pact, Vilna and Memel," *The Nineteenth Century and After*, CXVII (May, 1935), 585-596.

————. "The Baltic Situation," *Fortnightly Review*, CXXII (July, 1924), 42-51.

————. "The Baltic States: Some Personal Impressions," *The Central European Observer*, X, No. 39 (September 23, 1932), 549-551.

————. "British Policy in the Baltic," *Fortnightly Review*, CXL (October, 1933), 397-406.

————. "The Peace of the Baltic," *Fortnightly Review*, CXXX (November, 1928), 647-657.

————. "Poland and the Baltic," *Fortnightly Review*, CXXIX (January, 1928), 90-99.

Model, Michel. "Le Traité d'entente et de collaboration des états baltes," *L'Europe Nouvelle*, XVII, No. 867 (September 22, 1934), 956-958.

Monfort, Henri de. "L'Aspect européen de l'expérience baltique," in *La Pologne et la baltique: Conférences données à la Bibliothèque polonaise de Paris* ("Problèmes politiques de la Pologne contemporaine," Vol. I), pp. 123-143. Paris: Gebethener et Wolff, 1931.

Mousset, Albert. "Les Marches septentrionales de l'Europe: Une enquête aux pays baltes," *L'Europe Nouvelle*, XI, No. 558 (October 20, 1928), 1414-1417.

"National Disarmament Policies: Moscow Conference for Limitation of Armaments," *European Economic and Political Survey*, I, No. 16 (April 30, 1926), 11-15.

Ørvik, Nils. "Scandinavian Security in Transition: The Two-Dimensional Threat," *Orbis*, XVI, No. 3 (Fall, 1972), 720-724.

"Political Alignments in the Baltic," *European Economic and Political Survey*, I, No. 18 (May 31, 1926), 8-17.

Puaux, René. "Karlis Ulmanis, Latvia's Dictator," *Living Age*, CCCL (June, 1936), 323-325.

Rauch, Georg von. "Die baltischen Staaten und Sowjetrussland, 1919-1939," *Europa Archiv*, IX, No. 17 (September 5, 1954), 6859-6867.

Rimscha, Hans von. "Die Baltikumpolitik der Grossmächte," *Historische Zeitschrift*, CLXXVII, No. 2 (April, 1954), 281-309.

Rodgers, Hugh I. "Latvia's Quest for an Eastern Locarno, 1925-1927," *East European Quarterly*, V, No. 1 (March, 1971), 103-113.

Ronimois, H. E. "The Baltic Trade of the Soviet Union: Expectations and Probabilities," *American Slavic and East European Review*, IV, No. 10/11 (December, 1945), 174-178.

"Russian Foreign Relations," *European Economic and Political Survey*, II, No. 19 (June 15, 1927), 633-639.

Rutenberg, Gregory. "The Baltic States and the Soviet Union," *American Journal of International Law*, XXIX, No. 4 (October, 1935), 598-615.

Scala, Otto Erwin von. "Der lettländisch-estländische Zollunionsverrtag--ein Vorbild für ein deutsch-österreichisches Zoll- und Wirtschaftsbündnis," *Nationalwirtschaft: Blätter für organischen Wirtschaftsaufbau*, I, No. 1 (1927), 62-68.

Schram, Stuart R. "L'Union sovietique et les états baltes," in *Les Frontières européennes de l'U. R. S. S. 1917-1941* ("Cahiers de la fondation nationale des sciences politiques," No. 85), pp. 26-166. Paris: Armand Colin, 1957.

Simpson, J. Y. "Great Britain and the Baltic States," *Nineteenth Century and After*, XCIV (October, 1923), 614-621.

Spender, Hugh F. "Security and Disarmament: Cross Currents at Geneva," *Fortnightly Review*, CXXVIII (November, 1927), 600-609.

Taska, Arthur. "Dominum maris baltici und die Sowjetunion," in *Pro Baltica: Mélanges dédiés à Kaarel R. Pusta*, pp. 203-212. Edited by Jüri G. Poska. Stockholm: Publication du Comité des Amis de K. R. Pusta, 1965.

Tibal, André. "La Politique d'après-guerre des états riverains de la baltique," in *La Pologne et la baltique: Conférences données à la Bibliothèque polonaise de Paris* ("Problèmes politiques de la Pologne contemporaine," Vol. I), pp. 99-121. Paris: Gebethener et Wolff, 1931.

Ungern-Sternberg, Roderick von. "Bevölkerungensprobleme Lettlands," *Osteuropa*, XII (December, 1936), 155-173.

Volkmann, Hans-Erich. "Probleme des deutsch-lettischen Verhältnisses zwischen Compiégne und Versailles," *Zeitschrift für Ostforschung*, XIV (December, 1965), 713-726.

Westenberger, Hans. "Die handelspolitischen und wirtschaftlichen Beziehungen Deutschlands und Lettlands bis zum Abschluss des deutsch-lettländischen Vertrages vom 28. Juni 1926," *Osteuropa*, I (1925/1926), 656-667.

Williams, Warren E. "Die Politik der Allierten gegenüber den Freikorps im Baltikum, 1918-1919," *Vierteljahrshefte für Zeitgeschichte*, XII (April, 1964), 147-169.

Ybarra, T. R. "The Self-Extermination of Self-Determination," *New York Times Book Review and Magazine*, October 23, 1921, pp. 6-8.

Zienau, Oswald. "Die sowjetrussisch-lettischen und -estnischen Handelsbeziehungen," *Osteuropa*, V (January, 1930), 250-260.

III. Newspapers

Frankfurter Zeitung, 1922-1934.
The (London) *Times*, 1920-1934.
New York Times, 1920-1934.
Riga Times, 1925-1928.
Vossische Zeitung (Berlin), 1921-1934.

IV. *Bibliographies and Guides*

Mid-European Law Project, Library of Congress. *Legal Sources and Bibliography of the Baltic States: Estonia, Latvia, Lithuania.* ("Praeger Publications in Russian History and Communism," No. 23). New York: Frederick A. Praeger for the Free Europe Committee, 1963.

Ozols, Zelma Aleksandra. *Latvia: A Selected Bibliography.* Washington: Karl Karusa, 1963.

Schwändt, Ernst. *Index of Microfilmed Records of the German Foreign Ministry and the Reichs' Chancellery covering the Weimar Period, deposited at the National Archives.* Washington: National Archives, 1958.

Soviet Foreign Relations and World Communism: A Selected, Annotated Bibliography of 7,000 Books in 30 Languages. Compiled and edited by Thomas T. Hammond. Princeton, New Jersey: Princeton University Press, 1965.

Thomson, Erik. *Baltische Bibliographie 1945-1956.* Würzburg: Holzner Verlag, 1957.

United States. Department of State, Historical Office. *A Catalog of Files and Microfilms of the German Foreign Ministry Archives, 1920-1945.* Compiled by George O. Kent. Stanford: The Hoover Institution, 1962-1964. Vols. I, II.

Index